Risk, environment and society

ISSUES IN SOCIETY
Series Editor: Tim May

Current and forthcoming titles

Zygmunt Bauman: *Work, Consumerism and the New Poor*
David Byrne: *Social Exclusion*
Graham Crow: *Social Solidarities*
Mitchell Dean: *Governing Societies*
Gerard Delanty: *Citizenship in a Global Age*
Steve Fuller: *The Governance of Science*
Les Johnston: *Crime, Justice and Late Modernity*
David Knights and Darren McCabe: *Organizational Change*
Nick Lee: *Childhood and Society*
David Lyon: *Surveillance Society*
Graham Scambler: *Health and Social Change*
Piet Strydom: *Risk, Environment and Society*

Risk, environment and society
Ongoing debates, current issues and future prospects

PIET STRYDOM

OPEN UNIVERSITY PRESS
Buckingham • Philadelphia

Open University Press
Celtic Court
22 Ballmoor
Buckingham
MK18 1XW

email: enquiries@openup.co.uk
world wide web: www.openup.co.uk

and
325 Chestnut Street
Philadelphia, PA 19106, USA

First Published 2002

A catalogue record of this book is available from the British Library

ISBN   0 335 20783 9 (pb)   0 335 20784 7 (hb)

Library of Congress Cataloging-in-Publication Data
Strydom, Piet, 1946–
    Risk, environment, and society : ongoing debates, current issues, and future
prospects / Piet Strydom.
        p. cm. — (Issues in society)
    Includes bibliographical references and index.
    ISBN 0–335–20783–9 (pbk.) — ISBN 0–335–20784–7
    1. Risk—Sociological aspects.   2. Risk perception.   3. Risk-taking
(Psychology)   I. Title.   II. Series.

HM1101 .S77 2002
302′.12—dc21   2002024606

Typeset by Graphicraft Limited, Hong Kong
Printed in Great Britain by St Edmundsbury Press, Bury St Edmunds, Suffolk

We knew the world would not be the same.

J. Robert Oppenheimer, 1945

Now it is the totality that has become the problem and the task. It ushers in a complete transformation of history. The decisive thing is that there is no more 'outside'. The world closes. It is the earth's unity. New threats and opportunities appear.

Karl Jaspers, 1955

The irony is that one species should combine the insights of a Newton with the fears and appetites of fools.

Stephen Toulmin, 1968

. . . organizing our collective responsibility to the future, a task required of us today for the first time . . .

Karl-Otto Apel, 1986

A first step has already been taken in that these problems are no longer reserved for the supposed experts, but have been given over to worldwide legitimation controversies.

Jürgen Habermas, 1999

Contents

Series editor's foreword

Collectively, the social sciences contribute to a greater understanding of the dynamics of social life, as well as explanations for the workings of societies in general. Yet they are often not given due credit for this role and much writing has been devoted to why this should be the case. At the same time we are living in an age in which the role of science in society is being re-evaluated. This has led to both a defence of science as the disinterested pursuit of knowledge and an attack on science as nothing more than an institutionalized assertion of faith with no greater claim to validity than mythology and folklore. These debates tend to generate more heat than light.

In the meantime, the social sciences, in order to remain vibrant and relevant, will reflect the changing nature of these public debates. In so doing they provide mirrors upon which we can gaze in order to understand not only what we have been and what we are now, but to inform possibilities about what we might become. This is not simply about understanding the reasons people give for their actions in terms of the contexts in which they act and analysing the relations of cause and effect in the social, political and economic spheres, but also concerns the hopes, wishes and aspirations that people, in their different cultural ways, hold.

In any society that claims to have democratic aspirations, these hopes and wishes are not for the social scientist to prescribe. For this to happen it would mean that the social sciences were able to predict human behaviour with certainty. One theory and one method, applicable to all times and places, would be required for this purpose. The physical sciences do not live up to such stringent criteria, while the conditions in societies which provided for this outcome, were it even possible, would be intolerable. Why? Because a necessary condition of human freedom is the ability to have acted otherwise and thus to imagine and practise different ways of organizing societies and living together.

It does not follow from the above that social scientists do not have a valued role to play, as is often assumed in ideological attacks upon their place and function within society. After all, in focusing upon what we have been and what we are now, what we might become is inevitably illuminated: the retrospective and prospective become fused. Therefore, while it may not be the province of the social scientist to predict our futures, they are, given not only their understandings and explanations, but equal positions as citizens, entitled to engage in public debates concerning future prospects.

This new international series was devised with this general ethos in mind. It seeks to offer students of the social sciences, at all levels, a forum in which ideas and topics of interest are interrogated in terms of their importance for understanding key social issues. This is achieved through a connection between style, structure and content that aims to be both illuminating and challenging in terms of its evaluation of those issues, as well as representing an original contribution to the subject under discussion.

Given this underlying philosophy, the series contains books on topics that are driven by substantive interests. This is not simply a reactive endeavour in terms of reflecting dominant social and political pre-occupations, it is also pro-active in terms of an examination of issues which relate to and inform the dynamics of social life and the structures of society that are often not part of public discourse. Thus, what is distinctive about this series is an interrogation of the assumed characteristics of our current epoch in relation to its consequences for the organization of society and social life, as well as its appropriate mode of study.

Each contribution contains, for the purposes of general orientation as opposed to rigid structure, three parts. First, an interrogation of the topic that is conducted in a manner that renders explicit core assumptions surrounding the issues and/or an examination of the consequences of historical trends for contemporary social practices. Second, a section that aims to 'bring alive' ideas and practices by considering the ways in which they directly inform the dynamics of social relations. A third section then moves on to make an original contribution to the topic. This encompasses possible future forms and content, likely directions for the study of the phenomena in question, or an original analysis of the topic itself. Of course, it might be a combination of all three.

Our actions rely on routines that enable us to orientate ourselves. Familiar settings and known others are core to a common set of understandings that we deploy in our everyday lives. In the process, nature is often taken as something upon which we act, but not necessarily something that acts upon us. Storms, floods, fires, etc., certainly occur, but the forward march of progress is assumed to encompass an increasing mastery of the elements thereby thwarting their destructive powers and accompanying risks. Yet a simple separation between nature and culture is increasingly open to question. Quite simply, not only are the resources upon which we are dependent being used up at an unsustainable rate, but that use is highly skewed towards rich nations, such as the United States.

It is also widely assumed that the deployment and development of high technology is an indicator of progress. Similarly, our landscapes are being transformed by what are frequently hailed as testaments to human ingenuity, while over time there have been changing roles in society in terms of the state, science and religion. These transformations, however, have produced a complexity in which risks are not localized and irregular, but more frequent and general in their consequences. Thus, insurance companies seek to calculate their policy premiums according to the probability of having to meet subsequent claims, but disasters occur with devastating results that were not predicted and perhaps not even insured against. In these instances, not only are reactions to such events important to understand, but so too are the lessons that may be learnt for the ways in which we live together and relate to the environments of which we are all a part.

How these risks are understood utilizing what intellectual resources, and with what consequences for how social relations are organized, are core topics for Piet Strydom. In interrogating these issues he has produced an important contribution to our understandings of risk, environment and society. He starts the study with an observation that seems to be ignored by those who are privileged by current arrangements: that is, we are now facing an era of 'self-endangerment, self-injury and potential self-destruction'. These topics are then surveyed in relation to phases in changing perceptions of risk, the idea of risk itself and the current literature on risk and society. Nevertheless, he is not content to rest the discussion at those points. One of the novelties of this book lies in taking this literature into a terrain where it is subjected to interrogation according to its implications for contemporary social, economic and political arrangements.

Both in relation to 'expert' cultures and public debates, communications concerning risks have increased considerably in recent history. It is clearly important to understand the extent to which any increase in objective risk interacts with cultural differences in the perception and communication of such risks. This takes us squarely into the realms of realism and social constructionism. These background theories, after all, inform the manner in which risks are identified and acted upon, as well as reacted to and not even anticipated.

These issues took the analysis of risks to the social conditions of its constitution. The contributions of writers such as Ulrich Beck and Niklas Luhmann are considered in the light of this focus, as are the lexical and conceptual histories of risks and their means of classification. Here we move into the expert cultures, which – often bolstered by psychological, anthropological and cultural sociological work in this area – dismiss the claim that we are facing any escalation of risk in late modernity. However, those such as Beck insist on the qualitative differences that are now faced in social, spatial and temporal terms.

For Piet Strydom the implications of such writings necessitate a turn towards the social constructed forms of public discourse about risk, but without losing the reality of risks themselves. An analysis of historical changes in the deep-seated cultural structures that inform changing public perceptions of risk then leads him on to the role of the public sphere. Those he moves with on this journey include Jürgen Habermas and Karl-Otto Apel. Here we find changing forms of communication and the role of social movements producing definitional struggles within the public sphere, as well as the appropriate actions to take in response to risks. What is then required is an analysis of the role and forms of communication in terms of the potential to produce understanding and inform actions. One example upon which he draws to illustrate this process concerns the production of GM foods.

What are raised by these discussions are issues relating to consensus and conflict, as well as citizenship, sustainability, reflexivity, responsibility and inequality. Once again, he does not shy away from these discussions and turns to the idea of 'cognitive institutionalization', bearing in mind the need to examine the conditions under which risks are defined and acted upon. The United Nations Environmental Programme conferences on such topics as 'the human environment' and 'a charter of rights against industrial hazards' are considered in light of this perspective.

Attention is then turned to new ways of thinking about the relations between risk and society. Drawing upon the cognitive turn in sociology, he takes its role firmly into a tradition that calls for a diagnosis of our times according to publicly raised issues. Its purpose is to understand the cognitive structures that inform perceptions of risk as well as seeking to dispel illusions, but without succumbing to a dismissive understanding constituted by either a detached materialism or idealism. This pragmatically based realism can then contribute to publicly based collective responsibility in view of the problems that are now faced in contemporary society. It is because of this focus, accompanied by the consequences of not facing up to these challenges, that this book deserves to be widely read and discussed.

Tim May

Preface and acknowledgements

This volume started to take shape when Tim May invited me to write a book for the 'Issues in Society' series. I wish to thank him for this opportunity and to endorse his well-deserved reputation as a congenial, persuasive and effective editor. The ideas and arguments were gathered and developed during the 1990s. Contexts were provided both by courses or seminars I offered to undergraduates and postgraduates at University College Cork (UCC) and by various research projects. The majority of these were projects within the European Union (EU) Environment Programme of which I had been the responsible scientist while being a director of the Centre for European Social Research. Lately, I have been engaged in research on technological citizenship in the context of an interfaculty project on identity formation at UCC. Numerous visits to the European University Institute in Florence in the first half of the 1990s and extended research sojourns spent in Frankfurt in 1990 and again in Berlin and Frankfurt in 1998 added greatly to my understanding of the issues involved. Through exchanges, comments and criticisms in these different contexts, many people helped to shape these reflections.

Klaus Eder undoubtedly made the most direct impact on the way in which I am carrying forward a shared intellectual background. As for the concept of responsibility, I am deeply indebted to Professor Karl-Otto Apel, whom I wish to thank for his limitless generosity. To Professor Jürgen Habermas I am most grateful for his encouragement to pursue reflections on the public and the concept of triple contingency. But had it not been for Gerard Delanty's intervention and our constant exchanges, the book would not have come into being. In the 1990s, I was for a number of years virtually in constant discussion with Pat O'Mahony, Ger Mullally and Seamus O'Tuama. In the current research context at UCC, I must single out the latter, with whom I have been working on technological citizenship, and our research assistant Eluska Fernandez, who supplied me throughout with invaluable material. Besides Tim May, the first version of the manuscript was read, commented on and criticized also by Gerard Delanty, Mauricio Domingues and Pat O'Mahony in instructive ways for which I am grateful. Finally, I wish to thank Professor Karl-Otto Apel, Klaus Eder and Tom Burns for providing me with some of their sought-after writings.

The gathering and development of the ideas and arguments informing the book owe something to various grants obtained earlier from the European Commission and the Arts Faculty Fund, UCC. The writing of the book itself benefited directly from research funded by the Higher Education Authority. The positive vanishing point of the book, and thus much of the inspiration allowing its completion, was drawn from the town of Kinsale on the south coast of Ireland, where the book was substantially written. The beauty of its surroundings could not but lead one to imagine something beyond an avaricious and vain, authoritarian paternalist civilization of self-endangerment and ecological disaster. I dedicate this book to my children, Hanno and Maria, and to people of their age and younger, who will, I hope, later in the twenty-first century see a closer approximation to this imagined reality than I.

Introduction

This book, which is my attempt to establish the current level of knowledge about the theme 'risk, environment and society' and to give it some social scientific depth, could have been called 'the metamorphosis of danger' instead. It is widely recognized that we are today living in a civilization of self-endangerment, self-injury and potential self-destruction. Central to this self-understanding are not only a growing awareness of environmental destruction and the grave problem it entails for all life on earth, but also the global expansion of a new culture of the perception and communication of risk. Indeed, a wide-ranging discourse has emerged that is concerned with risk as well as more broadly with our civilization's failings. It is increasingly compelling us to take the motivations and consequences of our decisions and actions into account and to deal intelligently and in a justifiable way with the accompanying uncertainty and ambivalence. This has brought about a change in the conditions and therefore also the mode of constitution and organization of society. A new society is emerging that will in all probability come into its own during the next three to four decades. This nascent constellation is captured by such self-descriptions as 'the age of the environment' (von Weizsäcker), 'civilization of the gene' (Moscovici), 'biotech century' (Rifkin), 'runaway world' (Giddens) and, above all, 'risk society' (Beck). Both publicly and in the social sciences, this self-description has struck a resonant chord. It is from the underlying intuition according to which there is a new, historically specific link between risk, environment and society entailing an unprecedented metamorphosis of danger that this book proceeds. Its concrete starting point, however, is the public discourse that has become such a characteristic feature of our time.

Public discourse and the social sciences

During the last three decades of the twentieth century, we have witnessed a dramatic increase in public communication, debates and controversies about risks, and for the foreseeable future we can expect a continuation of this trend. The question of risk was first raised in the context of expert debates. Due to the fact that knowledge claims became objects of contestation, and collective agents (for example science, industry, the state, and social movements) began to compete and conflict with one another before a growing and increasingly attentive audience, however, public debates and controversies became the order of the day. While it occurred against the background of a growing awareness of risks in an ever widening range of spheres of life, in the course of time a gradual shift took place in the thematic focal point of this public concern with risk. Originally having arisen in the nuclear industry, it shifted first to global environmental problems and then to risks and potential risks generated by genetic engineering. As is suggested by a variety of ongoing campaigns and controversies, nuclear and global environmental risks still figure strongly in current debates and can be expected to continue doing so. The emphasis today, however, nevertheless is and will probably for some time to come remain on genetic engineering – what many a scientist, technologist, industrialist and government regard as the technology and industry of the future.

The social sciences entered the discourse about risk only relatively late. This occurred only once competition, contestation and conflict among the social agents involved caused risk to become a public issue. At this stage, questions arose that required social scientific answers. Due to which factors do particular interpretations of risks become dominant within different social groups or units? To what can polarization, controversy and conflict be ascribed? How did risk, despite such polarization and conflict, nevertheless become identified and collectively accepted as the most pressing secular problem faced by contemporary advanced societies? What are the conditions of the production of risk? What is involved in the collective identification and definition of risk? How is risk socially constructed? What consequences follow from the collective recognition of risk as the central issue of our time for the way in which society is constituted and organized? Does the ascendance of the risk issue indicate that we are entering a different type of society and, hence, a new era?

Mary Douglas was among the first social scientists to open the way toward understanding the new phenomenon of a growing awareness and public concern about technology-based environmental dangers (Douglas and Wildavsky 1982). But these questions proved too much for her anthropological approach, for their complexity under contemporary conditions requires the 'finesse' of 'the more social of the social sciences' (Douglas 1994: 12; see also Douglas 1986: 4). It is against this background that James Short (1984) issued his timely impassioned call for sociology to focus on a 'social transformation of risk analysis'. Sociologists responded by formulating social theoretic positions and advancing interpretations, albeit different and even conflicting ones, that truly transformed risk analysis. Ulrich Beck's (1992, 1995) theory of the risk society, as is well known, proved to be the most incisive contribution and thus captured the imagination. Yet of almost equal importance is Niklas Luhmann's (1989) analysis of 'ecological communication' and his sociology of risk (Luhmann 1993). In addition to transforming the field of risk studies, however, their respective contributions indirectly also raised questions about the public role of the social sciences, sociology in particular. As one of the voices in public communication, as a participant in debates and controversies about risks, what role does sociology play in the construction of the nascent society of the twenty-first century?

This book is an analysis of the public debates and the concurrent theories of risk as well as of contemporary society. It derives its central theme from the debates and theories. Their concern is with high-risk, science-based technologies and therefore with what are called 'high-consequence risks' (Giddens 1991: 4) or 'technological-ecological risks' (Bechmann 1993b: 251). On the one hand, public communication about environmental problems gives rise to a discourse in which distinct groups compete and conflict in the course of struggles to define in a collectively acceptable way what risk amounts to. In response to this, theories have been developed to make sense of the social or discursive construction of risk and, by extension, the constitution and organization of a new society. This is where our task becomes the analysis of contemporary society conceived as a 'risk society' (Beck 1992). On the other hand, there are real problems such as nuclear radiation, the Chernobyl disaster, holes in the ozone layer, the greenhouse effect, global warming and finally genetic engineering turning anthropological constants into variables and thus invalidating our most cherished assumptions about the human condition. To them correspond debates and theories about the status and role of science and technology as being of central importance in contemporary society, yet as having gone beyond their traditional institutional boundaries toward transforming society itself into a laboratory. In this case, the question of the production of risks leads us to an analysis of contemporary society as the 'experimenting society' (Krohn and Weyer 1989: 349). Starting from public discourse, then, this book focuses on high-consequence nuclear, global environmental and genetic risks, and makes the problem of their production as well as conflict and consensus about them the object of investigation.

The societal significance of risk

Theoretically, it is assumed here that risk must be understood in conjunction with a theory of society and, hence, societal transformation processes. Social theory is a reflection on the changeable structural features of society that constitute the limits and thus in a sense determine social relations, collective self-understanding and conflicts at a particular point in time. In addition to a theory of the transformation of society, it also provides an analysis and diagnosis of the present. In her anthropological approach, Douglas proceeds from the assumption that the members of all societies, irrespective of whether tribal or modern, classify their reality according to the distinction between purity and dirt or danger. By contrast with this proposal to understand the late-twentieth-century concern with high-consequence risks in terms of ahistorical anthropological universals, however, Beck, Luhmann, Giddens, Eder and others all proceed social theoretically. Their writings invariably point to the necessity of a theory of society, including a theory of contemporary society. Each in his own way, these authors all recognize that risk has never been more prominent as a theme than it is today and, accordingly, they seek to explain and clarify the phenomenon by placing it in the context of contemporary society. All of them appreciate that risk has for the first time only recently acquired significance for society as a whole, and that this forces us to rethink society as well as our basic social scientific concepts. It is only when risk is approached as a phenomenon of societal significance that it is possible to understand it adequately at all.

Together, the centrality of the problem today and the universal extension of risk consciousness indicate that risk is the signature of contemporary society. It stands for the fundamental process of social change leading to the society of the twenty-first century. Simultaneously, it is the repository of the basic experiences and problems of society. Risk points toward the new form of the processing of problems, or the new mode of the constitution of society that is transforming existing institutions and making possible a new mode of organization. It distinguishes the emerging society from other societies. On the one hand, it draws attention to the high-risk, science-based, high technologies of our time and, on the other, conjures up the new and qualitatively different danger potential harboured by the high-consequence risks facing us today. Risk also invokes a fundamental cultural change, involving a different understanding of nature, of the relation between society and nature, and – as both Beck (1992) and Giddens (1991) appreciate – even of the self. Above all, however, it implies a new, future-oriented, planetary, macro-ethics of responsibility (Jonas 1984; Apel 1987) which has already begun to take effect in the form a new cultural structure or model of our time (Strydom 1999d). It has begun to coordinate the activities of social actors and collective agents who communicate competing and conflicting interpretations of risks, and provides cultural tools and legitimation for the development of new identities, legal norms and institutions in the economic, social and political fields.

Important considerations follow from the fact that risk has significance for society as a whole. It means, to begin with, that risk is not simply an objective problem that could be solved by a troubleshooting engineer by means of appropriate scientific and technical knowledge. Simultaneously, it is a whole new climate of ideas, feelings and norms. It is a new discursive culture of perception, communication and collective attempts to identify, define and resolve an unprecedented problem turned into a public and political issue. As such, it involves a process of the social construction of reality. This implies that risk provides both the opportunity and the means for the transformation and reproduction of society. It is closely tied – and this is crucial for rethinking the basic concepts of sociology along cognitive lines – to a new way in which we today classify, interpret and order the world in which we live, a new way in which we bring society into being and arrange it in a more or less collectively acceptable manner. Risk is the key to the constitution and organization of contemporary society. From a historical perspective, therefore, it is comparable to the phenomena of domination or violence in the early modern period and of poverty in the high modern period respectively. The difference that risk is at present making to the constitution and organization of society is of the same order as the thoroughgoing and far-reaching evolutionary changes introduced by the collective problems of domination or violence and poverty in previous epochs. In this lies the societal significance of the contemporary phenomenon of risk.

Theoretical approach

The approach adopted in this book is, generally speaking, a continuation of various attempts in recent decades to correct a number of serious deficiencies in the social sciences (Dierkes and Wagner 1992; Adam et al. 2000). They go back to the neglect of different dimensions of society, such as technology, transformation and time, but especially the blind spot that occluded nature since the birth of these disciplines. Both technology and the relation between society and nature are given a central place in the book. Transformation and time, on the other hand, are incorporated through a replacement of the traditional emphasis on simple, causal, stable, linear relations by a concern with more complex, non-linear relations unfolding through time in a particular historical situation and dependent on cultural structures. It is this concern that demands that the problem of the relation between constructivism and realism, rather confusingly treated in the debate about risk, is clearly stated and resolved.

Theoretically, this approach is specifically developed through a cognitivist communication and discourse theory of society that focuses on the manner in which a common world is shaped through joint action and interaction. This theory is able to deal with the construction of the social world without losing its relation with reality. In keeping with the concept of 'communicative action' (Habermas 1984, 1987), it takes into account both meanings or textual representations of reality and the social actions or relations by which they are generated. The cognitive dimension is vital to retaining a firm grip on reality, since it not only organizes experience and structures action and communication, but also has roots in natural historical or evolutionary processes. While this theoretical approach finds inspiration in Habermas, it involves drawing insights from Touraine, Bourdieu and Luhmann and bringing together a variety of strands deriving from critical theory, social movement studies, the sociology of knowledge, social studies of science and technology, cultural studies, frame and discourse analysis, and cognitive science. Above all, however, it is an attempt to make a contribution to what may be regarded as the new cognitive sociology, yet a significant part of the rationale for this is the revitalization of critique.

The outcome is an integral and coherent analysis of contemporary society. While being critical, it does not persist in projecting a purely normative point of view. Rather, an awareness of ambivalence is maintained. By following the metamorphosis of danger, possible ways of dealing with some typical obstacles that we are facing in contemporary society, politics, ethics and social science are envisaged. A socio-cognitive critique, targeting both the status quo and utopianism, is developed that asks disillusioning questions about the orientations, actions and goals of all those participating in the constitution of contemporary society. That the social sciences themselves are by no means exempt from this questioning is apparent from the concern throughout with the role that they play in bringing into being and organizing the society of the twenty-first century.

Given the incisiveness of his contribution to the field, Beck unavoidably occupies a prominent position in the account offered in this book. It should be borne in mind, however, that the theoretical approach I put forward here goes well beyond his position. Let me single out two respects in which this difference impacts on the structure of the argument. In line with the criticism of Beck's neglect of the material conditions behind risks (see, for example, Rustin 1994), I include a chapter on the societal production of risk focusing on the material conditions of the risk society as encapsulated by what is called the 'experimenting society' (Krohn and Weyer 1989). Extending the criticism that Beck's analysis of the risk society in terms of individualization overlooks the intersubjective lifeworld (Habermas 1992: 199), I devote another chapter to the theme of communication, the transformation of the public sphere and the role of the public under these new conditions of contingency. The fact that I adopt a position that seeks to mediate realism and constructivism explains not only my twofold concern with material conditions and public communication in these two chapters. It also makes clear why I find it necessary to go beyond the exterior of such material conditions as science, technology, industry, capitalism and the state toward the cultural cognitive structures or models giving them direction.

Structure of the book

Like the other volumes in the current series, this book falls into three parts. Part one offers in Chapter 1 an accessible overview of the risk debates from which the contemporary concern with risk arose between the 1950s and the present. It follows this up with an analysis of background theories and epistemological positions in Chapter 2, and the most important theoretical directions presupposed in contemporary risk debates in Chapter 3. Part two picks up on the major structural dimensions previously highlighted and subjects them to a more penetrating analysis in four chapters. Chapter 4 deals with the question of what risk is, Chapter 5 with the societal production of risk in the experimenting society, Chapter 6 with the discursive construction of risk in public communication, and Chapter 7 with the cultural foundations and institutional dynamics of the risk society. In Part three, which is reserved for an original contribution to the topic, I attempt to rethink the risk society in terms of communicative rather than simply reflexive modernity. This is complemented with an outline of a corresponding cognitive sociological approach accommodating both constructivism and realism that could be useful in researching and analysing contemporary society. A special concern here is to provide a basis for a new concept of critique that could assist in the revitalization of the public role of the social sciences. The conclusion, which is devoted to a brief review of the main argument of the book, closes with the question of theory and practice or what the social sciences could contribute in the face of the risk society.

PART ONE

Problems, debates, frameworks and theories

The risk discourse: the contemporary concern with risk

In accordance with the theoretical and methodological approach adopted in this book, I begin with a descriptive analysis of a series of international debates and controversies – collectively 'the risk discourse' – that started in the 1950s and 1960s. It is from these communicative events that the concern with risk as related to the environment and, hence, society as a whole for the first time clearly emerged. An analysis that begins at this level offers us the opportunity to gain access to the phenomenon of risk in both its material and symbolic manifestations. While there are numerous environmental dangers, hazards or threats that have come to be recognized as risks (Perry 1981; Brown 1989; Simmons 1991; Nelkin 1992; Yearley 1996; Hewitt 1997), I shall follow the debates and controversies since the 1950s along a certain line of thematic development. From the relatively general viewpoint taken here, one can observe a shift in problem from nuclear energy through global environmental problems to biotechnology – notwithstanding the fact that older problems are not displaced by later ones but rather periodically reassert themselves. At a somewhat deeper level, however, it is possible also to discern the different phases through which these communicative events passed, involving distinct issues, participants, relations among participants, roles played by the public, modes of communication, paradigms of risk research, disciplinary approaches and discursive structures. Beyond and above content, therefore, I shall also present a rough periodization, from the beginnings of risk research to the emergence of a full-scale public discourse about risk, as well as a structural analysis of the debates and controversies.

The risk discourse embraces four phases, stretching from the 1950s to the present, that cover a trajectory from narrow, technical expert debates concerned with the accurate calculation of risks to broad public controversies in which also voluntary associations and social movements participate before an increasingly aware public audience. The first phase was epitomized by

Table 1.1 The risk discourse

Phase/period	1: 1950s	2: 1960s	3: 1970s	4: late 1970s to present
Dominant new theme	Nuclear energy	Nuclear energy	Global environmental problems	Biotechnology
Content of debate	Safety and risk	Opposition to nuclear power and risk assessment	Opinions and psychology of the opposition	Relations of participants, and construction of facts/reality
Risk research paradigm	Safety research/risk assessment: control	Risk comparison/social acceptance of risk: expertise	Surveys/risk perception/ risk communication: understanding	Transcending risk research: conflict and consensus
Participants	Experts and regulators	Experts, regulators, first stirrings of opposition	Experts, regulators, new social movements	Experts, industry, regulators, state, associations, movements
Major discursive frames	Techno-corporatist safety	Techno-corporatist safety, emergence of survivalism	Survivalism vs cornucopian-Prometheanism	Sustainable development: ecological modernization vs reflexive modernization; collective responsibility; ecological citizenship
Mode of communication	Inner access	Mobilization	Outer initiative	Full-scale public discourse
Role played by public	Excluded from expert debates	Emergence of public concern	Growing public concern expressed by voluntary associations and social movements	Recognized third party observing the participants and evaluating their contributions
Disciplines	Systems theory/ analysis, business management, decision and game theory, cost–benefit analysis	Innovation and diffusion theory, risk analysis	Risk analysis, empirical social science, psychometric and cognitive psychology	Risk analysis, cultural theory, sociology, political theory
Discursive logic	Techno-corporatist assumptions	Questioning and breakdown of old assumptions	Stark conflict between different sets of assumptions	New cultural forms of legitimation mitigating yet allowing continuation of conflict

the risk assessment debate. The second turned on the question of the comparison and social acceptability of risks. The third saw the emergence of opposition to scientific-technological risks and the concomitant attempt of risk analysts to explain the public perception of risks psychologically. The fourth, finally, is characterized by an ongoing process of contestation over the social construction of risk in a reconstituted public sphere in which democracy is often invoked against the attempts of scientists, technologists, risk analysts, managers and politicians to restrict the discursive process and thus to displace risks. The structural analysis of the different phases of the risk discourse, summarized in Table 1.1, focuses on some of the theoretically most important dimensions and thus lays down markers for the development of the subsequent chapters.

First phase: nuclear energy, safety research and the risk assessment debate

The extended discussions that followed in the wake of the development of an atomic weapon at Los Alamos, the bombing of Hiroshima and Nagasaki, and Soviet and American atomic tests in 1949 and 1954 respectively, indeed provided a pervasive background for the risk discourse. But other developments were required first before the real sense of Karl Jaspers's (1955) appreciation that the bomb marked the beginning of a new global epoch was more generally grasped. The contemporary risk discourse goes back to the 1950s, to the forced development of the nuclear industry and the concomitant raising of questions about the safety or security of civil nuclear technology and its destructive potential. Some trace the discourse back to the Chicago School of geography in the mid-1940s (Burton et al. 1978), while others locate its starting point in Starr's famous article on social benefit and technological risk published in 1969 (Bechmann 1993a). A little investigation shows, however, that it was the debate about risk in the civil nuclear industry that took a significant turn in the 1960s and 1970s when it became politicized, acquired a public dimension and broadened into the current fully fledged public risk discourse.

Almost immediately after the Second World War, the United States and Britain decided in favour of a civil nuclear generating capability. Beginning in 1950, the US Atomic Energy Commission (AEC) set out to harness nuclear technology as an energy source. But it was only after President Eisenhower's proposal of 'Atoms for Peace' that this programme was officially launched. The first demonstration plant was planned to go on line in 1958 in Shippingport, Pennsylvania (Hohenemser et al. 1977). Since Britain lagged behind, its project was a spin-off from the desire to produce nuclear weapons and bask in the attendant political prestige (Simmons 1991). In the course of the development of the Shippingport project, we witness a new departure in the United States. There the atomic programme called forth scientific research into the risks entailed by the industrial use of nuclear power. Incidents in the early 1950s at American installations contributed to this departure. Whereas the Americans turned toward risk research, the British by contrast moved eagerly ahead on an inadequate knowledge base, ignoring warnings regarding a possible Wigner energy release that could have prevented the accident of 1957 in Cumbria.

Guided by the idea that serious damaging effects could follow on an unexpected event of very low probability, this classical safety research – 'risk research' or 'risk analysis', as it came to be called – was motivated by economic and political concerns. The environment itself played little or no part in these considerations. Those responsible for the production, marketing and regulation of nuclear energy felt compelled to consider the potential dangers, hazards or threats inherent in the new technology as economic and political investment risks. Experts, the majority of whom were in the employ of private firms, were hired to undertake research into the problems faced by the utilization of nuclear power. Where the state administration became involved, it was also mainly from the point of view of the advancement of the new technology, the construction of power stations in accordance with safety standards, and control by safety experts. The task of the risk researchers was to anticipate and quantify the dangers, hazards or threats accompanying possible accidents and side-effects of civilian nuclear power, and thus to transform them into classifiable and calculable risks. It is this practically oriented, scientific concern with the consequences of nuclear technology that earned risk research the more specific title of 'risk assessment' or, more covertly, 'technology assessment' (Otway and Pahner 1976).

Among the experts charged with doing risk research were engineers, planners, economists and psychologists. Initially, social scientists such as anthropologists, sociologists and political scientists had no part in the process. This is reflected in the principal disciplines out of which risk analysis originally grew (Evers and Nowotny 1987). The first is the combination of systems and planning theory, originally deriving from the military sector and space research, that made possible the analysis of systems failures and the calculation of the probability of risk as well as the extent of damage and loss. The second is the complex of business management, planning theory, decision-making theory, game theory and cost–benefit analysis. In this case, the focus is on choosing between alternatives according to their different cost–benefit probabilities calculated in monetary terms. The third and final disciplinary area informing risk analysis, introduced to compensate for the limitations of formal theories and models, is the descriptive theory of decision-making behaviour. It allows the analysis of the actual behaviour of actors with a view to establishing the so-called 'risk behaviour' of human beings – a risk regarded as most significant yet virtually impossible to calculate.

The first risk study was undertaken in the United States at the request of the AEC and published about a year before the first plant went on line. The WASH 740 or 'Brookhaven Report' on *Theoretical Possibilities and Consequences of Major Accidents in Large Nuclear Power Plants*, which was updated in 1965, projected rather disturbing conceivable consequences of reactor failure. In 1975, it was followed by another major study, the *Reactor Safety Study* or 'Rasmussen Report' (Hohenemser et al. 1977). In an age that saw the increasing emulation of the leading countries in the area of civil nuclear energy generation, developments in the United States were closely, albeit with a certain time lag, followed in Germany. In both cases, we observe a parallel shift from an initial deterministic to a probabilistic concept of risk. The original American study proceeded from a deterministic concept, in which case concrete examples of breakdowns or accidents were reviewed in order to analyse the consequences. For instance, it was assumed that to prove the safety of a nuclear reactor it was sufficient to show that an unexpected event, such as a burst pipe in the main cooling system, could be controlled and managed. Under pressure from the US Congress, however, this theoretical assumption was replaced by a probabilistic concept of risk. Here the actual or hypothetically projected breakdown of single components is employed to calculate the probability of failures or accidents and to relate them to sequences of unexpected events. This approach obtained its most sophisticated form in the American *Reactor Safety Study* and the *Deutsche Risikostudie* of 1979 commissioned by the German Federal Minister of Research and Technology (Evers and Nowotny 1987). These studies provided industry with the typical argument according to which a nuclear catastrophe is indeed not impossible yet extremely improbable. In Britain at the time, Lord Rothschild (1978) accordingly ventured to argue that uranium power generation is in fact one of the safest sources of energy available.

As far as the risk discourse is concerned, both the disciplines informing the research and the resulting studies on risk in the nuclear industry are revealing. First of all, it is clear that the first phase of the discourse, what may be called the 'risk assessment debate', was essentially an expert debate. It was largely conducted by expert risk analysts such as engineers, economists and planners, typically joined by lawyers in Europe, within a context insulated from public view. Between the 1950s and 1970s, these experts multiplied and consolidated to such an extent that they were able to form a community of risk analysts, first in the United States but then extending internationally. It represented a new branch of interdisciplinary studies with its own institutional trappings, such as professional organizations, scientific journals and conferences (Covello and Mumpower 1985; Douglas 1986). In the course of the 1960s, this trend was strongly stimulated by public administrators who received it favourably and helped its widespread diffusion in planning and decision-making circles. It is important to note that it was the safety researchers and analysts conducting these expert debates who were responsible for introducing such words as 'risk', 'risk assessment' and 'risk analysis', thus indelibly stamping the vocabulary and language of the twentieth- and twenty-first-century risk discourse. The fact that the risk analysts initially enjoyed a monopoly expert position, however, unmistakably indicates the inherent limits of the first phase of the discourse.

Many questions can and indeed have been asked about the status of the claims advanced by risk analysts. Historically, the criticisms fall into two categories. On the one hand, critics pointed out the methodological flaws plaguing technical-economic risk studies, particularly as revealed by their typical objectivism. This was increasingly the case after the abandonment of a deterministic concept of risk in favour of a probabilistic one, for this brought home even to the technically trained that judgement, opinion, discretion and choice unavoidably entered what is ostensibly objective scientific research (Otway and Thomas 1982). If risk assessment possesses a psychological, social or political dimension, how could a purely natural scientific and even an economic risk analysis redeem its claim to being objective at all? Important as such questions are, much more interesting from the viewpoint of the development of the risk discourse beyond its first phase were questions that left the confines of scientific methodology so as to embed the risk assessment debate in its wider context. Invariably, these questions invoked the controversies about nuclear technology as well as other new risk-laden innovations which at the time started to occur with an increasing frequency. Not only did they cast doubt on the rather limited technical or instrumental rationality advanced under the banner of risk research, but also the critics pointed toward a broad social or socio-political rationality. In this, the critics were supported by new developments such as the first stirrings of public concern about grave contemporary risks, its consolidation into interest groups, voluntary associations and social movements, and the politicization of risk assessment. Slowly it started to become clear to a growing number of people that risk does not simply call for the mastery and control of social processes (such as public opinion formation, political decision-making and consumption) by focusing on and manipulating a narrow, arbitrarily selected band of dangers and uncertainties. Rather it gives rise to a range of issues that are relevant well beyond the core scientific, economic and political institutions of society. These issues clearly started to divide the citizenry at large into distinct, competing and even conflicting social groups whose different perspectives, interests, orientations and activities needed political mediation and thus transformation into properties of society as such.

Once the limits of the risk assessment debate was reached, once the public and its organizations such as interest groups, voluntary associations and especially social movements appeared on the scene, the dynamics of the risk discourse underwent a change. A shift of focus occurred from the probability of objectively calculable risks to the new question of the social acceptability of risks. As the mode of operation and assumptions of the risk researchers were exposed, the expert risk assessment debate made way for the second phase of the risk discourse.

Second phase: nuclear and environmental opposition and the social acceptability of risk

The shift from the experts toward the public set the tone of the second phase of the risk discourse. It meant the entry of another social actor as well as of an audience, the contextualization and hence broadening of the discourse, and a significant change in the approach of the experts. In addition to the emerging public concern, a second characteristic feature of this phase was the first sounding of the major new theme of global environmental problems. It eventually became more prominent than the nuclear theme, yet not displacing but rather enhancing it whenever it made another appearance (for example Chernobyl in 1986, THORP in 2000).

Although the anti-nuclear movement attained a high visibility only in the wake of the energy crisis of 1973–74, the opposition to the civil use of nuclear power underwent limited yet by no means insignificant developments already in late 1950s and 1960s (Hohenemser et al. 1977; Rucht 1990). The year 1965 marks the turning point when the distrust of nuclear power began to be generalized into a distrust of high technology and to be linked to threats to the natural environment. Since then, the development of the anti-nuclear movement and the formation of new environmental groups as well as revitalization of traditional environmental organizations ran parallel and mutually reinforced each other. The first onslaught against commercial nuclear power followed in the late 1960s upon the disclosure of routine radioactive emissions from power plants. By 1970, Earth Day in particular, environmental awareness culminated in a sudden but deep and apparently irreversible change of mentality which inaugurated the so-called 'Green Seventies'. During the following two years, the first large environmental coalition, the Consolidated National Intervenors, took up position at the AEC hearings which exposed serious deficiencies in risk research and regulation. The Union of Concerned Scientists took the lead in questioning AEC safety measures, and soon after Ralph Nader as well as the Sierra Club took up opposition to nuclear power. Against this background, Friends of the Earth played its part during the following years in transforming nuclear power into a symbol of high technology, unbridled and destructive growth, and centralized political control. These various developments effectively drew attention to the difference between data about risks produced by experts, on the one hand, and the meaning of such data to individuals and social groups, on the other, and thus stimulated the emergence of a public response to the risk assessment debate. It is interesting to note that the very time of the emergence of public concern was the incubation period of the later widespread interest in the public sphere. During this period, Habermas (1989) was in the process of writing his influential book on the public sphere that was published in 1962.

A range of different factors cleared the way for the emergence and growth of social movement activity and public concern, some of which merit mention here. A broad contextual factor, the cultural dynamic originally set free by the French Revolution, was manifested at the time in the form of a value change among blacks, youth, students and other sections of the population (Turner 1969; Inglehart 1977). It is remarkable, however, that experts, albeit dissident experts or counter-establishment scientists, played a crucial role in the process of consciousness-raising. For these purposes, they could of course draw on available critical – both conservative and neo-Marxist – philosophical and social scientific analyses of science and technology, such as those of Heidegger (1977), Ellul (1964) and Marcuse (1964). At the time of the Sputnik I launch in 1957, the German Nobel prize-winner for physics, Max Born, criticized space exploration as a triumph of the mind that in fact represented a failure of reason. Then, in 1962, the American biologist Rachel Carson published her *Silent Spring* in which she extrapolated the damaging long-term consequences both for the environment and health of the unchecked use of toxic chemicals in agriculture. In the course of the decade, this alarming analysis was followed by a spate of comparable publications in different fields by such authors as Barry Commoner, Paul Erlich and Gordon Rattray Taylor. The message of these counter-experts was that the self-recuperative powers of nature were no longer sufficient to correct the exhaustion of raw material resources, the growing costs and risk of energy production, and the increasing environmental challenge. At a deeper level, one could mention the paradigm change in twentieth-century science that started to make itself felt at this stage. The new understanding of the physical process as self-organizing not only was accompanied by a reflexive turn in theoretical knowledge and an appreciation of objectivity as being dependent on theoretical construction, but also contained the startling insight that human beings form part of nature rather than simply being its masters (Moscovici 1977; Merchant 1990; Eder 1996a). Various incidents and events that received media coverage, from the Marcoule protest in France in 1958 through the Unesco Biosphere Conference in 1968 to the AEC rule-making hearings, provided concrete focal points for the developing awareness and mobilizing activities. It is possible to continue listing relevant factors, but the main point is that they conditioned or contributed to the emergence and growth of social movement activity and public concern, and thus the beginnings of public scrutiny by environment, consumer and other citizen groups. Later, it would become apparent that these events marked a fundamental change in the modern understanding of reality. The 'implosion of modernity' (Nowotny 1996: 151), as it is called, captured the erosion of the boundary between society and nature and the recognition of the newly emergent unity of the socio- and biosphere.

The politicization of risk research and risk assessment through the entry of different groups and the public called forth a multiple response from the experts which underwent a mutation as the new set of debates unfolded. Initially, an attempt was made to account for the opposition to nuclear energy and other technologies by means of innovation and diffusion theory. Based on historical evidence, researchers proceeded from the theoretical assumption that the person who is unwilling or unable to adopt innovations is typically attached to the status quo, conservative and of relatively advanced age (Katz et al. 1963; Rogers 1963). In addition, such persons were often assumed to exhibit a lack of knowledge of an innovation and its possible consequences and to be alienated (Douvan and Withey 1954; Erskine 1963), such as the Luddite or machine-breaking farm labourers in nineteenth-century

Britain. As research on the nuclear opposition developed through the 1960s and well into the 1970s, however, these assumptions were shattered (Renn 1984). It turned out that protesters against technological innovations and their risks were neither conservative, nor alienated and even less ignorant, but rather educated, informed about innovation and aware of its potential negative consequences. Rather than fixing on the adoption of innovation, like the diffusion researchers, the theorists of the emerging anti-nuclear and environmental movements by contrast stressed the consequences and side-effects of new technologies for human health and the social and natural environment. The tension and emerging conflict between these diametrically opposed positions gave rise to a perception of ambivalence and a feeling of uncertainty about technological advancement, and the first signs of a breakdown of confidence and trust in institutions became visible. For instance, questions were increasingly raised about the dual role of the AEC as both promoter and regulator of nuclear power generation, leading some to speak of the 'unhappy marriage between development and regulation' (Hohenemser et al. 1977: 32).

Risk analysts adopted a different strategy in the face of public concern and the emergence of a risk conscious opposition to technology. It was aimed at a pragmatic compromise in the context of the public debate. It consisted of two arguments, 'risk comparison' and 'revealed preferences' or 'revealed behaviour', as they were called. The leading proponent of this approach was the risk analyst Starr (1969). This strategy rested on assumptions about the calculability of risk and the price that society is willing to pay for safety. Risk comparison is a way of describing the risks of hazardous technologies by comparison with other better known risks. Besides expressing the magnitude of a risk, however, it sought to persuade the audience regarding how large a risk should be and thus to imply its acceptability. A good example of this twofold, explicitly descriptive and implicitly rhetorical, argument is as follows: first, 'the cancer risk of living at the boundary of a nuclear power plant for five years equals the cancer risk of eating 40 tablespoons of peanut butter (due to aflatoxin)', and second, 'if you are willing to eat 40 tablespoons of peanut butter over the next five years, then you should be willing to live near a nuclear power plant' (Roth et al. 1998: 57). The revealed preferences argument, second, was used to give risk comparison historical depth and thus to make the rhetorical component more compelling. It proceeded from the assumption that there is a direct relation between compliant behaviour and acceptable risk, so that what an individual, group or society is willing to accept as a risk can be inferred from observable past behaviour. Past behaviour reveals genuine risk preferences, and to the extent that past behaviour is compliant it is indicative of acceptable levels of risk. Risk analysts believed that with such a demonstration they were in a position to persuade the public to adopt new technological innovations and to accept the risks entailed by them.

As regards the second phase of the risk discourse, it is important to note that by embarking on the comparative risk approach the experts unintentionally recognized the entry of the public and its organized form, and thus brought about a change in the discursive context. In the preceding risk assessment debate, the basic issue was the mastery and control of hazards accompanying new technology. At this stage, the very approach adopted by the experts, both theoretically and methodologically, implied the necessity of taking into account the response of those affected by a given risk rather than leaving it up to the experts alone to determine it decisionistically. Inadvertently, they raised the question of the social or collective acceptability of risk. A spate of publications sporting either 'acceptance' or 'acceptability of risk' in their titles appeared at this stage and continued for some time (Douglas 1986). This issue not only came to characterize this phase of the risk discourse, but also forced the dynamic of the discourse toward its next phase.

The strategic sense of the risk comparison-revealed preferences approach was to allow the experts to retain the initiative by fixing on objective risk levels and thereby to lead the opposition and public to accept risks. Yet a barrage of criticism, which started almost immediately, exposed both the logical and ethical flaws of the experts' argumentation. The critics, among them psychologists (Slovic et al. 1979) and risk researchers (Otway and Cohen 1975; Covello et al. 1982), pointed out that what was actually at stake was less what people had come to accept than what they really wanted. Rather than a matter of actual levels of risk, it was one of how risks are being perceived. Being aware that the older objectivistic risk research had the undesirable side-effect of provoking uncertainty, scepticism, mistrust and even anger among members of the public, the critics envisaged a new departure that could assuage the increasingly strained relations among those who produce, regulate and bear technological risks. Of the two orientations that were possible here, the psychological approach gained currency and would play a leading role in the third phase of the risk discourse. The remaining sociological and political approach, which is concerned less with the individual than with society, the legitimacy of risk decisions and decision-makers, and the kind of society in which we want to live, had to wait for a more favourable opportunity to make an acknowledged contribution to the discourse. Examples of the latter approach dating from the 1960s are Habermas (1971) and Touraine's (1971) incisive and subterraneously influential analyses of science, technology, politics and protest.

Third phase: public concern and the problem of risk perception

The third phase of the risk discourse was inaugurated, not by an expert dispute about scientific or technical questions, but by the growing criticism and opposition to new technology and its consequences and side-effects. At the time, therefore, a shift from a technical-economic dispute to a conflict of values and worldviews was clearly perceptible. While the newness and magnitude of the nuclear risk weighed heavily with many, it became apparent in the course of time that the nuclear power issue came to function as a symbol for the problems of the late twentieth-century scientific-technological, industrial, consumer society. When global environmental problems such as the global commons and water and air pollution became agenda items in the late 1960s and early 1970s, therefore, the new social movements and the public did not have any difficulties seeing the relation between the different issues. All embodied dangers, hazards or threats, albeit to different degrees, that formed the correlate of the 'anxiety' (Luhmann 1989: 127), 'dread' (Slovic et al. 1979) or 'pain' (Offe 1986: 108) experienced by members of society. Some suggest that this is the very same emotional anxiety, ironically, that inspires the rational expert perspective (Wynne 1989a). But it should be noted that only certain sections of the population possessed the necessary action orientations and motivation to support or join the newly formed social movements of the time. They were those who were subjected to people processing through administration and planning, including risk research, and consequently underwent a learning process which allowed them to experience open contingency and the permanent possibility of anxiety (Eder 1986; Halfmann 1988). Rather than just being a motivating and orienting factor of certain participants, however, anxiety began to frame this phase of the risk discourse. Not only public criticism and opposition could be linked to it, but equally also the new directions taken by the experts. Approaching it from the vantage point of crisis theory, Habermas (1976) pinpointed, among other things, the perceived problem of a precarious ecological balance as stimulating a 'legitimation crisis', a public questioning of assumptions and institutions which solicited counter-strategies from risk analysts and authorities.

Gradually building up since the early 1960s in the United States, criticism, opposition and environmental consciousness made their appearance also in other western countries. By the late 1960s and the early 1970s, these phenomena found support in an influential train of argumentation that used the population biological and ecological concept of 'carrying capacity' to project a graphic image of looming tragedy. The predicament of humankind was that there were definite limits to growth beyond which scientific, technological, industrial society was already moving to such an extent that it began to reveal itself as unsustainable. This line of argumentation about unavoidable limits or finite resources, so-called 'survivalism' (Dryzek 1997: 23), drew the apocalyptic horizon of environmentalism and provided a focal point of public anxiety. It was forcefully, even sensationally, advanced through such metaphors as 'the tragedy of the commons' (Hardin 1968), the 'population bomb' (Ehrlich 1968), 'ecological economic thermodynamics' (Georgescu-Roegen 1971), 'limits to growth' (Meadows et al. 1972) and 'steady-state economics' (Daly 1977). By contrast with the projection of imminent tragedy, the experts were quick to propound counter-arguments of abundance and ingenuity.

On the one hand, the experts sought to refute the assumption of the finite capacity of the planet to support life and, on the other, they wished to expose the reputedly illiberal, authoritarian and potentially even tyrannical political philosophy of some of the ecologically minded. Pitting abundance against scarcity, their alternative was a combination of cornucopianism and Prometheanism (Dryzek 1997). Whereas the former conjures up nature as an unlimited storehouse of resources by means of the mythological image of a goat's horn overflowing with fruits, the latter draws on the mythological figure of the demigod who stole fire from Olympus to portray humans as capable of finding ingenious solutions to any problems. The fact that, besides technological innovation, the market mechanism and the invisible hand were assumed to be basic givens, explains why economists played the leading role in advancing this counterattack. The core of the economic argument is price as the measure of scarcity. Thus Barnett and Morse (1963) showed by means of long-term trends that the real price of natural resources keeps falling and that such resources are in effect becoming more abundant with time, and in Britain Beckerman (1974) defended the projection of economic growth into an indefinite future. With the publication of his *The Ultimate Resource* in 1981, Simon (1996) established himself as the leading American proponent of the cornucopian-Promethean school, and in collaboration with Kahn three years later produced one of the best known of its documents (Simon and Kahn 1984). During the 1980s, particularly under President Reagan, this school had a huge impact on American environmental policy, leading to the disabling of essential Environmental Protection Agency (EPA) regulatory functions and a reversal of US commitment to global environmental accords. Judging by its energy policies and its reaction to the Kyoto Agreement on Global Warming and the UN Biological Weapons Treaty, this seems to be repeating itself under the George W. Bush administration. The tug-of-war continues. On the one hand, economic optimists still press their argument in terms of the pricing system. On the other, environmentalists retort that their assumptions conceal the fact that market pricing provides a systematic incentive to producers to impose negative externalities on the environment, thus lowering their costs by causing pollution, hazards and risks (Yearley 1996; Jacobs 1997).

Besides engaging with survivalism, the experts followed a second strategy more closely associated with risk research in response to the rise of public criticism and social movements. Initially, it took the form of survey research on both sides of the Atlantic, but subsequently it was transformed into much more sophisticated psychological studies. Survey research into the attitudes and opinions of the public (Hohenemser et al. 1977; Renn 1984; Evers and Nowotny 1987) was instigated mainly by private initiative in the United States and Canada and by the state and the Commission in Europe. Invariably, the starting point was the misgivings of managers and politicians about public attitudes and the arguments mustered to articulate public anxiety and criticism – for instance, in voter referenda such as the California initiative of 1976 calling for a public decision on the effectiveness of all safety systems. The surveys concentrated mainly on the issue of nuclear energy technology, but some attention was also given to problems attaching to technology more generally and to the relation between technology and the environment. As research subjects served representative sections of the population or people resident in the vicinity of operating or planned nuclear power plants, but at times protest movements were also included. Many studies showed that there was a certain correspondence between the respective positions assumed by the public and experts on what makes for anxiety and uncertainty. Major themes and expectations animating the public were precisely those brought to the fore by expert debates about risk assessment and social acceptability. At the same time, however, the surveys revealed that the public discourse covered a broader range of issues than could be attributed to the influence of the experts. A cultural dynamic involving collective learning was at work. It not only transformed action orientations and values, the perception of dangers and the evaluation of scientific-technical progress, but also conditioned the formation of voluntary associations and social movements willing to jettison conventional political behaviour in favour of protest (Inglehart 1977; Touraine 1981, 1983; Habermas 1984, 1987). Some were convinced that they could demonstrate this fundamental shift (Dunlap and van Liere 1978). It separates the traditional syndrome of commitments to mastery of nature, abundance, growth, progress, prosperity, science and technology, private property rights and a laissez-faire economy from the new worldview rejecting anthropocentrism and stressing limits to growth, a steady-state economy and a balance of nature.

Corresponding to the conflict between cornucopian-Prometheanism and survivalism, or between the 'Dominant Social Paradigm' and the 'New Environmental Paradigm', studies on both sides of the Atlantic found that the evaluation of technology went in two distinct directions, depending on cultural orientations and values (Evers and Nowotny 1987). For instance, those who were positively disposed toward economic growth exhibited a willingness to accept nuclear power plants, whereas those who put a premium on environmental protection had a predilection for rejecting nuclear technology. Another important finding of the surveys concerned the confidence and trust of the public in experts. Many studies showed that the degree of public confidence and trust in those making technical decisions was not high by any standard. The public perceived a connection between economic interests and scientific-technological development and implementation, and expressed a preference for an increase in public participation, albeit not without an appreciation of the relative powerlessness of the public. Whereas 'anxiety' and 'uncertainty' were frequently used words in the third phase of the risk discourse, the increasing appeal to 'participation' since the mid-1970s is indicative of the growth and impact of the environmental movement. The public and organizations emanating from it became increasingly aware not only of technological hazards, but also of decision-makers and established power structures.

In the course of the 1970s, risk research underwent a significant development that became virtually synonymous with the third phase of the risk discourse. Psychological research into the perception of risk and judgments associated with risk-related options became the order of the day. Until the early 1980s, consequently, psychometric analysts (Otway and Fishbein 1976; Slovic et al. 1979) largely dominated risk research. This new departure arose due to a number of different considerations. First, risk experts increasingly appreciated the impossibility of establishing criteria of social acceptability and thus shifted their attention to the perception of risk. Second, psychologists proposed to compensate for the methodological limitations and superficiality of opinion surveys by developing attitudinal and cognitive methods of inquiry. Whereas the former would clarify the factors underlying attitudes toward technology and classify them into different groups, the latter involved a search for mental models and modes of thinking predisposing individuals toward different ways of perceiving and evaluating technology. A final consideration is of a political rather than a scientific or methodological kind, as later revealed by two disillusioned risk researchers. They realized that 'risk research, especially in the area of risk perception, is being used . . . as a tool in a discourse . . . whose hidden agenda is the legitimacy of decision-making institutions' (Otway and Thomas 1982: 69).

In the face of growing public anxiety, criticism, resistance and social movement activity, researchers took the psychology of the technology opposition as their new object of investigation. Both attitudinal and cognitive research were aimed at discovering why the public was unwilling or incapable of incorporating the objective analysis of technological risks into its own perceptions and judgements. The research proceeded from assumptions that public perception was based on misunderstanding, error, biased experience, lack of information, ignorance or on fundamentalism, mob rule and even malice. These assumptions found expression in a more or less pronounced elitism, arrogance and contempt toward the public, which often continued to persist in such bodies as the Royal Society (Wynne 1989b) and the European Commission (Wheale and McNally 1993). In the course of time, the experts' strategy of playing their own purported rationality out against the irrationality of the public became a topic of extensive criticism and proved to be one of the major mechanisms responsible for the erosion of public confidence and trust in institutions and decision-makers.

However meaningful the psychometric research, it soon became apparent that both its methodological approach of psychological reduction and its covert strategy of symbolic politics were limited, if not in error. On the one hand, the supposition of an ignorant or irrational public led risk experts to proceed to a set of related approaches, all aimed at stimulating learning processes which would bring the public round to accepting given risks. These approaches, from the provision of scientific advice through scientific literacy to educational programmes, were later consolidated under the title of 'risk communication' (Plough and Krimsky 1987) and implemented on both sides of the Atlantic, but the results were as dismal as ever. The public

remained unmoved, the basic problem being the inability of risk commun-
icators to grasp the necessity of replacing top-down decisionistic, scientistic,
technocratic, bureaucratic or educational communication by a constructive
debate among all those involved in a risk controversy (Leiss 1996; Fischhoff
1998). On the other hand, the psychological reduction of complex cultural
and social phenomena allowed the criticisms of social scientists with a perspective broader than the psychological one, such as anthropologists, sociologists and political scientists, to be heard and taken seriously for the first
time. Appreciating the context dependence of risk perception, these social
scientists understood the impossibility of making sense of complex, culturally structured social processes from a psychological perspective. Among
these processes are the mobilization of social movements, the formation of
collective identities, the transformation of social problems into collectively
recognized issues, the logics and dynamics of controversies and social conflicts, and the social construction of reality in the sense of the transposition
of perceptions, values and actions into properties of society. Although a
tradition of sociological critique of science and technology represented by
Gehlen, Schelsky, Marcuse and Habermas was waiting in the wings, it was
an anthropologist (Douglas and Wildavsky 1982), assisted by a risk analyst,
who initially succeeded in capturing the attention. Not only did Douglas
confront risk research directly in its own terms, attacking its individualistic
and abstract context-independent assumptions, but also she put forward an
imaginative and for many a convincing cultural theory which showed how
perception is filtered by available value, orientation and attribution systems. Disillusioned risk researchers (Otway and Thomas 1982; Otway 1987),
who knew that risk research dominated by experts had ended in failure,
sensed that even more than such ahistorical cultural structures were at stake.
But it was only after the passionate appeal of Short (1984), the then president of the American Sociological Association, to transform risk research
sociologically that sociology gained entry to the risk discourse and started
to play a significant role in it. The anthropological and sociological broadening of the risk debates, which followed in the wake of the entry of the
public and social movements, coincided with the transition from the third
to the fourth phase of the risk discourse.

Fourth phase: full-scale public risk discourse

During the 1980s a remarkable turn took place in the risk discourse. The
change was underway already in the late 1970s and early 1980s, but the year
of the Chernobyl disaster, 1986, graphically marks the turning point. It
was during this period that the differences, antagonisms, conflicts, anxiety
and acute uncertainty caused by the breakdown of generally shared, taken-
for-granted assumptions about nature, social institutions, science, technology, expertise and progress were for the first time mediated and to a
degree mitigated. Increasingly, risk researchers recognized that objectified

risks had to be seen in relation to the culturally structured, social perception of risk, and that this implied that the relevance of a different form of knowledge, the social knowledge represented by the public and social movements, had to be acknowledged besides expert knowledge. In 1977, some leading risk researchers found it possible after a survey of the situation to conclude:

> Our immediate prognosis is for extension rather than diminution of the opposition to nuclear technology. . . . Our own bias is to keep the nuclear option open, but to proceed cautiously; to press vigorously for solutions to immediate problems; but to forgo at this time the implementation of plutonium recycle and the breeder.
>
> (Hohenemser et al. 1977: 33)

Another leading risk expert even saw fit to submit that 'what counts as fact is conditioned by political, organizational, and peer pressure' and, further, that 'the true experts on questions of value regarding the risks of technology are the people whose lives are affected' (Otway 1987: 125). Rather than remaining caught up in the vicious circle of the expression of anxiety, the fundamentalist moralization of the risk issue and the radical rejection of technology, correspondingly, social movements embarked on the search for sovereignty and demanded participation in decision-making (Halfmann 1988). As is confirmed by developments internationally (Morrison 1980; Schnaiberg 1983; Eyerman and Jamison 1991; Fréchet and Wörndl 1993; Eder 1996a; Kriesi and Giugni 1996), the movements entered a phase of institutionalization and legitimation in which they exhibited a new orientation. Their institutionalization coincided with a significant transformation of the public sphere (Eder 1995, 1996b). Instead of outright antagonism and conflict, they were increasingly drawn into discursive conflict with both opponents and regulators. This is also the period during which changes in the state became visible (Jessop 1994; Habermas 1996). As regards its form and function, a shift occurred from the social welfare state to the security or preventive state. Being hollowed out and weakened by the dual process of localization and globalization, it was increasingly compelled to deal with collective dangers over and above taking care of order and just distribution.

The fact that the participants at this stage in the risk discourse were able, if not to settle their dispute, then at least to continue it with resources allowing reasoning, indicates the emergence of new enabling and legitimizing cultural forms as well as new practices in the transformed public sphere. These developments provided the conditions for late-twentieth-century and current endeavours to deal collectively with an open history and a higher degree of contingency, uncertainty and ambivalence. The new practices are communicatively conflictual ones constituting what came to be called 'the social construction of reality', including in particular 'creative', 'participatory', 'discursive' or 'deliberative democracy' (Burns and Ueberhorst 1988; Dryzek 1990; Habermas 1996; Held 1996). The new cultural forms include what the Brundtland Report publicized internationally as the officially sanctioned yardstick of 'sustainable development' (World Commission on Environment and Development 1987; Redclift 1992; Szerszynski et al. 1996), as well as the new concepts of rights, citizenship and collective responsibility associated with and extending it (Jonas 1984; Apel 1988; Frankenfeld 1992; Galtung 1994; Christoff 1996a). Significantly for the opening years of the fourth phase of the risk discourse, sustainable development succeeded in interrelating the two discursive strands that so harshly conflicted during the preceding phase, survivalism representing ecology and cornucopian-Prometheanism representing the economy. Rather than excluding all differences, tensions and conflict, however, it channelled them as early as the late 1980s into the competing and conflicting variants of 'ecological modernization' (Jänicke 1985; Hajer 1995) and 'reflexive modernization' (Beck 1992; Beck et al. 1994). In this field, we witness the continuing struggle between the experts and regulators, on the one hand, and non-governmental organizations (NGOs), social movements and significant sections of the public, on the other. The former often seek to secure and repair the acceptance of the status quo without asking any serious questions, while the latter, sometimes penetratingly and at other times too rhetorically, question the relations, forms of power, social control and supposed legitimacy involved. Whenever new developments take place, new issues appear or new actors enter, the logic of discourse in the new public sphere divides the participants and pits the antagonists against each other in highly polarized debates before it brings about any coordination.

Through their criticism of the psychology of risk perception, Douglas and Wildavsky (1982) made a decisive contribution to the opening and development of the fourth phase of the risk discourse. They showed that, far from being individual, both perception and judgement are mediated by variable cultural patterns that are themselves tied to distinct structural forms of social organization. Depending on whether located in the institutional culture of the market (such as business people), bureaucracy (for example state regulators) or a collective (such as members of the environmental movement), people entertain a particular set of values, orientations and goals which leads them to perceive and evaluate risks in their own distinctive way. In confronting risks, each group defends the particular moral order or societal state it regards as worthy of maintaining or bringing into being. This cultural anthropological intervention in the discourse proved highly meaningful and productive. By systematically identifying the social and cultural structures that serve as selection frameworks for different social groups, it made possible an appreciation of unavoidable differences and divisions in any and every society, and thus also of the highly visible battle fronts drawn around the risk issue in late-twentieth-century society. These insights into risk perception and selection had the effect of broadening the discourse and allowing the different participants to assume more justifiable positions. They were able to improve their understanding both of themselves and their partners and opponents – sometimes, indeed, in the service of refining their own strategic action. Such improvement of self- and mutual understanding and thus the possibility of effective communication, for instance between engineers and social scientists, even became the goal of representatives of the Douglas school (James and Thompson 1989). For this reason, Douglas's cultural theory has been taken up enthusiastically in the UK by both the Royal Society and regulators (Löfstedt and Frewer 1998: 6–8). But it has also been criticized and seriously challenged, both theoretically and empirically.

Sociologically, at any rate, the limitations of the contribution of the Douglas school were immediately apparent. While acknowledging Douglas's contribution, James Short (1984) briefly stated and anticipated a number of important criticisms. He found Douglas and Wildavsky's view of 'sectarian voluntary associations' such as the environmental movement inadequate since they overemphasized confrontation, polarization and conflict to the neglect of the role of such associations in mediation, social integration, social change, cultural and social pluralization, and democratization. Short also took exception to Douglas and Wildavsky's politically inspired evaluation of such phenomena – their 'ideological commitment' and 'advocacy' of a partisan position (Short 1984: 717, 721). He further considered Douglas's idea of risk as a 'social construction' as falling far short of its sociological potential. He therefore reverted to the sociological tradition of 'the social construction of social problems' which combines an analysis of the 'claims-making' activities of interest groups and social movements with accounting for the 'emergence of social conditions as a social problem' (Short 1984: 720). Of special sociological concern here is the process whereby those who define a situation from the perspective of very different interests nevertheless find it possible to come together in their search for solutions to mutually threatening conditions. Far beyond Douglas's static and under-complex anthropological position, Short proposed the extension of social constructivist analysis by the inclusion of an analysis of the mass media. Finally, he also suggested that the cultural dimension of social constructivism needs to be developed, perhaps by learning from cognitive psychology's concern with 'classifications of the world' and analysing the 'framing' of social problems on the basis not of purely technical but rather the much broader 'social rationality' (Short 1984: 720, 718–19).

Risk researchers and analysts indeed did not leave the new avenues opened by Douglas and Short unexplored. Characteristic of the fourth phase of the risk discourse are various attempts, beginning in the 1980s, to go beyond the confines of traditional risk analysis – from technical calculation to social mediation, from expert accuracy to social construction in public discourse. Mazur (1987) drew attention both to the effect of the sheer amount of news coverage in the media on public reactions and to the agenda-setting function fulfilled by the media in making particular issues salient to the public. Kasperson et al. (1988) proposed a broader framework, incorporating the media, which can be used to account for the degree of social amplification that a risk receives under given conditions. The media allow the selection of a risk-related event and its interaction with psychological, social, institutional and cultural factors or processes in ways that can either amplify or attenuate the individual and social perception of the risk involved. From the social constructivist perspective, the mechanism of amplification and attenuation of risk not only is too simple and too static, but also lacks a grasp of the processes of social interaction underlying it. This position indeed surfaced among risk researchers (Gould et al. 1988). Yet the full appreciation of what is meant by the fact that the participants in any risk debate entertain fundamentally different values and priorities, and that risk is socially constructed in the process of the discursive interrelation of their competing and conflicting definitions, had to await social scientific developments far beyond the tradition of risk analysis. As part of such a broader approach, a trend emerged according to which social construction was regarded as a process whereby society deals with uncertainty (Evers and Nowotny 1987) and ambivalence (Bauman 1992).

By calling for the sociological 'demystification' and 'transformation' of risk analysis and the creation of a 'sociology of risk' instead, Short (1984) above all pinpointed the most basic limitation of Douglas's position. It suffers from the fact that it remains under the spell of the tradition of risk analysis that has its roots in classical safety research and is guided by the question of a socially acceptable level of safety. What is sociologically required, instead, is a shift from the safety question to the question of the societal conditions of the constitution of risk. Of all the sociologists who started working in the area of risk in the late 1970s and 1980s, Beck is the one who grasped this most clearly. His rightly famous book, *Risk Society* (1992), which should be read together with its sequel *Ecological Politics in an Age of Risk* (1995), is squarely focused on the conditions of the constitution of risk in contemporary society. It had a transformative impact on the social sciences, and it reshaped both ecological debates in political, NGO and social movement circles and the broader public risk discourse. As a best-seller, *Risk Society* contributed to consciousness-raising about risk, science and technology, the environment, and the nature of contemporary society among large numbers of the lay public. Beck's contribution thus marks the terminus of the trajectory leading from classical safety research and the expert debate about risk assessment in the 1950s and 1960s to a full-fledged public discourse about risks and risk-related matters. This is confirmed by the publications of a diametrically opposed theorist such as Luhmann (1989, 1993) and like-minded authors such as Giddens (1990, 1991) and Eder (1993a, 1996a).

Characteristic of the fourth phase of the risk discourse is the entry of sociology along a broad front. This is clear from the fact that behind Beck's decisive intervention and those of other leading authors stands a whole complex of interrelated creative departures in sociology with interdisciplinary connections dating from the 1970s and 1980s. Together, these different strands account for the central sociological concern with social actors, communication, discourse, the logic, dynamics and structuration of such processes, the problems of conflict and consensus emerging from them, the role of the media and the public in the articulation and resolution of such problems, and the accompanying cultural and institutional innovations under conditions of increasing complexity, contingency, uncertainty and ambivalence. First of all, there is the sociology of knowledge that has been revitalized by the wide-ranging impact of Heidegger and Wittgenstein (Apel 1967; Bloor 1983) as well as later especially of Kuhn (1962; Barnes 1982; Fuller 2000). Sociologically crucial, however, was Berger and Luckmann's (1967) phenomenological and Garfinkel's (1967) ethnomethodological elaboration of the sociology of knowledge into the theory of the social construction or social negotiation of reality. Then there is the new sociology of scientific knowledge or social studies of science that inquires into the networking, social practices, ritualized behaviour, coding processes and so forth that go into the collective production of scientific knowledge (Nowotny 1973; Bloor 1976; Mendelsohn et al. 1977; Latour and Woolgar 1979; Knorr 1981; Knorr-Cetina and Mulkay 1983). The closely related sociology of technology (Perrow 1984; Pinch and Bijker 1984; MacKenzie and Wajcman 1985; Weingart 1989) should also be mentioned here. To these innovations should be added the emergence of environmental sociology (Catton and Dunlap 1978). Beck's work further exhibits the impact of the sociology of social movements, particularly its focus on the problematization of issues and on collective learning, knowledge production and identity formation (Melucci 1980; Touraine 1981; Habermas 1984, 1987; Melucci 1985), which allowed him to go well beyond the rather confining concentration of the constructivist sociology of science and technology on the micro-dimension. Above all, however, Beck continues the German tradition of critical theory. But perhaps the most characteristic core of Beck's thinking, which paradoxically at the same time is its most promising yet least developed dimension, draws on the nascent cognitive sociology of our time. Central here is the multiple cognitive transformation of the sociology of knowledge and, indeed, of sociology itself (Knorr-Cetina and Cicourel 1981) by phenomenological sociology and ethnomethodology, the new sociology of scientific knowledge, the critical theoretical (Habermas 1972, 1984, 1987; Bourdieu 1986) and systems theoretical (Luhmann 1995) communication theory of society – most of which presuppose the emergence of the cognitive sciences since the late 1950s (De Mey 1982; Varela et al. 1993; Bechtel and Graham 1998). This particular development provided the spearhead for the social sciences' proper entry into the risk discourse, and it also represents their best prospect to make an adequate contribution to that discourse as it unfolds in the future. Culturally constituted and socially effective cognitive structures not only allow connections to be established among the social, psychological and cultural levels, but also are central to the very process of social construction, while not excluding a reference to reality. The cognitive turn places the social sciences in a propitious position to develop an integrated, culturally sensitive approach to nature, the environment and risk, which alone can prevent their being made subservient to the natural sciences.

The fully developed public risk discourse had been anticipated by the explosion of communication around events such as the AEC hearings in 1971 and the Flixborough industrial accident in 1974, both of which played a significant role in the initial arousal of public concern (McGinty 1976; Hohenemser et al. 1977). But the discourse took on its proper shape only with chemical and nuclear industrial disasters such as Seveso in 1976 and Three Mile Island in 1979. Subsequently, it acquired its characteristic serrated profile, which is defined by periodic drastic increases in communication around dramatic events, due to large-scale disasters such as Bophal and Chernobyl and other accidents and events involving oil tankers, car ferries, passenger aircraft, nuclear power, environmental issues, food pollution, genetic pollution, and so on. Despite the dependence of the discourse on dramatic events and increases in communication involving different issues, however, it is by no means the case that the vicissitudes of the fickle public and media attention cycle cause important issues to disappear and to be forgotten completely (Downs 1972). A high-level shift of problem from nuclear power generation through environmental issues to biotechnology is certainly observable over time, but even as the latest issue looms ever larger, the older ones come back to life with almost predictable consistency. While the late 1960s and early 1970s saw the introduction of global environmental problems over and above nuclear energy, the former did not replace the latter as a salient issue – despite the fact that the battle against nuclear energy had been won for the time being in the United States and Germany. Not only did distrust of nuclear technology fit well with a concern about threats to the environment, but also nuclear energy was recontextualized by the new developments, with the result that it attained a special symbolic status which it retains in the discourse up to the present. The international controversy in 2000 involving Britain, Japan, Germany, Ireland and the Nordic countries about the THORP reprocessing facility at Sellafield after the revelation of the falsification of safety records at the plant is a case in point, as is the 2001 controversy about the MOX plant. Similarly, the ascendancy of biotechnology as a risk problem has by no means prevented global warming from becoming an explosive issue in the twenty-first century. The exposure of the fragility of contemporary civilization by the terrorist attacks on the United States has even redirected attention on all of these different risks at one and the same time.

The question of risk attaching to genetic engineering and, by extension, to biotechnology was initially raised in the United States after the first successful recombinant DNA experiment of 1971. While providing the kernel of the controversy that spread also to Europe, it was not until the mid-1980s that a broad public debate about the issue ensued. Contributing factors were the sharp increase in scientific research after the Asilomar conference of 1975, which ended a moratorium on experimentation, and the rapid transfer of rDNA knowledge from science to commercial firms between 1981 and 1983 (Ravetz and Brown 1989; Gottweiss 1995; Rifkin 1998). The visibility of the new technology was further enhanced by the EU providing biotechnology-specific funding under numerous programmes since 1982, and governments embarking on support programmes for applied biology and biotechnology (Wheale and McNally 1993). In the mid-1980s, the turning point of the new biology, various international and supranational bodies, such as the G7 states, the Council of International Organizations of Medical Sciences and the Council of Europe, organized conferences or established institutions and steering committees focusing on biotechnology and bioethics (Paul 1994). While observers of the British scene in the late 1980s found evidence only of an embryonic development of public reaction to the potential impacts of biotechnology (Ravetz and Brown 1989), the situation elsewhere was quite different, and in Britain it also changed in the following decade. Opposition to genetic engineering had appeared already in the United States, and in Germany the second half of the 1980s experienced an extraordinary upsurge of discussion groups, citizens' initiatives and social movements. Gottweiss (1995) talks of a wave and identifies some 60 organizations engaged in challenging the established practices and politics of genetic engineering. Internationally, a new social movement started to emerge in the 1990s in the biotechnological field focused specifically on the issue of the patenting of life – the so-called 'anti-biotechnology patents movement' (McNally and Wheale 1999). In the forefront of the articulation of public concerns, demonstrations at patent offices and international summit meetings, the drawing up of petitions and declarations, and legal challenges against patents on life were and still are such organizations as Friends of the Earth and Greenpeace. To them should be added Genetic Resources Action International (GRAIN) and Rural Advancement Foundation International (RAFI). In the UK, they are joined by the British Union for the Abolition of Vivisection, Compassion in World Farming, and No Patents on Life (McNally and Wheale 1999). The anti-risk movements have been a decisive factor in driving the various risk debates into a full-fledged public discourse. Not only do they represent the organized wing of the public who take up certain problem perceptions and judgements of the public and articulate them in the public sphere. More so than any of the other participants, whether experts or regulators, they simultaneously also proceed in such a way that they preserve and improve the public sphere itself, thus creating the conditions for being able to continue appearing in, transforming and building up the public sphere in the future.

In the last years of the twentieth century and the beginning of the new millennium, the risk discourse unfolded around a series of more or less sensational scientific and technological developments in the area of genetic engineering. They stretch from human reproductive technologies through the cloning of animals to genetically modified (GM) crops and foods. The issue of genetic pollution (Yearley 1996) at the root of the environmental and health risks posed by genetically modified crops and foods provided the focal point of perhaps the biggest and most surprising flash point around which communication concentrated and flared up dramatically. Having had their suspicion aroused by the BSE (bovine spongiform encephalopathy) fiasco in Britain, the European public, consumers, environmentalists and social movements focused their attention on the US biotechnology industry which was forcing its way into Europe. Previously, names such as Marcoule, Wyhl, Gorleben, Windscale/Sellafield, Harrisburg and Chernobyl were regarded as the symbols of the most embittered social conflicts in advanced modern society. At the turn of the millennium, this symbolic quality accrued to the biotechnology industry, particularly the giant Missouri-based Monsanto corporation which was unexpectedly brought to its knees by the European anti-genetic engineering movements, media and consumers (Borger 1999). A somewhat subtler dimension which drew sections of the public other than consumers into the discourse is the political one.

The early 1990s witnessed an increasing awareness of the democratic deficit in the EU and its key institutions (Paul 1994). In the biotechnological area, particularly bioethics or human technology, it arose in the wake of the Science and Technology Options Assessment report on *Bioethics in Europe* of 1992 and the circulation of the preliminary draft of the Council of Europe's *Bioethics Convention* in 1993. Although the European Parliament in 1989 called for an independent commission, the committee that eventually reported on research and development in genetic and cellular manipulations largely consisted of prominent proponents of bioethics. This raised questions about the purported neutrality of the committee and its ability to maintain recognized ethical standards limiting medical research. The report also brought the powerlessness and fragility of the European Parliament into focus. The latter had to defer to experts, some of whom are expressly disparaging of Europe's democratic institutions (Byk 1992, 1999), and apparently engaged in its own disassembly by participating – by contrast with its stance in 1989 – in the biogenetic redefinition of human rights. A similar light was shed on the Parliament in its relation to the Council of Europe by the practices surrounding the drafting of the preliminary Bioethics Convention. Not to mention strenuous efforts to avoid attracting public attention, documents were circulated in closed circles excluding even parliamentarians (Paul 1994). More recently, the *Guardian* made a number of related revelations. Not only did the then US president, Bill Clinton, on behalf of the corporate world put pressure on the European Commission and the then holder of the EU presidency, Tony Blair, to open up Britain and the rest of Europe to US genetically modified crops and food. At the same time, Blair agreed to the US demand through a procedure that excluded his cabinet colleagues responsible for the environment and GM crops from participating, and thus opened himself to having such labels as 'corporate prime minister' and 'US corporate stooge' attached to him (Hencke and Evans 2000; Monbiot 2000). More generally, the tension and conflict displayed by these various cases is a duplication of the continuing tug of war between ecological modernization and reflexive modernization which is so characteristic of the fourth phase of the risk discourse. On the one hand, experts and economic and political actors pursue the techno-corporatist advancement of the biogenetic programme. On the other, they are questioned and opposed by significant sections of the public, who register concern about the implications and possible consequences of this programme, and by voluntary associations and social movements, who publicly communicate, moralize and politicize this concern.

The discursively important developments mentioned above called forth also a reflexive self-questioning on the part of social scientists. Recent developments prompted the question of whether contemporary society is not being reideologized by means of the new biology. Some saw social processes, the subject matter of the social sciences, as increasingly being reconceptualized in biogenetic terms and, concurrently, their political regulation as being progressively understood as being possible by biotechnical means (Paul 1994: 75; Jäger et al. 1997). Under these new conditions, Rifkin (1998) thought that he could already identify a paradigm change in sociology being spearheaded by sociobiology. According to him, advances in genetic engineering are accompanied by the development of a 'sociology of the gene' or 'eugenic sociology' – a new sociology that is helping to create the cultural climate and conditions for the emergence of a 'bio-society' (Jäger et al. 1997). The penetrating yet wide-ranging nature of these various questions suggests that they possess a significance that goes far beyond the social sciences. They certainly force sociologists to ask what the proper role of sociology in contemporary society is. As proponents of the sociology of the risk society, in any event, they make a small yet by no means negligible contribution to the risk discourse. The question, however, is the precise nature of this contribution.

Summary

In the phase-like unfolding of the risk discourse, to summarize and conclude, the shift at the top-line thematic level from nuclear power through global environmental problems to biotechnology was less important than the progressive broadening of the discourse. From a restricted and exclusive expert ethos of risk calculation and assessment it shifted to a more open ethos of wide-ranging participation in the discursive construction of risk through public communication. Rather than being exclusively dominated by experts and regulators, the risk discourse has been shaped increasingly by social movements and the public. Over and above expert modes of communication of restricted inner access or mobilization of the public through paternalistic risk communication, the movements and public took initiative from the outside to contribute significantly to the generation of a public discourse about risk. This meant not only the breakdown of a hierarchical and linear mode of reasoning and modelling, which was based on the epistemological connection between determination and prediction, but also a confrontation with an emergent reality of intricately networked processes with non-linear dynamics. Both a higher degree of complexity in the process of the constitution and organization of society and much greater contingency now asserted themselves. As regards the logic of the discourse, or the unfolding of its structures, we witness the gradual questioning and erosion of the initially taken-for-granted techno-corporatist assumptions of scientists, technologists, corporations and regulators, followed by pronounced anxiety and uncertainty and an extended, rather stark, conflict during the 1970s and 1980s between social groups adhering to opposing sets of assumptions. It is only in the wake of the increased mediation of the conflicting groups and communicative structures in the new public sphere on the basis of the emergence of new cultural and institutional forms that the conflict has become more channelled and transformed into somewhat more constructive contestation. Since the logic of discourse turns on an ongoing process involving division besides coordination, however, highly polarized debates around new developments can nevertheless be expected periodically. The unfolding of the phases of the risk discourse was accompanied by different disciplines and theoretical approaches. The social sciences entered only relatively late. The highly discursive and mediated nature of the current phase, to which is central a process of contestation over the social construction of reality, not only maps out various new substantive tasks for sociology, but also offers it the opportunity to reinvent its various functions under novel conditions.

Having offered an overview of the risk discourse, it is to a more systematic analysis of its theoretically important structural dimensions in the following chapters that I now turn.

2

Background theories and frameworks of understanding

The unfolding of the risk discourse since the late 1950s, as we have seen, was accompanied by different ways of thinking and, by extension, a series of different social scientific approaches. The first tentative contributions were made in the 1960s and 1970s by innovation and diffusion theorists and survey researchers respectively. Their work assisted risk analysts in their attempt, which later proved abortive, to facilitate the social acceptance of risks. Social scientists were able to make their rightful contribution, however, only when problems of conflict and consensus intensified to such an extent that attention had to be given to the risk issue in its wider cultural, social and political context. This became possible in the late 1970s and 1980s, so that by the end of the decade social scientific contributions started to increase quite dramatically.

At this stage, it is possible to present the major theoretical directions that grew out of this social scientific efflorescence – on the one hand, the critical theory of the risk society and, on the other, the sceptical theory of the contingent society. Before doing so in the next chapter, however, I propose to review the general background theories and epistemological frameworks that inform social scientific work on, indeed, any thinking about the environment, risk and the risk society. This will allow us to paint a clear picture of the major theoretical directions, but by bringing out their basic assumptions it will at the same time also help us to obtain a more detailed and considered understanding of the differences and clashes within and between these directions. Most important among the general background theories are human ecology, rational choice, cultural theory, systems theory and the theory of modernity. The epistemological assumptions made by social scientists vary between realism and constructivism, which leaves us with the task of having to disentangle the confusing contemporary debate.

Background theories: from human ecology to the theory of modernity

Human ecology

The oldest and broadest of the general theories providing a background for the contemporary social scientific concern with the relation between society and nature in general and risk in particular is what is known as human ecology. The concept of ecology, which etymologically derives from the Greek *oikos* meaning household, was formulated by the German evolutionary biologist Ernst Haeckel in the nineteenth century (Onions 1976). It named a new discipline that studied the relations of plants and animals with their habitat. Some twenty-five years later, the concept was incorporated into sociology, the first social science to do so, and applied to human beings in relation to their habitat. On this basis, the leading sociologist of the Chicago School, Robert E. Park (1936), proposed to call the new branch of sociology 'human ecology'. Rather than the relation of human beings with nature and the problems resulting from their impact upon it, however, it formed the core of the Chicago School's urban sociology, being concerned with the social and spatial movement of people in their urban habitats. Although human ecology was conceived in terms of the ecological model, processes such as migration, social differentiation and segregation thus in effect distracted the attention from deeper and more pervasive relations with the environment. The Chicago School of geography, on the other hand, sought to analyse both the impact of natural hazards and the reactions of those affected by them (White 1945). Despite its obvious limitations, the tradition of human ecology kept alive a fecund starting point for a new sociological departure in the 1970s.

The basic idea of human ecology was that of an ecological interrelation between social actions, processes and institutions and the human environment, and the need to explain the formation of social patterns, institutions, values and lifestyles. Under the changing conditions of the early 1970s, this tradition provided Catton and Dunlap (1978) and Dunlap and van Liere (1978) with a reference point to conceive of a new human ecology or an environmental or ecological sociology. At a more specific level, it allowed them to formulate ideal-typical models of the past and present that together shed light on contemporary social change. According to them, a fundamental change of beliefs, values and attitudes, a change of worldview or paradigm, is well underway. Up until the 1960s, a constellation of beliefs, values and attitudes prevailed in the United States and other western countries that they call the 'Dominant Western Worldview' or the 'Human Exemptionalist Paradigm'. Based on deep-seated anthropocentric assumptions according to which nature exists solely for human use, this worldview included a belief in abundance and progress, devotion to growth and prosperity, faith in science and technology, and commitment to a laissez-faire economy, limited state intervention and private property rights. By contrast, the 'New Environmental Paradigm', which emerged in the 1960s and was displacing the traditionally dominant paradigm, is made up of a series of novel ideas. Among them are limits to growth, steady-state economy, balance of nature, and so forth. According to Dunlap and some of his associates (Dunlap and van Liere 1978; Dunlap and Mertig 1996), this new paradigm has gained considerable popularity in academic and intellectual circles as well as widespread acceptance among the general public. In the form of environmental consciousness, indeed, the new ecological understanding has recently spread so far beyond the borders of rich western countries that it can legitimately be considered a global phenomenon.

Although its proponents have largely confined themselves to programmatic statements and research on attitude and value change and the spread of environmental consciousness, the new human ecology has enjoyed a relatively wide reception. This was facilitated by a noted critical discussion (Buttel 1986, 1987). Its major impact has been on the institutionalization of the new sub-discipline of environmental sociology. The theoretical core of human ecology is the relationship and interchange between ecological conditions and cultural and social patterning in different spatio-temporal contexts. In the 1990s, the Uppsala school extended human ecology and is at present pursuing it further (Dietz et al. 1990; Burns and Dietz 1992, 1997). In its latest version, a promising degree of refinement has been achieved by combining environmental constraints and selectivity, both physical and social, with 'bounded constructivism' through the incorporation of cognitively structured and knowledgeable agency (Burns and Dietz 1997). A comparable step has been taken in the context of British critical realism. Basing himself on Bhaskar (1978, 1989), Sayer (1984), Benton (1985) and the early Marx, Dickens (1992) proposed to develop a 'green social theory' which seeks to re-establish a connection between society, nature, human actors as organisms with natural histories, and historically developing deep mental structures. Both these schools bring into focus in a new way important matters pertaining to human ecology as a background theory – questions about the relations among culture, society and nature, about creative human agency, about cognitive structures, and about evolutionary theory.

Rational choice

If human ecology adopts a holistic perspective embracing society and nature, rational choice decomposes this whole in favour of emphasizing the individual rational actor, or *homo economicus*. While rational choice theory forms the foundation of contemporary economic theory, it has been incorporated into sociology (Coleman 1993) and provides a range of widely employed arguments in the debates about environmental risks. It seeks both to explain the emergence of contemporary environmental problems and to propose solutions to them. On the basis of a parsimonious model of rational individual action, it spells out a range of interaction models that are used to analyse the increasingly complex relations between actors. Central to this approach is a concern with the aggregation at the macro-level of largely unintended consequences of actions executed by individuals at the micro-level. Environmental problems and risks are thus portrayed as the result of unavoidable dilemmas or paradoxical social situations in which the self-interested actions of the rationally calculating actors create conditions potentially affecting all the participants in a negative way. Action gives rise to an external effect that clouds the utility of other actors without any possibility of regulating or neutralizing the impact on the context of social relations.

Analogous to such a 'prisoner's dilemma', the structure of decision-making prevailing in contemporary market institutions generates wide-ranging ecological problems of the over-exploitation of freely accessible yet simultaneously scarce resources, such as air, water, fish, and so on. This dilemma of common goods is what is known as 'the tragedy of the commons' (Hardin 1968). A further dimension of such a social dilemma is that, while it involves an inescapable process of collective self-injury, the individual remains powerless in the face of the impacting external effects. Individual efforts directed at an external effect (such as leaving the car in the garage) not only have high costs for the individual (time and money involved in taking the train), but also achieve virtually nothing in terms of collective utility (reduction of CO_2 gases). It is by thus starting from the structural conditions of paradoxical social situations that rational choice theory explains the social production of local and global environmental problems, hazards and risks. Likewise, solutions to such problems are also devised on this basis. Typically, this takes the form of the internalization of external effects by means of market economic instruments. The best known example is environmental or green tax. The basic assumption of this approach turns on a high degree of confidence in the efficacy of the market. Although this confidence was considerably strengthened by the collapse of the planned economies of the former Eastern Bloc countries, the fixation on the market also reveals the limits of rational choice theory.

On rational choice theory's basic premises, it will never be possible to eliminate socially produced problems completely. Nevertheless, various authors (Smith 1982; Axelrod 1984; Elster 1989) have demonstrated in extension of rational choice theory that there is more to society than rationally calculating individuals who face social dilemmas and in response give rise to a process of collective self-injury. Over and above uncooperative individual decisions, there is evidence of cooperative relations among individuals. Their existence points toward evolutionarily stable strategies which themselves presuppose social institutions and cultural rules. These underpinnings of cooperation could stretch from externally imposed regulations or sanctionable conventions to more deeply embedded cognitive structures and cultural models. Once we acknowledge the latter end of this continuum, we burst the narrow limits of the rational choice framework.

Cultural theory

Cultural theory is a holistic approach compared to rational choice in so far as it gives pride of place not to the individual but rather to configurations of cultural patterns which make action, interaction and mutual understanding and social interpretation possible. By contrast with the holism of human ecology, where the major emphasis is on nature, however, the principal stress here is culture. Nature itself becomes something strictly cultural. Cultural theory builds on a long and unbroken yet often submerged tradition in which the formal dimension of rules is at times prioritized and at other times the substantive dimension of meaning. Douglas, a major representative of this theory in the study of risk, has sought to bring together her own selection of the classical texts in her book *Rules and Meanings* (1973). In any event, it can be traced to Kant's concern with the categories by means of which the mind comes to know reality, on the one hand, and to Hegel and Marx's shift of emphasis to action and the process of social construction, on the other. In the first part of the twentieth century, it was creatively restated by authors representing a disparate range of disciplines such as philosophy (Husserl, Heidegger, Wittgenstein, Merleau-Ponty), sociology (Durkheim, Mannheim, Schutz), anthropology (Evans-Pritchard, Malinowski), social psychology (Mead) and psychology (Bartlett, Piaget). In one way or another, these authors were interested in the cognitive structures, cultural models and knowledge that guide and give form and content to communication and social forms of life. Following upon a period of submergence, this tradition underwent an unexpected revival and more widespread reception since the 1960s. Central to this efflorescence was the insertion, through the intermediary of the sociology of science, of a phenomenologically and cognitively transformed sociology of knowledge at the very heart of sociology, and the transposition, through the intermediary of the sociology of social movements, of this cognitively transformed processual sociology from the micro-level to the macro-level of society. On this basis, social scientists could consider the structuring and organization of society in terms of knowledge in all its forms, not just epistemologically secured scientific knowledge. Simultaneously, they could also conceive of the constitution of society as a process of social construction that is given form by cognitive structures at the psychological, social and cultural level.

Depending on emphasis, the cultural theoretical perspective on environmental problems or risks takes a different direction. Where rules are emphasized, a more structural and hence more static approach is the result. Douglas's publications, which owe much to Durkheim, are exemplary of this tendency (Douglas and Wildavsky 1982; Douglas 1986, 1994). The basic assumption in this case is that what counts as a risk in a particular group is dependent on the underlying cultural structures, themselves rooted in social structures, which make available the necessary classifications, hierarchical ordering principles and knowledge by means of which the group members are able to perceive and identify the risk in question. Where meaning is emphasized instead, as in the case of phenomenological and hermeneutical approaches, the focus is on specific social groups in their unique risk contexts. Observing criteria such as age, gender, ethnicity, lifestyle or sexual identity, analysis seeks to make comprehensible the meaningfulness of the perception and definition of risk and the risk avoidance or even risk taking strategies of those involved. Although the more traditional phenomenological and hermeneutical approaches respecting the subjectivity of actors go far back to authors such as Dilthey, Husserl, Heidegger and Schutz (Luckmann 1978; Bleicher 1980), it is only very recently that social scientists have begun to undertake risk studies of this kind (Aggleton et al. 1995; Schulze 1997; Lupton 1999). There is still a third cultural theoretic approach in the literature taking up a position midway between the rule-oriented and the meaning-oriented directions. It is more concerned with change and flux in structures and meanings and at the same time sees culture as in principle imbued with power. It is for example represented by Ewald (1986, 1989, 1991; see also Dean 1999) who, inspired by Foucault (1991), adopts a post-structuralist approach to risk. He proceeds from the assumption that risk is not something in reality, but rather a category of the mind whereby human beings understand and order reality. Of first concern, therefore, are the cultural rules or forms of knowledge that make risk conceivable, such as statistics, accounting, epidemiology, management, psychology and sociology. But these forms of knowledge are always placed within the context of discourses about risk and thus seen in relation to both the techniques used to discover risks and the political rationalities and programmes employed to order, regulate and manage them. This perspective allows the appreciation of the role that risk plays in the subjection of populations to surveillance, regulation and discipline and the encouragement of individuals and communities to regulate themselves in accordance with given norms of governance.

Systems theory

Like human ecology and cultural theory, systems theory contrasts sharply with rational choice in so far as it, seeking to avoid reductionism, gives priority to larger complexes of relations and connections rather than to the individual or the actor. But the fact that it regards such complexes abstractly as a system, instead of interpreting it more substantively as either nature or culture, distinguishes systems theory from human ecology and cultural theory. At the outset, it should be stressed that very different versions of systems theory have been brought to bear on the question of risk. Some feel that systems theory's potential is yet to be more fully explored (Diekmann and Jaeger 1996). Claval (1992) points out that, although systems theory at first allowed the synthetic consideration of environment and society, it involves such complexity and such large data requirements that the results shattered the initial hopes attached to it. It should be emphasized, however, that systems theory has had a beneficial sobering effect on social theory in the past few decades. Not only did it make clear that the increase in the complexity of society has costly consequences for the dynamics of the organization of society, but also it demonstrated the need for a relational perspective on society.

While Rapoport (1996) outlined a general systems theoretical perspective on environmental sociology, other more specific versions have been put forward by social theorists. To varying degrees, the four mentioned below have been applied to an analysis of the environmental risk field. The most important and extensive contribution has been made by Luhmann in books dealing with ecological communication and risk (Luhmann 1989, 1993; see also 1990a). After having been influenced initially by Parsons's reception of general systems theory, he radically reformulated his functionalist systems theory in the early 1980s under the impact of new developments in biology and cybernetics. The result was his so-called 'autopoietic systems theory' (Luhmann 1995), which assumes the differentiation of society into function systems and then follows the processes whereby society as a social system constantly creates itself. The work of such representatives of the Uppsala school as Burns and Dietz is based on a version of systems theory that, unlike Luhmann's, makes room for human agency and transactions between agents. This is what is called the 'theory of actor-system dynamics' of which Burns's 'rule system theory' is a central component (Burns et al. 1985; Burns 1986). A third substantial systems theoretical contribution, which is highly critical of Luhmann, is Münch's (1996) comprehensive analysis of risk politics that forms part of the revitalization and extension of Parsons in the form of neo-functionalism. By contrast with autopoiesis and the autonomy of function systems, it stresses the interpenetration of the subsystems of society. Nowotny's (1996) so-called 'endosociology' is also a departure from within systems theory. Besides these four examples, it is noteworthy that there is also a pronounced element of systems theory in Beck's thinking. This was strengthened by his adoption in 1988 of Luhmann's idea of a complex self-referential system beyond control and its critical reversal under the title of 'organized irresponsibility' (Beck 1995). Perrow's (1984) demonstration that accidents are a normal rather than extraordinary feature of high-risk technology could also be mentioned under the rubric of systems theory. According to his analysis, it is incontrovertible that the systemic structure of high technology has become so complex that risk is now a constitutive feature of contemporary technical and social organization. This account represents a sociological elaboration of an aspect of the non-linear dynamics of contemporary reality.

For Luhmann (1989, 1993), ecological problems and risks derive from the form of differentiation of modern society and consequently decision-making in different function systems. Correspondingly, such problems present themselves to different function systems and cannot be dealt with at source. The increasing communication that is generated by ecological problems and risks in contemporary society attests to the fact that the future is unknowable. Despite this unnerving increase in complexity, contingency, ignorance and uncertainty, the autopoiesis of society nevertheless steams ahead. Burns and Dietz (1997) are much more specific in that they lead the production and reproduction of hazards and risks back to technologies, policies and social practices as well as to structural conditions such as competitive systems. Capitalism, the state and science and technology thus call forth a response from the public, social movements and NGOs. From this result cultural dynamics involving both power exertion and conflict that constitute a process of construction of national and global society and culture which is more fundamental than regular political competition and economic conflict. Münch (1991, 1996) rejects both Luhmann's autopoietic view of autonomous function systems and Beck's reversal of it. On the basis of the institutionalist concept of systems interpenetration, by contrast, he develops a context sensitive, comparative analysis of distinct societal modes of risk control in Germany, France, the UK and the United States. Whatever its limitations, this is doubtless a contribution toward the development of the ability to distinguish among different 'realizations of risk societies' that Beck (2000: 227) has called for. In her 'endosociology', Nowotny (1996) starts from the internal breakup of modern society and the erosion of the boundary between society and nature to pinpoint the intensification of the internal perspective which brings the unity of the bio- and sociosphere into focus. Under these novel conditions of complexity, contingency, uncertainty and ambivalence, risk became its key metaphor because the processes whereby contemporary modernity is constituted are subject to the unpredictable and uncontrollable evolution of reality.

Theory of modernity

It is by no means unusual for social scientists who focus on social systems to incorporate assumptions regarding modern society into their thinking. Systems theory, in other words, often shades over into the theory of modernity. This is more or less the case with the above-mentioned systems theorists. For Luhmann, functional differentiation marks the emergence of modern society. A comparable historical dimension is present in Burns and Dietz, who stress the significance of such modern phenomena as capitalism and science; in Münch, who accepts that it is a central task of sociology to understand modernity; and in Nowotny, who focuses on the implosion of modernity. Like human ecology, rational choice and cultural theory, however, the dominant thrust of systems theory is to offer a general theoretical account rather than being historically specific. This is where the theory of modernity or modernization theory enters. At its core lies a reference to modern society and the historically specific form it assumes. As regards contemporary society, two varieties of the theory have been developed since the 1980s. Both focus on the new phase in the development of modern society in which the environment and risk have acquired central significance. The first version is ecological modernization and the second reflexive modernization.

Although the concept of 'ecological modernization' was coined and promoted by Huber (1982, 1995), Jänicke (1985) and Spaargaren and Mol (1991, 1992; Spaargaren 1996), for many in the English-speaking world it has become synonymous with the name of Hajer (1995, 1996), a critical analyst of the trend. He traces the basic idea, which emerged in the period beginning in the late 1970s, to secondary policy-making institutions such as the Organization for Economic Cooperation and Development (OECD), the United Nations Environment Programme (UNEP) and the Brundtland Commission. Environmental problems such as air pollution, acid rain, ozone layer depletion and global warming played a significant role in providing an impetus toward this new departure, which by 1984 was generally recognized as an alternative policy option. Although Hajer links it to the idea of sustainable development, it is evident that ecological modernization is a much more specific and focused articulation of it. Rather than just asserting the reconciliation of the competing values of ecology and economy, it assumes that economic growth and environmental protection are fully complementary, so that the latter is not merely good for the former but in fact essential to it. While in the early 1980s the idea seemed an unattainable and even naively idealistic goal, the late 1980s and 1990s saw it increasingly being incorporated into the standard practices of both government and industry. Environmental degradation was increasingly seen not as the first sign of an impending doom but rather as a stimulus to meaningful and profitable innovation, and accordingly governments and industry set to work to internalize the ecological consequences of their activities. They started to appreciate that efficiency prevents pollution, that the anticipation of consequences pre-empts belated cures, that growth could be sustainable rather than destructive, and that environmental problems could be regulated to society's benefit. In Germany, for instance, the adoption of the precautionary principle in the 1980s led to the environmental fine-tuning of the law, and in 1989 the Netherlands launched its National Environmental Policy Plan, with other countries such as Japan, Norway and Sweden following suit.

As implied by such developments, ecological modernization entails the restructuring of the basic institutions of society, from the capitalist economy and the state through science and the media to consumption and the public. Central to such a transformation is a 'new way of seeing, with new constraints and new opportunities' (Hajer 1995: 262) that has a deep-seated structuring effect both on the interpretation and understanding of the world and on the activities of a significant number of agents. This new set of cognitive structures nevertheless allows a range of different scenarios and forms of realization of ecological modernization, which means that different ecological modernities could come into being. Hajer (1995: 281) distinguishes different possibilities which vary between a 'techno-corporatist' and a 'reflexive' version, or between a 'weak' and a 'strong' version (Christoff 1996b). The former is characterized by an economistic, industrial, technical and instrumental orientation, a closed or hierarchical technocratic-bureaucratic style, unitary or hegemonic knowledge and solutions, and restriction to the national or, at best, the privileged developed context. By contrast, reflexive ecological modernization entails a radicalization of ecological modernization. Its has an ecological, holistic, institutional and communicative orientation, unfolds through an open deliberative democratic and reflexive institutional style, fosters the mediation of a plurality of concerns and knowledges, and has a global vision. It is quite conceivable that both of these versions of ecological modernization could share a common understanding of environmental problems and risks. Once reflexive ecological modernization goes beyond the focus on gradual decline in order to incorporate the possibility of environmental catastrophe, however, it distinguishes itself radically from techno-corporatist ecological modernization. This is precisely what Beck does when he theoretically links strong ecological modernization and reflexive modernity and places it in the context of the risk society. Giddens's (1990, 1991, 1999) work on risk and Eder's (1996a) on post-environmental reflexive modernity continue along this same trajectory. Not surprisingly, the shift represented by Beck, Giddens and Eder is forcefully opposed by proponents of ecological modenization such as Mol and Spaargaren (1993; Mol 1996).

Before considering Beck, however, I wish to mention a somewhat different yet related development that falls within the theory of modernity: the so-called 'governmentality' approach to risk (Ewald 1989, 1991; Castel 1991; Dean 1999) inspired by Foucault (1991) and introduced earlier. In accordance with the historical centrality of the strong French state, this approach adopts a very specific and quite narrow perspective, and it assumes the form of a theory of modernity by bringing it to bear on the transformation of contemporary society. It traces the shift from the welfare regime of the social state that is spearheaded by a trend towards 'reflexive government' (Dean 1999: 176). Risk is significant in this context in that it functions as a 'governmental rationality' (Gordon 1991; Dean 1999: 176). It is constructed through knowledge, techniques, practices and programmes as a governable entity, and at the same time it allows government to subject the population to surveillance, regulation and control and to force individuals and communities to be free and to take responsibility for themselves. Dean (1999) argues that it is the analytics of government dimension of this approach, which contrasts sharply with and is more adequate than Beck's theory, which constitutes its proper contribution. This contribution is doubtless important, but from a sociological point of view Dean's claim is not entirely convincing. The significance of risk as a mode of constitution of society that can be analysed at the micro-level does not and cannot invalidate the sociological concern with the macro-dimension of society. What is of more interest regarding the further development of risk sociology, in my view, is the governmentality approach's methodological orientation toward 'mentalities', the 'condition of forms of thought . . . made practical and technical' (Dean 1999: 16, 17, 18). This dimension provides a point of contact with the broad cognitive problematic hesitantly raised by various other authors and, given its importance, I shall return to it again and again in the course of this book, particularly in the final part.

Beck's work demonstrates yet another significant dimension of the theory of modernity as a background theory. His theory of reflexive modernization does not only show that previously achieved levels of modernity are running up against limits and that we have entered a transitional phase in which the foundations of industrial society or the welfare regime of the social state are being eroded and transformed. The larger part of his work is indeed taken up by working out some of the details of what is happening to science, politics, democracy, the state, consumption, the family, identity and above all industry under the new conditions. What makes his analysis unique in the field and lends it a particular poignancy is his theory of contradiction (Beck 1995; see also Breuer 1989; Rustin 1994) or contradictory institutionalization (Habermas 1987). Beyond and above this, however, Beck's deployment of reflexive modernization against industrial modernization and, especially, his emphasis on the catastrophic potential of contemporary risks are of epochal significance. His aim is to construct a new 'model for understanding our times' (Beck 2000: 226). This does not mean that he is merely interested in making available a more 'general understanding' (Dean 1999: 179) that could be useful to ecological modernization or governmentality theorists in improving what they are engaged in doing. More than that, he is deliberately setting out to continue and renew the age-old sociological task of developing a diagnosis of society (*Theory and Society* 1995; *American Journal of Sociology* 1996; *Kölner Zeitschrift für Soziologie und Sozialpsychologie* 1998). The 'risk society' was his initial choice as a placeholder for this societal diagnosis. Whatever its merits and demerits, which will be considered in due course, this diagnosis has already proved fruitful in that it has focused the question and generated a debate about the self-understanding of contemporary society, how it should orient itself, and its relation to its future.

Epistemological frameworks: realism and constructivism

Without exception, each of the background theories mentioned above makes a series of basic assumptions, irrespective of whether they are stated explicitly or not. These assumptions vary from a realist epistemology, on the one extreme, to a constructivist epistemology, on the other, in each case allowing a distinction between a strong and a weak version. In the course of the emergence of the social scientific concern with the environment and risk, particularly in the 1980s and 1990s, the question of epistemology proved to be a controversial one (Delanty 1997). Even as late as the year 2000, Beck still considered it necessary to make his own epistemological position clear. Since the debate inadvertently gave rise also to a good deal of confusion, it is not possible here to ignore the epistemological question.

Table 2.1   Major theoretical and epistemological positions

Epistemology	Theory	Theorist
Strong (naive) realism	Human ecology or environmental sociology	Catton, Dunlap
	Ecological modernization	Huber, Jänicke, Spaargaren and Mol
Weak (critical/ reflexive) realism	Green social theory	Dickens
	Sociocultural evolution plus bounded constructivism	Burns and Dietz
	Endosociology	Nowotny
Weak constructivism (constructivist realism)	Reflexive modernization	Beck, Giddens, Eder
Strong (naive) constructivism	Rational choice	Esser
	Cultural theory	Douglas
	Autopoietic systems theory	Luhmann
	Governmentality	Ewald

Table 2.1 provides a schematic overview of the four major epistemological classifications and relates each to corresponding theoretical positions and theorists.

When environmental sociology made its appearance in the United States during the 1970s and 1980s, the so-called 'revolutionary era of environmental sociology' (Gramling and Freudenburg 1996), major contributors – for instance, Dunlap, Catton, Buttel and Schnaiberg – saw it as their task to bring the environment back in. To accomplish this task, in their view, social scientists were required to overcome their deeply ingrained antipathy to physical environmental variables, to appreciate that physical limits and resources are real, and that there are real connections between human activity and environmental degradation. As their opponents they saw not so much classical and neo-classical authors, such as Durkheim and Parsons, who focused on society to the exclusion of nature, as those traditions and authors who promoted the idea of the social definition of the situation or the social construction of reality. The sociology of knowledge, phenomenological sociology, symbolic interactionism, the social problems tradition and ethnomethodology were all targeted since they provided the methodological and theoretical means whereby it was possible to 'socially construct away' (Gramling and Freudenburg 1996: 352) real physical variables and environmental problems. What had to be recognized, by contrast, was that such variables and problems are brute facts that impress themselves on us by their sheer weight. They are determined solely by nature and can be discovered and revealed only by the sciences. Here we witness the core of the realist epistemology of environmental sociology. It often takes the form of naive realism – that is, there is a reality given out there made up of observable brute facts – which is underpinned by a strong naturalism – that is, nature is the ultimate determining force. From this viewpoint, it is necessary to assimilate the social sciences to the natural sciences. There are of course others who represent a more sophisticated form of realism. Dickens's (1992) extension of the critical realism of Bhaskar, Sayer and Benton to the environmental field is an example. While Bhaskar (1989) draws certain limits around naturalism in the case of the social sciences and thus represents a weaker version, Benton (1985) – and, following him, Dickens (1992) – insist that nature and society can be studied not only on the basis of the same epistemology but also with the same methods. But Dickens then also stresses the importance of historically developing deep mental structures. Another example is the Uppsala school's (Burns and Dietz 1997) incorporation of bounded constructivism into evolutionary theory, which suggests a weak realist epistemology.

It is largely sociology based on naive realism and strong naturalism that has joined forces with the natural sciences in the late 1980s and 1990s in efforts to manage the resources of the planet by techno-corporatist expertise using strategies of prediction and control (Szerszynski et al. 1996; Macnaghten and Urry 1998). This was the case particularly after the publication of the Brundtland Report. While the natural sciences provide the hard facts about the state of nature, the environment and environmental problems, the social sciences have the subservient role of having to identify the impact of nature on society and, conversely, of society on nature. In this underlabourer role, the realist social sciences have become institutionalized in major research programmes on the environment at the national, European and international level – this, to be sure, at the peril of the erosion of the intellectual and institutional structure of the social sciences (Dierkes and Wagner 1992). Judging from some European environmental research, the expectation that the social scientist should don the cap of the social engineer in order to provide appropriate responses to the problems described by the natural sciences weakened somewhat in the course of the 1990s. Whether it is significant, however, is an open question.

Just why the sociology of knowledge, phenomenological sociology, symbolic interactionism, the social problems tradition and ethnomethodology are disturbing to realists becomes immediately apparent when one considers the provocative treatment that such directions give objective conditions. In a famous paper on 'Competition as a cultural phenomenon' presented in 1928, Mannheim argued that what is accepted as reality, whether in everyday life or in science, depends on a process of public interpretation in which the different participants all compete for the correct social diagnosis or definition: 'Sociological analysis shows that this public interpretation of reality is not simply "there"; nor, on the other hand, is it the result of "systematic thinking out"; it is the stake for which men fight' (Mannheim 1993: 406). Here Mannheim not only draws on Heidegger, but also takes cues from the Frankfurt School's view of synthesis as a practical, provisional normalization of continuing oppositions rather than a final reconciliation of contradictions (Kettler and Meja 1988). Starting from the observation that what is real for one society or group may not be real for another, Berger and Luckmann (1967) likewise focused on what is taken for granted or 'what passes for "knowledge"' in a given situation. They proposed that sociology should analyse the process of 'the social construction of reality' whereby what is taken for granted becomes established in the first place (Berger and Luckmann 1967: 27, 15). Following the lead of Blumer (1971), symbolic interactionists (Downs 1972; Spector and Kitsuse 1973, 1977; Mauss 1975; Tuchman 1978; Gusfield 1981; Schneider 1985; Hilgartner and Bosk 1988) advanced a similar position on social problems and established a link with environmental problems such as dangerous toxic chemical wastes. According to Blumer, far from being an objective and identifiable condition, a 'social problem exists primarily in terms of how it is defined and conceived in society' (Blumer 1971: 300). As soon as a problem such as an environmental hazard or risk is no longer treated as a simple mirror of an objective condition, but rather as a collective construct emanating from a process of communicative competition and conflict among participants who define the problem in different ways, questions arise that realism cannot answer. Why do only a fraction of the large number of serious objective problems ever become recognized and dealt with as problems? Why do some conditions become defined as problems, commanding a great deal of collective attention, whereas other, equally hazardous or harmful ones are not? Why do objective problems that were with us already for a considerable period become recognized as environmental hazards only at a particular point in time? The basic insight behind these questions, which is so disturbing to realists, is that what is at stake in environmentalism is less the survival of humankind than the cultural foundations and institutional organization of contemporary society. It is this insight that is at the heart of the constructivist epistemology. Both its impact and scope were considerably enhanced by the new sociology of science. It showed that even the purportedly hard and factual knowledge base of objective conditions provided by science is a matter not of truth but of claims which become established in the course of conflicts and negotiations among scientists and between scientists and policy-makers (Bloor 1976; Mendelsohn et al. 1977; Latour and Woolgar 1979; Knorr 1981; Knorr-Cetina and Mulkay 1983; Weingart 1983; Aronson 1984; Jasanoff 1987; Wynne 1988; Yearley 1996).

A recent influential sociological version of rational choice has been presented on the basis of a constructivist epistemology. Taking cues from symbolic interactionism, phenomenology and social psychology, Esser (1990, 1996) incorporated the famous Thomas theorem of 'the definition of the situation' into rational choice theory. Although acknowledging that people define or construct their situation under conditions over which they do not have full disposal, he ultimately emphasized the individual actor's selection of a model of the situation and mode of information processing. Like the realist model of the individual scientist observing external reality and gaining objective knowledge about it, this individualist assumption raises questions about the collective human processes in the context of which the individual is in the first instance at all able to observe and exercise a choice. This is where the most directly influential presentation of constructivism in the environmental and risk field enters: Douglas's cultural theory. Her work made a broad impression since it attacked realism, together with its individualist assumption, at its very root by proposing 'to dispose of the contention that selection of dangers could be determined by direct assessment of the physical evidence' (Douglas and Wildavsky 1982: 14). Obviously stimulated by the resurgence of the sociology of knowledge, she put forward the thesis that risk is a collective construct, or, more precisely, that: 'Risk should be seen as a joint product of *knowledge* about the future and *consent* about the most desired prospects' (Douglas and Wildavsky 1982: 5, original emphasis). Although scientific knowledge contributes, risks are more heavily aesthetic, moral and political constructs that are formed through cultural frameworks of understanding which are themselves in turn grounded in different forms of social organization.

Although Douglas (1994) later insisted that risks are real, this is a defensive strategy that should not be allowed to conceal the fact that she at crucial junctures in fact holds an extreme constructivist position. This is borne out by Douglas and Wildavsky's (1982) lengthy and systematic analysis of risk and culture, particularly their treatment of the environmental movement. That they believe that there are no real risks is self-evident. According to them, the anti-nuclear movement and Friends of the Earth 'identify the risks the world faces from the pollution of nature' since this allows them to 'serve their purpose best'. By referring to 'global issues', 'invoking general doom' and speaking 'on behalf of the whole of mankind', (Douglas and Wildavsky 1982: 125), the movements are able not only to mobilize sect members but also to unjustly blame and attack industry. By contrast with Douglas, Ewald (1989, 1991; see also Dean 1999) is unequivocal in his adoption of a strong constructivist epistemology. He explicitly accepts that there is no such thing as risk in reality and, therefore, that anything could be constructed as a risk. As such, risk is in turn something that could be employed to further construct and order reality. He does not shrink back from regarding risk as a category of our understanding by means of which reality is approached and dealt with. This extreme form of constructivism is what has been called 'neo-Kantian or idealist constructivism' (Sismondo 1993) with reference to Latour and Woolgar's (1979) work. The political implications of Ewald's work, however, are the opposite of Douglas's pronounced conservatism – despite her claim to be neutral. Starting from biology, neuropsychology and psychology, Luhmann (1990b, 1992) developed a sophisticated version of constructivism based on the systems theoretical distinction between system and environment. While he assumes that the recursive constructive process is itself a real process that maintains an oblique contact with reality, reality is nevertheless de-ontologized in the sense that an ontological representation of reality is epistemologically irrelevant. This means that, cognitively speaking, all reality is constructed, but constructed reality is not the reality to which reference is made. On this basis, he regards the debate between realism and constructivism as sterile and believes that he has managed to go beyond this impasse. Judging from his writings on ecological communication (Luhmann 1989) dating from a slightly earlier period, however, there is little doubt that he embraced an extreme form of constructivism in his sociological analysis. His treatment of the new social movements is remarkably similar to that of Douglas and Wildavsky. According to Luhmann, the new social movements are not communicating about objective problems in their environment at all, but through communication constitute both themselves and the problems they are addressing. It is not surprising, then, that one commentator thinks that the main problem of his approach is that it is 'overly constructivist' (Halfmann 1988: 25).

Epistemologically speaking, ecological modernization in its dominant version can be linked to realism. What is more, the techno-corporatist form that it assumes as well as the research it has instigated and the institutional changes it has wrought indicate that it is close to a strong, naive realism, which is in turn backed up by a strong naturalism. This means that ecological modernization is accompanied by a tendency to give priority to the natural sciences and, conversely, to cast the social sciences in a natural science mould and to assign them to a subservient position. In proportion as neo-liberalism has played a central role in politics and policy since the late 1970s, the bond between ecological modernization and a strong realist epistemology was fortified and invigorated. The only condition under which ecological modernization would move away from strong realism is where it was transformed, to use Hajer's (1996) distinction, from institutional learning or a technocratic project into cultural politics. But this begins to shade over into reflexive modernization.

The epistemological assumptions underpinning the theory of reflexive modernization have proved to be rather controversial. Beck's position in particular has been subjected to criticisms from all sides, realist and constructivist, left and right. For instance, Breuer (1989) effectively criticized his realism by objecting to his apparent stylization of objective dangers rather than critics, protestors and the media as the opponents of high technology. Rustin (1994) effectively criticized his constructivism by objecting to his idealism and hence neglect of real material powers such as capitalism as the cause of environmental problems. From a Durkheimian position not dissimilar to Douglas's, Alexander and Smith (1996) vehemently attacked Beck's reputed objectivism and concomitant lack of a cultural theory. Some three years after he had reasonably clarified his position, Lupton (1999: 28), a follower of Douglas, still saw fit to claim that Beck 'tends to waver between a realist and a weak constructionist approach' – while herself failing to appreciate that Douglas's own position is marred by gerrymandering. Szerszynski et al. (1996) delivered their more thoughtful criticisms in the course of attacking strong realism as manifested in environmental sociology and national and international research programmes and institutions, on the one hand, and strong constructivism, on the other. Environmental problems are neither simply shaped by real processes in nature alone, nor mere social constructions. Seeking to go beyond these sterile alternatives, they leaned on Beck yet felt that he had not gone far enough. To the extent that he regarded the environmental crisis as a social rather than a natural crisis, they found him to be 'excessively social constructivist'. At the same time, they also criticized him for 'a curious realism' in so far as he saw the real physical riskiness of high technologies as having driven industrial society beyond its limits (Szerszynsky et al. 1996: 7).

Since the publication of his first two risk books, Beck (1996, 1999) has taken pains to clarify his epistemological stance. Although it may not satisfy a philosopher, the clarification does go far enough to confirm that he rejects both 'naïve realism' and 'naïve constructivism' in favour of giving priority to a 'social constructivist view' and relating it to a 'reflexive realism'. At this stage, there can hardly be any doubt about Beck's epistemological position. It is not the same as Bhaskar's (1989) weak critical realism, and, although closer to it, is still a remove away from Habermas's (1999a) weak naturalism – to which my own position as put forward in Chapter 8 is related. Rather, it lies on the constructivist side of the continuum, between both Dickens and Burns and Dietz, on the weak realist side, and Douglas, Luhmann and Ewald, on the strong constructivist side. Away from the extremes, Beck falls in the middle area where the most creative thinking is being done today. Beck himself identifies here first with 'constructivist realism' and then 'reflexive realism' (Beck 1999: 26). It is my contention, however, that Beck's work immanently calls for being explicitly brought closer to a weak realist epistemology, and thus theoretically for its unstated evolutionary theoretic assumptions to be articulated without a displacement of the constructivist component.

Summary

In this chapter, I have reviewed the most important theoretical frameworks against the background of which social scientists are today attending to questions concerning the environment and risk, from human ecology through rational choice, cultural theory and systems theory to the theory of modernity. These background theories were then located within the contemporary epistemological framework that accommodates a strong and a weak version of both realism and constructivism. This analysis clarifies the range of theoretical and epistemological components that are employed by social scientists working in the field of risk, environment and society. Having first isolated these components and then having indicated some of the relations among them, it is now possible to identify and present the major theoretical directions that are in contention today.

3

Major theoretical directions

According to Scott (2000: 34), there are 'two systematic attempts by social scientists to wrest the issue of risk away from specialists (risk analysts) and place it on a wider social scientific and public agenda'. One is Beck's sociological theory of the risk society and the other is Douglas's cultural theory of risk. Scott prefers the latter and, although a sociologist himself, uses it to culturalistically criticize and dissolve Beck's theory of the risk society. Lupton (1999) achieves something comparable, but then she at least does so from a cultural studies perspective. In his identification of these two directions, Scott ignores the most sophisticated, systematic social theory of risk, namely that of Luhmann. In addition, he overlooks a crucial matter when he juxtaposes Douglas and Beck. Both Beck and Luhmann not only acknowledged the relevance of Douglas's cultural perspective and took it up in their work, but also each in his own way took the further step of transforming her debilitating attachment to the psychology of perception and static structuralism. Whereas Douglas represents a neo-classical approach that is unable to transcend the familiar themes of the risk discourse, both Beck and Luhmann put forward post-classical approaches that consider contemporary society in new ways. Besides the theory of the risk society and the cultural theory of risk, the French governmentality approach could be singled out as a significant theoretical direction. While I by no means want to deny the potential of this theoretical departure, for present purposes it cannot be treated as a major direction. Not only does it operate in terms of a sociologically too narrow governance perspective, but also thus far it has had little impact in the environmental field (see for example Darier 1996). It has largely found historical application (Ewald 1986), and as far as contemporary society is concerned it remains confined as yet to the analysis of neo-liberal prudentialist politics and policy (Castel 1991; Dean 1999). Were it to become relevant in the field of ecological risk, it would have to broaden its focus on government and experts considerably to include social movements and the public, as is suggested by the trajectory of the risk discourse since the 1950s.

The best starting point for the identification of the currently most important directions in the area of risk and the risk society is the social scientific debate that forms part of the contemporary risk discourse. Taking substantive, theoretical and practical considerations into account, I propose to give attention to two theoretical directions that can be regarded as the major contending tendencies in the field of risk and the risk society today. Competing and conflicting at both epistemological and theoretical level, they are not uniform positions, but as directions actually cut across the dimensions of the typology presented in Chapter 2. The first direction maintains a critical stance and thus seeks in some sense to retain a diagnostic view of contemporary society. The second, by contrast, is of a sceptical nature and denies any possibility whatsoever of grasping society as a whole, thus closely resembling the postmodernist or post-structuralist decomposition of totalities and uniformities. The leading theorist of the former is Beck, but it is in some sense or another also represented by Giddens, Eder, Wynne, Dickens, Hajer and Nowotny. The fountainhead of the latter is Luhmann, and he is supported or followed in one way or another by Japp, Bechmann and – in Britain – Blühdorn. By contrasting and comparing these two directions, it is possible to highlight two lines of multiple tension and overlap that are of acute relevance in the contemporary social sciences. At the same time, it also gives us the opportunity to begin to identify the different strands of the sociology of risk and of contemporary society.

In the following, therefore, I propose to concentrate on the critical theory of the risk society and on the sceptical theory of the contingent, hypothetical or paradoxical society.

Critical theory of the risk society

Ulrich Beck is the leading proponent of the critical theory of the risk society which, notwithstanding differences of varying magnitude, is also represented by Nowotny (1987, 1996), Eder (1988, 1993a, 1996a), Wynne (1989a, 1989b, 1996), Giddens (1990, 1991, 1999), Dickens (1992) and Hajer (1995, 1996). As we have seen, Beck is the author who most decisively redirected the risk discourse by replacing the rather narrow guiding question of an acceptable level of safety by the much wider and more penetrating question of the societal conditions of the constitution of risk. He was able to do so only on the basis of a fundamental societal change dating from the 1970s that took the form of an endogenization process (Nowotny 1996). Through it the boundary between nature and society was blurred and the natural environment was incorporated in society itself. This allowed Beck to see risk as an index of the attendant problems of industrial production that gave rise to the global ecological crisis. Although apparently manifesting themselves in the form of external problems, environmental problems for him are actually internal societal problems that are created by human beings themselves – risks or so-called 'manufactured uncertainties' (Beck 1999: 105, 112, 140). Environmental problems and the concomitant risks are not simply dangers and hazards threatening society from the outside, but they concern an internal crisis of science- and technology-based industrial society, affecting both its production process and its core institutions. Beck achieved this radical redirection of the risk discourse by means of a theory of modernity possessing two distinct yet closely related components. The first is his theory of modernization and the second is his theory of institutional contradiction. Initially put forward in 1986 in *Risk Society* (Beck 1992), both were elaborated two years later in *Ecological Politics in an Age of Risk* (1995). The latter, important to note, was to a significant degree a critical sociological reaction to Luhmann's *Ecological Communication* (1989), originally published in the same year as Beck's first book, yet strangely this is not reflected in the English translation. Elaboration, modification and refinement, often suggested or compelled by both sympathetic commentators and critics, ensued in the following years. Beck brought the results together in *World Risk Society* (1999).

The changes in Beck's thinking are of both a theoretical and an epistemological-methodological kind. Theoretically, perhaps the major refinement concerns his initial all too pointed rationalism, which was highlighted by critics like Breuer (1989), Bonß (1991), Luhmann (1993) and Wynne (1996). In this respect, he introduced a number of modifications. Instead of propounding a hyper-Enlightenment interpretation of the modernization process, he tempered his concept of reflexivity by developing a greater appreciation for the complexity of society and incalculability and unpredictability of the socio-historical process. Instead of assuming a linear view for the most part, he came to understand the dynamics of knowledge and decision-making about risks as being of a non-linear kind. Instead of a purely positive concept of knowledge, he came to a realization of just how significant non-knowledge or unawareness is in conflicts about risks. Although not surrendering his view that decision-making is becoming a political issue, he became more sensitive to the complexities of democratic participation and decision making. Epistemologically, the criticism of his unreflective eclectic employment of extreme forms of both realism and constructivism, for instance by Szerszynski et al. (1996), led Beck to improve considerably on his position.

Beck's theory of modernity must be seen against the background of his critique of the social sciences, sociology in particular (Beck 1992: 82–3, 180–1, 1995: 13, 82–4). Not only has sociology become overspecialized, either researching detail problems or fixing on the classics, but also it is fragmented both by its division into numerous sub-disciplines and the complexity and instability of societal relations. Under these conditions, sociology has lost sight of the historical dimension of society and, consequently, turned away from synthetic interpretations of society and diagnoses of the present age. This abstinence indicates both a lack of sociological imagination and a blindness that render it incapable of appreciating the threatening dangers and catastrophic potential of contemporary society. Mainstream sociology abandoned its own most characteristic task of following the historical process and the concurrent vicissitudes of its object of study and thus of diagnostically determining the epochal quality and signature of the new age we are entering at present. Instead, it perpetuates sociological platitudes that blunt sociocultural criticism. When it does acknowledge physical, ecological and medical dangers, it leaves them to the natural sciences, without appreciating that natural scientific formulas are technically mystified forms of social power relations, expert and political decisions, legal norms, conventions, cultural values and an occidental understanding of science and technology. Not seeing the relation between science and the wider public sociocultural domain, sociology by the same token forfeits its own public role. As communication about risk increases in the public sphere, sociology's puzzling reticence grows more tenacious. What ought to happen, by contrast, is that sociology should take cues from public communication and discourse to develop a historically specific diagnosis and analysis of contemporary society. This should be done in a way that resonates with the public and has the potential of improving our self-understanding, of providing orienting knowledge and of influencing political perspectives on the future.

Risk society for Beck is an epochal concept. It refers to the historically new societal arrangement or the distinctive form of modernity that first made its tentative appearance in the 1960s and especially the 1970s and is at present still in the process of emerging, probably to come into its own in the next 30 years or so. It is a meaningful social theoretic concept that makes sense only in terms of a theory of modernization understood as a theory of the development of modern society. From the preface of his first book to his most recent publications, Beck is emphatic not only about the fundamental process of historical development and change of modernity from one form to another, but also about the historically specific nature or epochal quality of each of these forms. His central concern with developing a diagnosis in the sense of 'mov[ing] the future which is just beginning to take shape into view' (Beck 1992: 9) or a 'model for understanding our times' (Beck 2000: 226), which is explicit in the title of *Risk Society: Towards a New Modernity*, would be entirely meaningless unless it is seen in the context of such a theory. In a fairly sensitive critique, Goldblatt (1996) objects that Beck has not presented sufficient evidence to support his diagnostic interpretation of an epochal transformation to the risk society. If this is a request for more evidence, then it is acceptable, but if it is a questioning of the epistemological sense of a sociological diagnosis as such, as does Scott (2000) in his rather pointed culturalist critique of Beck, then it must be resisted. Beck stands in a well-established social theoretic tradition that maintains the methodological and theoretical necessity as well as the hermeneutical and practical urgency of this task (Brock 1991; *Theory and Society*

1995; *American Journal of Sociology* 1996; *Kölner Zeitschrift für Soziologie und Sozialpsychologie* 1998).

As regards his theory of modernization, Beck adopts a threefold model of the historical development of society, but his focal concern is of course the transition currently in process. Having been preceded by the civilizations of the pre-industrial period, we are today witnessing a break with 'classical industrial society' and a transition to the 'industrial risk society' (Beck 1995: 77–8). Giddens, who is also concerned with the uniqueness of modernity (1990), adopts a similar threefold view (1999), while Wynne (1996) denies such qualitative differences. Whereas industrial society took off in eighteenth-century Britain and reached its zenith in many countries around the globe in the two golden decades after the Second World War, the risk society for Beck is at best the future that has begun to take shape since the 1970s. The discovery of the human genome blueprint in the summer of 2000, for instance, effectively put in place one of the most basic foundation stones of the risk society. The elaboration of its potential and implications, not to mention giving it cultural, social and political form, will require decades, perhaps even the best part of the twenty-first century, to accomplish. Beck uses the adjective 'industrial' in each of the three historical phases, which suggests that he, like Giddens (1990), attaches central significance to industrialism in the process of modernization. In fact, he links it to the generation of the different kinds of risks to be found in industrial society and risk society respectively – proletarianization, exploitation, impoverishment, unemployment and work accidents in the former, and nuclear, chemical, environmental, biotechnological hazards and artificial catastrophes in the latter. But he emphatically rejects economic, technological and industrial determinism. In opposition to social theorists from Comte, Marx, Durkheim and Weber through Horkheimer, Adorno, Parsons and Gehlen to Foucault, Habermas and Luhmann, he insists that the apparently independent and autonomous system of industrialism has burst its own logic and limits and consequently has entered a process of dissolution. This radical turn marks the current phase in which modernization becomes reflexive. Instead of remaining confined to the elaboration of the various potentials and paths contained within industrial society, modernization now takes hold of the very social, political and cultural principles of industrial society, overturning and transforming them beyond recognition and extrapolating their new potentials in opposition to industrial society itself. Thus the process of reflexive modernization leads from industrial society to the risk society.

The latest phase in the historical development of modernity possesses its own new and unique epochal features and quality. Sociologically, it is vital that the epochal dimension be placed centre stage, unlike in the case of naturalistic objectivism, which is qualitatively insensitive, and cultural relativism such as Douglas's, which indeed proceeds qualitatively but overlooks the historically specific nature of society. Starting from the most prominent public debates, controversies and conflicts, Beck gains access to the new epoch through the insecurities experienced and expressed by the contemporary public, social movements, scientists, experts, politicians and others. Typically today, communication and conflict flare up around a particular type of danger, hazard, threat or risk. Neither natural disasters coming from the outside and thus amenable to externalization to God or nature, such as prevailed in the pre-industrial period, have this effect any longer. Nor do the specific uncertainties determinable with actuarial precision in terms of a probability calculus backed up by insurance and monetary compensation, such as were typical of industrial society, fall in this category. At the centre of attention today, by contrast, are what Beck calls 'late industrial mega-dangers' (1988: 121) and Giddens refers to as 'manufactured risks' (1999: 26). They are distinguished by the fact that they are dependent on human decisions, created by society itself, immanent to society and thus not externalizable, collectively imposed and thus individually unavoidable, objectively incalculable, uncontrollable and in the final analysis therefore no longer insurable. They are based on science and high technologies and thus presuppose the decomposition and recomposition and hence the changing of nature in highly potent yet equally highly unpredictable and uncontrollable ways. Nuclear, chemical, genetic and ecological risks are paradigmatic examples. In addition, these risk are embedded in socio-technical systems that are so complex that they generate non-linear dynamics which are in principle beyond full control and thus make large-scale accidents a normal or mundane phenomenon. The central position that Beck ascribes to such technological-ecological risks in his diagnostic interpretation explains why he alternatively refers to the present age as the 'scientific-technological civilization' (1995: 127), the 'atomic, chemical, genetic age' (1995: 1), the 'self-endangering civilization' (1992: 10), the 'risk society' (1992) or, in the light of the global nature of such risks, 'world risk society' (1999). Giddens's equivalent is the 'runaway world' (1999). For Beck, this qualitatively new epoch distinguishes itself both from all previous civilizations and from industrial society by its new level of technical disposal over life on earth and, in particular, by its historically unprecedented threat of total self-annihilation. Giddens is more reserved in this respect, preferring to give attention to a range of so-called 'disembedding mechanisms' (1990: 22). Although the threat of total self-annihilation makes us confront and see the whole, for Beck it alone does not constitute the historically new quality of the nascent society. This novelty comes to view fully only once the brute fact of this total threat is seen in relation to the social institutions that make it possible and, together with their cultural assumptions and political practices, lend contemporary risks their cultural, social and political character and explosiveness.

This brings us to the second major component of Beck's theory of modernity, namely his theory of institutional contradiction – something that is central to Eder's (1993a: 36–40) thinking but is less so in the case of Giddens, although he does regard modernity as 'double-edged' requiring 'institutional analysis' (1990: 7). Beck presents it in opposition to naturalistic objectivism and cultural relativism, both of which for different reasons overlook contradiction, by expressly developing an intermediate sociological position that acknowledges both the destructive potentiality of contemporary mega-dangers and the reflexivity it induces and stimulates. The social and political explosiveness of high consequence technological-ecological risks, which is visible in the enormous increase in communication and conflict around them, can be led back to immanent contradictions in and between the institutions responsible for dealing with such threats. First put forward in *Risk Society*, this theory was in particular developed in *Ecological Politics in an Age of Risk* in a critical appropriation of Luhmann. Surprisingly, only a few of Beck's commentators and critics show an appreciation for his notion of institutional contradiction and its theoretical significance (Breuer 1989; Brock 1991; Rustin 1994), and even fewer see the relation between Beck and Luhmann (Münch 1991; Miller 1994). Luhmann, as we shall see below, offered a systems theoretical account according to which modern society consists of functionally differentiated systems which are so highly specialized and autonomous that they are able to deal with societal problems only in terms of their own particular system logics. The economy does so in terms of prices, politics in terms of majorities, law in terms of guilt, science in terms of knowledge, and so on. For Luhmann this means not merely that modern society cannot deal with environmental problems, but that there are no such problems and that whatever communication the new social movements generate around such problems is only so much noise for the function systems. And if anything endangers society, it is this excessive communication and the resultant noise. Beck (1988: 166–74) takes this diagnosis on board, but, instead assuming the reality of high-consequence risks, critically reverses it to mean that contemporary society is incapable of solving its most pressing problems since the responsibility for their production and resolution is passed from one system to the other. For instance, who is responsible for agricultural soil contamination: the farmer, the fertilizer industry, government regulators, EU policy-makers, or the consumer of agricultural products (Beck 1992: 32–3)? This set of contemporary systemic conditions is what Beck takes as one of the major themes of his work under the title of 'organized irresponsibility' (1995: 5–69, 1999: 55, 2000: 227). Its contradictory nature, simultaneously involving both competence and unaccountability, provides the foundation for the periodic display of the highly conspicuous contradictions in and between the core institutions of modern society.

The 'central contradiction' in contemporary society for Beck (1995: 64) rests on the circumstance that there are mega-dangers or hazards that are on the one hand created in society itself, but on the other are neither attributable nor accountable nor even manageable within society. Being of a social and political rather than technical nature, he establishes contradiction with reference to rankings and claims made within and between institutions. Giddens proceeds less critically by talking in a more diffuse and ambivalent manner of paradoxes (1999: 29–31). As Beck sees it, the typical institutional pattern – whether science, industry, politics or law – is to make what has been produced in society on the basis of values, choices and decisions appear as though it is not of society at all. For this purpose, institutions use any means at their disposal, from probability calculations, actuarial predictions and statistics through the propagandistic inflation of opportunities and perpetuation of industrial fatalism to the cynical denial of any problems whatsoever and their frantic cover-up. Institutions engage in normalizing practices and issue safety assurances that are incommensurate with the magnitude and quality of the new mega-hazards we are facing. The challenges of the twenty-first century are being met with concepts and approaches dating from the nineteenth and early twentieth centuries – what Beck (1988: 9, 1995: 1) calls the 'century mistake' or 'paradigm confusion'. Periodically, however, the social and political explosiveness of disasters and failures such as Flixborough, Seveso, Three Mile Island, Bophal, Chernobyl, BSE, Sellafield-THORP and so forth uncovers this contradiction in all its starkness. The increase in communication and conflict reveals that the core institutions are not only out of keeping with institutionalized rights and norms, historical meaning complexes and cultural expectations, but also in need of drastic overhaul by the introduction of new institutions of attribution, responsibility and codetermination (Beck 1995: 84).

As people become aware of and understand the contradictory nature of institutions, the self-criticism of society intensifies. Such self-criticism above all applies to the bureaucratic apparatus responsible for safety, but it extends beyond immediate risk and safety questions also to other institutions such as science and politics. But it is not only the internal split in institutions that becomes articulated. Different actors, agencies and groups, for instance scientists, technologists, industrialists, politicians, social movements, lawyers and insurers, take up positions against one another, contradicting each other while competing and conflicting. In a recent example, industry, governments and farmers argued that no risk attaches to genetically modified foods, while the banking sector withdrew from investing in biotechnology and supermarkets banned GM foods from their shelves in view of the European public's perception of genetic engineering as a high-risk technology. Conflicts of this kind, which are typical of the risk society, possess a social theoretic significance for Beck since they demonstrate his concept of 'reflexive modernization' (1999: 109–32). Through conflict, society is compelled to become aware of and reflect upon the process of development in which it is engaged, what impacts and unintended consequences follow from it, what knowledge is used, how it is used and for what purposes, but also what knowledge is not used, what is dogmatically clung to, what is exaggerated, what is underplayed, what mistakes are made, what is omitted, as well as the sheer ignorance involved. Beck insists that his position is unique, compared to those of Giddens and Lash, in that he alone appreciates the significance of 'non-knowledge' or 'unawareness' (1999: 109–32). Be that as it may, self-criticism and conflict also explain why Beck's critical theory of contemporary society, like Eder's (1993a: 98–100,

138–9) which owes something to both Habermas and Bourdieu, is not a direct extension of the well-known critical theory of society of the Frankfurt School (Held 1980; Dubiel 1988). Instead of adopting a well-established normative standard and then applying it in a judgement and condemnation of society, Beck – like Eder – starts from the different criticisms voiced by the members of society themselves and critically analyses the intersecting lines of conflict. In this sense, his theory of the risk society is a critical 'theory of societal self-criticism' (Beck 1999: 80). But the sociological significance of societal self-criticism and conflict is still more far-reaching. Here we touch on his important concept of relations of definition and his social constructivism.

In so far as Beck (1999: 124–5) no longer accepts that risks are simply determined by nature or technology, but rather insists on the non-linear dynamics of the interweaving of different actors, agencies and groups in a process of communicative competition and conflict, he adopts a constructivist view. Like Eder's (1993a, 1996a) and Hajer's (1995) respective constructivisms, which are theoretically and empirically worked out in much more detail, his is a dynamic one differing sharply from for instance Douglas's static structuralist conception. Beck is emphatic that '[r]isks are social constructions' (1995: 92) that 'initially only exist in terms of (scientific and anti-scientific) knowledge about them. They can thus be changed, magnified, dramatized or minimized within knowledge, and to that extent they are particularly *open to social definition and construction*' (1992: 22, original emphasis). Risks are constructed in a process of social definition or what Beck calls 'definitional struggles' (1992: 29) or 'definitional conflicts' (1995: 131). This process takes place in the medium of communication or 'public discussion' (1992: 30) in the context of the 'communicative society' (1999: 101) – something, once again, that has received much more attention in Eder's work (1993a, 1996a). A plurality of 'argumentation craftsmen' (Beck 1992: 32) is involved, including experts and public relations officials from different sectors of society, such as scientists, politicians, lawyers, social movements and the mass media. In the process, we witness a multiplicity of antagonistic definitions advanced on the basis of the competing and conflicting rationality claims of the different actors struggling for more general acceptance by the public. A crucial component of the process of social construction in and through which risks are collectively defined is what Beck calls 'relations of definition' (1995: 61, 110, 129–33; 2000: 224–5; see also Goldblatt 1996: 165–6; Cottle 1998).

Formulated in analogy to Marx's 'relations of production' and Habermas's 'relations of understanding', this concept refers to the framework within which definitional conflicts and struggles transpire and risks are socially constructed. It consists of the perspectives, rationalities, knowledges, rules and institutions that structure the collective identification and definition of risks. Thus it is both a cultural and social or institutional framework, but one that simultaneously also supports power relations. In industrial society, the relations of definition coincided with the power relations of industrialism and thus gave expression to the generally adopted faith in science and progress (Beck 1995: 131). As communication penetrated the emerging risk society, however, the relations of definition became more visible and started to undergo change. As the 'self-critique of science' and the 'self-refutation of bureaucracy' (Beck 1995: 121, 73) progressed and society became more reflexive and self-critical, the relations of definition became democratized. Increased participation in the collective definition of risks had a multiple effect. It was accompanied by a questioning and relativization of scientific, technical and administrative rationality and knowledge; the recognition of social and cultural assumptions and of different rationalities and knowledges; and a growing appreciation of the communicative or discursive process and of the crucial role of the public in that process. Here Beck perceives an 'opening up' or 'reinvention of politics' (1992: 183–236, 1997), involving a thorough reconstitution and democratization of the relations of definition. Not only does it lead to the establishment of a 'world risk society' (1999). It also harbours the potential of eroding established institutional power (1999: 90–108) and the realization of both an 'ecological democracy' (1995: 180) and, more generally, of what he alternatively calls a 'new modernity', a 'responsible modernity', an 'alternative modernity' or even 'many modernities' (1992: subtitle, 1995: 171, 2000: 222).

Beck has a clear view of the new role that the social sciences, sociology in particular, should be playing in the nascent society of our time. There can be no doubt about that fact that this self-understanding of his places him squarely in the critical tradition in the social sciences and thus distinguished him sharply from Luhmann's sceptical direction. Under the conditions of the implosion of modernity, the social sciences must resist the temptation to rigidify in established routines, to grow silent or become cynical and, instead, remain open to the possibility of the transformation of cultural, social and political assumptions and structures. He thus seeks to spearhead a paradigm shift that would entail a reformation of sociology 'so that it can provide a new framework for the reinvention of society and politics' (1999: 2). The first requirement is that sociology must rid itself of its debilitating blindness in order to acknowledge the contemporary form of the human trauma of apocalypse. It must become alive to the 'dark side of modernity' (1992: 83) and bring the threatening self-destruction of society into full view (1995: 83). Once this has been achieved, sociology can make a contribution to the more general revival of enlightenment. In particular, it can contribute to the 'emancipation of science from its self-inflicted fate of immaturity and blindness with respect to risks' (1992: 180). Above all, however, sociology must inquire what the consequences of the new socio-historical consciousness, the new awareness of societal self-endangerment, are for the constitution and organization of society. There are various suggestive developments of social scientific significance. For one, a central theme of everyday public controversies and conflicts is the conscious, social, democratic development of technology. Another consideration is that the nature of contemporary mega-hazards and high-consequence risks is such that it demands and legitimizes the maximum level of democratic participation in dealing with these new phenomena and with the future. Yet a further development is the search for alternative routes into the future and their stabilization. The latter requires arrangements that expose the deficiencies of existing institutions, operate on the assumption that authority is possible only on the basis of good, legitimate arguments, and function in such a way that they allow their own transformation or supersession. For sociology, this raises the question of the urgent need for new institutional developments that are of a reflexive nature, particularly new institutions of attribution, responsibility and participation (1994: 28– 31, 1995: 84). The overwhelming insight gained from an investigation into the significance of self-endangerment, however, is an appreciation of the openness of the history of society that now begins anew (2000: 88), which demands of the social scientist to attend to the adventure of the incalculable and unpredictable social construction of reality (Beck and Bonß 1989). As regards this incalculability and unpredictability, however, Beck does not consider the possibility, as do for instance Eder (1988, 1993a, 1996a, 1999), Giesen (1991), Dickens (1992), Burns and Dietz (1992, 1997) and Nowotny (1996), that the theory of evolution might be of sociological importance. But he is aware that sociology is here not only theoretically, but also epistemologically and methodologically, on new terrain. Sociology is no longer in a position to provide knowledge that can be directly applied in the solution to problems (Beck and Bonß 1989). Nor can it any longer criticize and condemn society by taking up a position outside it or by having recourse to an abstract normative standard. And even less can it make ex cathedra statements about the content of the corrections needed to steer society onto the right course. It is up to those involved to decide on such matters according to the conditions under which they live. Sociology can make a contribution to the critique of society and to specific decisions about what measures to take only by starting from the critique that is in process in society itself. It has to remain alive to the reciprocal critique of sectional rationalities and groups in society, and thus to the intersecting lines of conflict of a society which has become reflexive and self-critical.

Sceptical theory of the contingent society

Niklas Luhmann, who put forward the most sophisticated and systematic sociology of risk, is the leading spokesman of the sceptical theory of the risk society. He accepts that today we live in a 'society . . . that has no choice but to run risks' (1993: 218), and occasionally he even uses the expression 'risk society' (1993: 28, 83, 103). But his view of contemporary society is much rather of a contingent (Luhmann 1998), 'hypothetical' (Bechmann 1993b: 266) or even paradoxical society. And not infrequently he describes himself as being 'sceptical' (Luhmann 1993: 157, 159). As the second major social theoretic direction, it has many similarities with Beck's, but the sharp differences are more conspicuous. Luhmann is as emphatic in his rejection of Beck's critical sociology, that is, his attempt 'to warn society' (Luhmann 1993: 5), as is Beck (1988: 167) in his repudiation of Luhmann's Kafkaesque systems theory emptied of all human beings but Luhmann himself. Luhmann even proposes to appropriate and redefine 'critical sociology' as one that operates with 'a heightened, not self-evident capacity to draw distinctions' (1993: vii–viii) rather than with critique. While this sceptical theory is also represented by Japp (1990, 1992, 1993), Bechmann (1993b) and Blühdorn (1997), in its politically conservative effect it is similar to Douglas's. In Britain, Blühdorn has been fighting on the rhetorical and ideological forefront for its advancement, vehemently attacking critical opponents such as Beck and Eder.

For Luhmann, the topic of risk can be developed only within the framework of a theory of modernity. He thus sees the increasing scientific and public significance of risk as an indication of the fact that modern society has recently undergone a momentous change entailing a new relationship to its own future. Action possibilities, contingency and the pressure to make decisions have all increased, but so too have uncertainty and the awareness that current decisions shape the future and generate the consequences of tomorrow. Consequently, contemporary society represents 'the future as risk' (Luhmann 1993: 37). Although Luhmann regards modern risk society as indeed owing much to the perception of the consequences of contemporary 'high technology' (1993: 83), it has been made possible by more deep-seated developments such as the expansion of possibilities through research and knowledge.

From its onset three centuries ago, Luhmann (1995) assumes, modern society is characterized by the structural principle of functional differentiation which unfolded through the gradual separation of autonomous function systems such as the state, law, economy and science. This growth in complexity did not merely bring with it an unprecedented increase in action possibilities, but changed the very structure of society itself. Neither could society any longer be normatively integrated through the shared action orientations, values and goals of the members, nor was it possible to avoid the disintegration of its regulative centre and its displacement by a decentred organization of society. Rather than morally rich normative structures, society was now guided by cognitive-instrumental expectations. The economy, science and technology, lately high technology, became the leading function systems. From them stem the most significant innovations. Science is of central importance, however, as it proceeds since the early modern period on the principle of curiosity in the sense of researching and producing knowledge about everything that is accessible to its methods. Crucial for an understanding of risk is the concurrent change in the time horizon of modern society. Not only did the difference between past and future obtain a new significance, but also on the basis of the loss of a unitary culture and the opening up and multiplication of new possibilities and orientations, the emphasis shifted from the past to the future. At that point, contingency became the dominant experience. It became increasingly apparent that metasocial guarantees, such as religion, values and nature, are produced in society itself and, consequently, that there was an overproduction of possibilities, that a new classification was necessary, that a selection among options was unavoidable and that decisions must be made on the basis of available knowledge under conditions of uncertainty. The novelty of modern society, for Luhmann, resides precisely in its loss of unity, expansion of possibilities, increase in knowledge, orientation toward the future and pressure toward decision-making.

It is against the background of such structural principles as functional differentiation, scientization, future orientation and decision-making that Luhmann delineates the uniqueness of contemporary society. Considering the primacy of the future, he identifies a series of divisions and controversies that in the early modern period centred around revolution and later around industrialization, but today are regrouping around ecology and related matters (Luhmann 1993: 48). More important, however, is his close analysis of the way in which modern society deals with the future through time-binding mechanisms and thus generates structures for the constitution and organization of society. His approach is a comparative one according to which a distinction is made among early modern, later modern and contemporary modern society. For each of these periods, he identifies a different yet functionally equivalent way of dealing with or binding time and thus of creating a degree of certainty – norms, scarcity and risk respectively.

In early modern society, norms were predominantly used to deal with time by determining in the present how those involved were to behave in the future (Luhmann 1993: 53–62). Such norms were typically embodied in a national system of law. Once access to scarce resources for the satisfaction of needs raised a quite different future-related problem, however, norms had to be supplemented by a different form of time-binding. Access to resources was regulated by the scarcity mechanism embodied in the economy or system of distribution. By monetarization, it allowed the acquisition, alienation and transfer of property in a flexible manner, which immensely improved provision for the future (1993: 62–5). Risk, according to Luhmann, is a form of time-binding of a very different kind. It emerged in response to a novel problem in a novel situation characteristic of late-twentieth-century society. By contrast with previous solidly structured social orders, contemporary society has to deal with an unpredictable and uncertain future that depends on decisions made under contingent and precarious conditions and, hence, cannot sufficiently be regulated by means of norms and distribution systems. Rather than order, contemporary society is faced with the problem of fatality. Instead of providing direct guidance, it has acquired a reflexive capacity – what Luhmann calls 'second-order observation' (1993: 68, 76, 219) – which allows it to appreciate that the decision-making on which the future depends is a risky procedure. Consequently, it develops a pronounced sensitivity to ecological problems. Whereas Luhmann aligns norms and scarcity with law and the economy respectively, it is remarkable that he neglects to specify any equivalent in the case of risk. He stresses that the future can be dealt with only in the medium of probability/improbability, but to this he adds that under current conditions the social dimension is obtaining greater weight or, at least, a different status than before (Luhmann 1993: 72). In his own account of the social dimension, however, he elaborates only on the familiar contemporary risk conflicts. Although mentioning the possibility of social agreement, his characteristic sceptical position that communication leads to dissent rather than consent shines through everywhere (1993: 116–17, 155). Bechmann (1993b: 258) is emphatic that the opposition between risk and danger generates more dissent than it opens possibilities for consent, while Blühdorn (1997: 143) foresees at best only aimless and ineffective debates. Luhmann (1993: 115) himself introduces the interesting theoretical concept of 'a recursive networking of all individual contributions to communication' and mentions writing and printing as early examples of such a development, but he declines to entertain what this might mean today. Considering current developments, one might surmise that a possible candidate for the missing institutional carrier could be the public sphere (Habermas 1989, 1996; Eder 1996b) or, more generally, some form of global governance – a topic receiving increasing attention today (Zolo 1997; Archibugi et al. 1998; Dower 1998; Habermas 1998). But Luhmann (1993: 79, 158–60) and, following him, both Bechmann (1993b: 260–2) and Blühdorn (1997: 141) emphatically reject the relevance of any form of intersubjectivity or global ethics, which would form one of its necessary components.

Considering that Luhmann treats risk as a form of time-binding, it is apparent that he does not regard it simply as an observable object, a real thing or a fact. Rather, it is a form of perception and understanding or what he calls a 'contingency schema' (Luhmann 1993: 17). It brings together and couples event and loss, and thus allows people in the first instance to identify something in reality. But because both event and loss are temporal contingencies rather than facts, something that might occur in the future, this form of perception and understanding makes it possible for people to differ in the way they see and interpret matters. Some see it as risk, others as danger. Thus, as Luhmann puts it: 'Temporal contingencies provoke social contingencies' (1993: 17). This is characteristic of contemporary society. During the nineteenth century and the first two-thirds of the twentieth, there was a certain unity between the temporal and the social dimensions, between the future and society. In the late twentieth century, by contrast, uncertainties in the temporal dimension infiltrated the social dimension. The future, which can be perceived only in the medium of probability, invaded society. At this level, we witness the difference and indeed widespread contemporary conflict between those who see and interpret potential loss in antagonistic ways – either as risk or as danger. On the one hand, there are those who regard potential loss as the consequence of a decision – a decision to take a risk and thus to avail of an opportunity or chance. On the other, there are those who regard such loss as externally caused and imposed on them – that is, as a danger – without consultation or their consent. Luhmann (1993: 101–23) thus sees the contingency schema that allows something to be interpreted either as a risk or as a danger as today typically taking on the form of a social difference and social conflict between decision-makers and those affected. Bechmann (1993a: xxii) even regards this relation as a structural conflict, a conflict inscribed in the very structure of contemporary society, that has to be regarded as characteristic of scientific-technological development. Sociologically, then, the theme of risk concerns less real things than the relationship between the time dimension and the social dimension, or between the future and society, and especially struc-ture formation. The latter includes new institutions and forms of social regulation for risky behaviour that are as yet difficult to anticipate.

Luhmann accepts that it was the spectacular upsurge of ecological risk generated by technological development that impelled the pronounced con-temporary awareness of the high degree to which society endangers itself and thus the characteristic risk consciousness of our time (1993: 71). But in contrast to Beck, who especially in his earlier writings suggested that deciding in favour of a proper technology and an adequate way of dealing with it would provide a solution, he traces the problem to the deeper level of the centrality of decision-making in contemporary society. The future is indeterminable not only because of the complexity of reality and our lack of knowledge, but above all because it depends on and is shaped by the process of deciding itself. To make a decision in the present is to run the risk of a loss in the future, but not deciding leaves one in exactly the same position (Luhmann 1993: 28). The uniqueness of contemporary society does not simply reside in its dependence on decision-making and its obses-sion with the future, therefore, but it is focused by the self-referential nature of decision-making in the present and hence the double-sided nature of risk. Luhmann thus builds the risk problematic into the paradoxical nature of modernity as such. This eventuates in his view of contemporary society as a society of contingency (1998) or a 'hypothetical society', as Bechmann (1993b: 266) calls it, for which risk serves as the emblem. The social theoretic core of the risk problem and, more broadly, of the risk society is that the transformation of modernity has led to a new paradoxical type of action of which high technology, with science behind it, is the paradigm case. Whether we make a decision or let it go, whether we act or wait, either way we run a risk since the consequences are equally unknown in both cases.

Over and above the beneficial sobering effect of Luhmann's systems theoretical account of the complexity of contemporary society, the scept-ical thrust of Luhmann's view of the contingent society, which is explicitly and even vociferously advanced by Bechmann (1993b) and Blühdorn (1997), is obvious – not unlike that of Smart (1998), who proceeds from postmodern-ist presuppositions. From this viewpoint, Beck's various proposals toward a solution to the problem of the self-endangerment of society appear as being part of the problem. The risks that Beck conceives of as decision-based, manufactured uncertainties duplicate themselves in their double-sided or paradoxical form precisely in the solutions he proposes to deal with risk. Irrespective of whether it is a matter of waiting for the self-destructive and self-critical tendencies of society to manifest themselves, reversing the burden of proof, establishing principles of attribution and liability, developing a network of reciprocal control measures, holding prior debates about consequences, strengthening the possibilities of contradiction and veto, and revitalizing enlightenment (Beck 1995: 169–83) – in the sceptical view, all these measures remain caught up in the unavoidable dilemma of risk politics. They only add to the central problem of decision-making, rendering it more complicated and difficult, without any prospect of discriminating between the good and the bad consequences (Luhmann 1993: 152–60). And what is more, from the sceptical viewpoint Beck completely underestimates the complexity of the situation. Even if the risks at issue in contemporary society are invariably dependent on decisions, in distinction to externally imposed dangers such as earthquakes or meteorite strikes, they are for the most part not attributable to any particular decisions. In this respect, Luhmann (1993: 26) specifically mentions damage to the environment. An irreversible shift in the ecological balance, such as global warming, becomes visible or a disaster, such as unprecedented flooding in Britain, occurs once a given threshold is overstepped. In the buildup toward the threshold, however, no individual decisions can be isolated, but only the accumulation of the effects of decision-making, the long-term consequences of decisions no longer identifiable, over-complex and indistinct causal relations, and so forth. Although it is apparent that without decisions having been made nothing of the sort would have happened, certain conditions bring about so-called 'second-order dangers' (Luhmann 1993: 26) involving considerable losses or damage that defy being linked to particular decisions.

The way in which society deals with the paradoxical problem it faces, according to Luhmann (1993: 76–82), is not by trying to solve it, but rather by accepting and elaborating it – which means multiplying and specifying the risks. The differentiation of society into a multiplicity of autonomous, operatively closed systems serves this purpose. Each of the systems, depending on whether it is coded as political, economic, scientific, legal or whatever, selects problems and treats them in its own terms. Through these systems, society possesses a range of differentiated and highly specific forms for heightening, normalizing and contextualizing risks. On the one hand, each system engages in and encourages risk taking through the pressure to make decisions, and thus it increases the riskiness of its operations. On the other, each limits such riskiness by bringing its own criteria or 'binary coding' (Luhmann 1989: 36–43, 1993: 76) to bear on the given situation. Science deals with it by developing knowledge according to truth or falsity; the economy approaches it through cost in terms of payment or nonpayment; the law rules on it according to whether it is legal or illegal; politics makes decisions in terms of the distinction between government and opposition and, secondarily, between conservative and progressive, and so forth. Although they are thus operationally closed, the systems could affect one another. This possibility grows in proportion as traditional safety nets such as a unified culture, morality, the family or community have become eroded, as is typical in contemporary society. Transfer effects are observable when a risk acceptable to a given system has an unpredictable or unsettling impact on other systems. In the recent past, for instance, the development of scientific knowledge and its technological application, say microbiology in genetic engineering, had serious consequences for both the economic and the political system. By providing structures that enforce the availing of possibilities or opportunities and hence risk-taking, the function systems together immensely increase the riskiness of all the operations in society. Everything then depends on the capacity of individual systems to tolerate, absorb and deal with eventualities. In fact, Luhmann leaves open the possibility that the various systems constituting contemporary society reproduce themselves in such a way that their continued existence cannot be ensured any longer – without our being able to do anything about it (Luhmann 1989; Miller 1994). Contemporary society, then, is characterized by the encouragement of the taking of risks, the reduction of traditional safety nets, and the abandonment of the consequences to an unregulated process of mutual accommodation of the function systems.

The nature of contemporary society, for Luhmann, not only explains why we today live in 'a society . . . that has no choice but to run risks', experience 'the future as opaque' and see it darkly in terms of 'potential and possibly no longer controllable losses' (Luhmann 1993: 218, 82). Simultaneously, it also shows why sociology is forced to adopt a position of 'abstinence' (1998: 1–7), compelled to 'adjust' to the process whereby the societal system realizes its own differentiation and autopoiesis. As a consequence, Luhmann insists, sociology has no option other than to jettison every concern with 'practical reason', 'ethics' and 'critique' in favour of confining itself to a strictly 'scientific description' and 'insight into the structures of modern society and the consequences thereof' (1993: 213, 212).

Summary

In this chapter, the two major contemporary theoretical directions in the social scientific field of risk, environment and society were analytically presented. Against the foil of the most important background theories and epistemological frameworks, the tensions and conflicts within but especially between the critical theory of the risk society and the sceptical theory of the contingent society were highlighted. What also became apparent, however, is that it is theoretically impossible to settle for any one of these two positions simply and purely. Whereas Beck, especially in his earlier work, was too naive and optimistic, Luhmann is too fond of the normatively devoid paradoxical complexities of society. The only way of dealing with the problem of the relation of the two theories, therefore, is to make theoretical choices on the basis of an evaluative position favouring the possibility of learning and of democracy, without excluding an awareness of obstacles and ambivalence, which is closer to Beck, Eder and Wynne than to Luhmann and some of his followers.

In any case, the above analysis not only offers us access to some of the most significant issues in the current social scientific debate, but also gives us a first grasp of the sociology of risk and the risk society. While Part two will be informed by the theoretical insights obtained here, it will be substantively developed in accordance with the major dimensions that are at issue for interested citizens and social scientists alike, as suggested by the analysis. It is therefore to the more systematic presentation and analysis of the cultural and institutional dimensions of contemporary society in the next four chapters that I turn now.

PART TWO

Cultural and institutional analysis

4

Risk – what is it?

Since the early 1960s, as was apparent from the analysis in Chapter 1, risk has been of central importance in expert, public and social scientific debates about technology and the environment. By the end of the 1980s, at any rate, many gained the impression that a fundamental change was taking place in the semantics of late twentieth century society. From a twenty-first-century perspective, the recent intensification of debates especially around genetic engineering, biotechnology and bioethics confirms that this impression was essentially correct. During this period, a new language, vocabulary and linguistic meanings made their appearance in debates and began to overlap with the dominant themes and topics of the preceding period. Like production, growth and wealth earlier, risk and related words now took on a prominence they never enjoyed before. This highly visible new societal semantics, which provides us with a valuable access route into contemporary society, raises a whole range of progressively deeper questions that I propose to explore in this chapter.

Beginning with an analysis of the semantic level, we shall review the history of the word and concept of risk and seek to uncover the cognitive schemata and cultural models that from a certain point of view explain the current prominence of the phenomenon of risk. On this basis, it will be possible to obtain a grasp of the current classification of risks – not only distinct semantic fields of risk, but in particular the difference between old and new risks. This is a necessary step in the understanding of the new quality ascribed to contemporary risks. Social scientists, however, are unable to content themselves with semantics, cognitive structures, cultural models and classifications of risks alone, and therefore questions about how risks figure in public debates will also be raised.

Risk semantics

During past decades, we have been witnesses of a change in the semantics of society and hence, as will become clear in due course, in its cognitive organization. A shift has taken place from an economic semantics to a risk semantics. It would of course be an exaggeration to say that the latter displaced the former, but there can be little doubt that the new risk semantics has begun to cover and even go beyond the older economic semantics. While the new social movements were the proponents of this momentous semantic change, it is the case that any historically specific societal semantics is rooted in cognitively processed experiences of everyday life. Any societal semantics thus embraces a reference to reality and the different images or representations that those involved have of reality. The economic semantics of the preceding period fed on the elementary experience of unequal access to generally desired yet scarce resources and values. For instance, some commanded wealth, whereas others suffered poverty. The new risk semantics, by contrast, is generated by experiences undergone in the face of high technologies and their consequences and side-effects, particularly in the guise of the environmental crisis. For some, nuclear, chemical and genetic technologies offer a chance warranting the taking of risks, whereas others suffer from the dangers involuntarily and without consultation imposed upon them. In fact, today even those who take such risks are beginning to experience that the dangers thus generated threaten themselves too.

The new semantics that has gained currency in public communication and publications of all sorts consists of a set of closely related words and meanings, including danger, hazard, threat and risk. Others such as safety, risk research or risk analysis, risk assessment, risk acceptance, risk perception, risk management, cleaner production, technology assessment and technology opposition equally belong to it. Still other crucial ones such as ecology and nature as well as sustainability and responsibility must also be reckoned to it. Less obvious yet closely related to it is also the widely employed word knowledge. A tabular comparison of this new risk semantics

Table 4.1 Comparative perspective on contemporary risk semantics

State society (16th–18th centuries)	Industrial society (late 18th–mid-20th centuries)	Risk society (late 20th–21st centuries)
Domination	Wealth	Risk
Violence	Poverty	Danger
State	Economy/industry	Ecology
Order	Production/growth	Safety/sustainability
Constitution	The social	Nature
Rights	Justice	Responsibility
Law	Money	Knowledge

with other historically distinct societal semantics from the past three to four centuries is illuminating. In addition to the economic semantics of the nineteenth and twentieth century mentioned earlier, Table 4.1 includes for the sake of comparison also the semantics of the early modern state society, which was characterized by a pervasive experience of domination and violence (Strydom 2000).

Considering that it is the key word in the new semantics of the late twentieth and the early twenty-first century, it would be worth our while to inquire briefly into the meaning of the word and to explore the concept of risk.

Lexical and conceptual history of risk

Although etymological dictionaries of the modern European languages typically contain entries for risk, it is freely admitted that the origin of the word is unknown and much debated (Onions 1976). One author for instance traces it to an Arabic root (Bonß 1991: 263), while others speculatively link it to Greek and Latin (Johnson and Covello 1987: i). As regards its use in Europe, one author locates it in fourteenth-century Spain and another discovers it in Italian documents dating from 1319 (Bonß 1991: 263). Basing himself on a French etymological dictionary article, Ewald (1989: 389; 1991: 198–9) traces the word *risque* to Italian and places it in the context of early modern maritime trade and insurance. *Risco* meant 'that which rips', from which 'reef' or 'rock' also derive, and thus referred to the 'risk that cargo runs on the high seas'. Johnson and Covello (1987: i) relate the modern word to the Vulgar Latin *resecum*, meaning 'danger', 'rock', 'risk at sea', and the Greek *rhiza*, meaning 'cliff', thus giving it a similar connotation of 'sailing around a dangerous obstacle'. In its older usage, risk had been understood as an objective danger embodied by a natural phenomenon or event such as a rock or storm. By contrast, the modern word is a neologism created by the theory of insurance and given institutional existence by the juridical definition of insurance (Ewald 1991: 199). Social theorists as different as Beck (1995: 76–8) and Luhmann (1993: 9) share this understanding with Ewald. Be that as it may, the modern word appeared in German in printed form for the first time in the sixteenth century (Luhmann 1993: 9), and it entered English in the seventeenth century via French and Italian (Onions 1976). Instead of the earlier 'run into danger', it then had the more differentiated meaning of 'a chance or peril of destruction or loss'. Rather than simply a *force majeure*, risk was during the next two centuries increasingly related to the consequences of human decisions and actions and seen as a specific mode of treatment of events which could affect individuals and groups. It is only in this context that the precariousness of the time dimension and especially the claim to rationality associated with the concept of risk became clearer.

According to Ewald (1986, 1989, 1991), risk became the central instrument in the creation of security by means of which the 'provident' or welfare state was brought into being and organized. By way of the calculus of risk, supported by population statistics, accident statistics, general settlement formulae and the general principle of monetary compensation for damages, the incalculable was rendered calculable so as to create present security in the face of an open, unpredictable and uncertain future. Even classical sociology and its concept of society, such as represented by Durkheim, and perhaps even Weber's notion of the process of rationalization, depended on these developments. As the core technology of insurance, risk presupposed the development of science, mathematics and particularly probability theory since the eighteenth century (Hacking 1990; Bernstein 1998). On the one hand, the concept of risk brought to awareness that more things might happen in the future than actually will happen, some of which may be positive and others negative. On the other, it advanced an explicit claim to rationality in that it purported to express eventualities in terms of probabilities. Due to this rationalist tradition, it is to this day still accepted that in certain contexts risk is a quantity that can be measured quite precisely by means of a formula. According to it, risk is equivalent to the probability of loss multiplied by the magnitude of loss divided by time (Bechmann 1993a: ix; Rayner and Cantor 1998: 91). As the trajectory of the risk discourse demonstrated, however, this rationalist or formal-normative approach, which typically informs risk management, suffers from severe limitations. Not only does its narrow technical definition block a better and broader public understanding of probabilities, but also it focuses on the avoidance of undesirable outcomes below the level that is relevant for societal technology choices. This implies that it ignores the question of fairness or justice connected with issues of safety (Luhmann 1993: 13–14; Rayner and Cantor 1998) – not to mention the question of responsibility.

Due to these limitations, risk became more broadly understood and employed in public communication in the late twentieth century. Its meaning cannot be confined to the actuarial formula of the formal-normative approach or, to put it differently, to calculation injunctions aimed at averting loss while rationally exploiting the available options. Even to expand it beyond engineering considerations of what is optimal and what is not so as to include considerations of what is desirable and what is not, as psychologists often do, does not capture the full meaning of the current concept of risk. Although everyday language seems to confound risk and danger, the very fact that it links the two gives a more accurate indication of the contemporary sense of the concept. As Luhmann (1993: 21) and Beck (1999: 137) both stress, risk is a two-sided matter. It gives rise to the distinct and even conflicting perspectives of those interested and those involuntarily affected. The risk society, in other words, is a society in which some take risks for the sake of possible benefits and others are compelled to face the dangerous consequences of such risk taking. It is precisely this broad understanding of risk, which has been achieved in the course of the risk discourse, that is captured by the culturally informed sociological approach. Both Beck and Luhmann have learned from this advance. It should be noted, however, that Douglas and Giddens take different positions here. Douglas (1994: 38–54) laments the fact that risk as a probability calculation aimed at reducing uncertainty is simply transcribed as unacceptable danger, as do the general public as well as Beck, and then put to the same primitive political uses as any term for danger. Her ideal is a hierarchical tradition, such as that of Japan, which would preclude the typically western politicization of risk. Giddens (1990: 34) claims that risk and danger are closely related yet not the same, but then in effect rejects the distinction when he submits that risk is precisely the danger that future loss could occur.

Scheme of safety and danger

Beyond questions of etymology and semantics, an adequate grasp of risk today requires that it be located in the context of the transformation of society since the 1960s and 1970s. Besides the wide range of historical events and processes to which social scientists have given attention in order to characterize the implosion of modernity and the new times in which we are living today, however, risk semantics presupposes the cognitive organization of society and everyday life (Strydom 2000: 59–67). Instead of fixing on external parameters, therefore, it is necessary to focus on the internal self-organization of society. Giddens writes that today 'thinking in terms of risk and risk assessment is a more or less ever-present exercise' (1991: 124). He is undoubtedly correct, and it seems to be all the more the case after the devastating terrorist attack on the World Trade Center in New York on 11 September, 2001. The question, however, is why. Social order in society and everyday life is the outcome of the human striving toward orientation and internal consistency. What has undergone a transformation in the recent past, from this perspective, are the relations that human beings maintain with themselves, with others, and with their social, cultural and natural world. On the basis of changes in reality and correspondingly in representations and interpretations of reality, people reconfigure this set of relations and cognitively attempt to create some degree of consistency among its various dimensions. The fact that change has taken place, that culture has become fragmented and that traditions and social norms have lost some of their force, by no means implies that the cognitive self-organization of society has broken down. Having become more complex and differentiated, it requires greater efforts from individuals, groups and organizations to engage in a process of cognitive self-organization and thus to give themselves a structure allowing them to maintain multiple relations, to evaluate each other mutually and the construct unique identities. Despite the implosion of modernity, the breakdown of metanarratives and the increase in possibilities, information, ambivalence, uncertainly and orientation problems, there is a hidden order below the confusing surface that can be traced to cognitive structures resulting from the search for orientation and consistency in this new situation.

The risk semantics of our time represents the most immediate level at which we are able to get a glimpse of the cognitive self-organization of contemporary society. As a fundamental semantics that is commonly yet quite differently used by a significant number of individuals, groups and organizations, it points toward the scheme or frame according to which reality is to an increasing degree cognitively structured, perceived and evaluated today. To identify this cognitive scheme or frame, let us penetrate beyond risk semantics to the conflicting concerns raised in the course of the risk discourse. On the one hand, experts early on expressed a concern about safety or security in the case of high technological innovations and developed a new strand of research that they hoped would assist in its furtherance. On the other, the public and social movements later through the communication of anxiety in the face of highly improbable yet potentially catastrophic circumstances gave expression to a new and pronounced awareness of danger. Together, these two opposing sets of orientations indicate the new scheme or frame that has come to play an increasingly important role in the cognitive self-organization of contemporary society. It is the cognitive scheme of safety or security and danger, as it may be called (Lau 1989: 418). Schemes or frames of this kind consist of cognitive structures. They are to be found in the minds of individuals who bring them into play in their actions through memory, but at the same time they also form part of culture in the form of models of reality which are collectively available. By employing the resources and rules contained in the mind and culture for the purposes of perceiving, interpreting and evaluating reality, individuals as well as groups and organizations are able to partake of the process of the cognitive self-organization of society (Strydom 2000).

It is interesting to note that cognitive schemes of this kind are central to social theory and, therefore, assert themselves in some form or another in the analyses of society presented by social scientists. The cognitive schemes of order and violence and of wealth and exploitation were in earlier epochs at the core of Hobbes's *Leviathan* (1973) and of Marx's *Capital* (1977) respectively. Similarly, the scheme of safety and danger at present provides the organizational core of the analyses of such leading authors as Beck, Luhmann, Giddens and others. Books such as *Risk Society*, *Risk: A Sociological Theory* and *The Consequences of Modernity* or *Modernity and Self-Identity* are replete with evidence of this kind. They exhibit their authors' consequential incorporation of contemporary cognitive structures and cultural models of reality as well as the impact of these structures and models on their selection, analysis, structuring and presentation of information and material.

Classification of the semantic field of risk

Psychologists, particularly the Oregon School following the psychometric paradigm (Slovic et al. 1979; Slovic 1987), were the first to develop a systematic classification of risks. Using psychophysical scaling and

multivariate analysis techniques, they produced a cognitive map of perceptions and attitudes toward a very wide range of hazards which could be
used to explain or predict reactions to risks and to improve communication
between policy-makers or decision-makers and the public. Individuals were
asked to judge the riskiness as well as the desired level of regulation of
diverse (from 30 to 81) hazards. These judgements were then related to a
range of properties of hazards that were hypothesized to account for risk
perceptions and attitudes, such as voluntariness, dread, knowledge, con-
trollability, benefit, number of deaths caused per annum, and so on. The
multiple elements of hazards that people purportedly perceive, weigh and
react to were finally subjected to factor analysis and thus, through the
correlation of different characteristics (for example, voluntary–controllable,
delayed adverse effect–not well known), condensed to a small set of higher
order factors. The researchers labelled the two principal factors that emerged
from the analysis 'dread' and 'unfamiliarity', and used them as axes to construct a 'factor space' (Slovic 1987).

This risk field consists of four cells in which the diverse hazards are
located according to whether they are dreaded or not (horizontal axis) and
whether they are unfamiliar or not (vertical axis). While the high dread/
known cell contains an old risk such as nuclear weapons, the new science-
and technology-based, high consequence risks such as air, water and soil
pollution, chemical pollution, nuclear reactor accidents, radioactive waste
and DNA technology all fall in the high dread/unknown sub-field. In
Slovic's mind, this classification applies to lay people who perceive hazards
in close relation to the various risk characteristics, typically bringing their
emotions into play and ignoring available information. The fact that
experts see riskiness devoid of emotion in terms of the available statistics
on expected annual morbidity he, by contrast, takes to explain why their
definition of risk conflicts with that of lay people.

Wynne (1989b) has severely criticized this psychometric classification of
risks both from a sociological and a policy viewpoint. By fixing on individual mental factors, the psychological approach overlooks the underlying
social judgements and institutional dimensions informing the divergence
between lay and expert evaluations of the riskiness of high technologies.
By the same token, it also consolidates the 'objective risk-subjective public
perception fallacy' (Wynne 1989b: 127), thus dismissing alternative social
judgements and foreclosing the opportunity of institutional innovation which
could bring both sides closer together in more mature and constructive risk
debates. In the light of Wynne's defence of the public against the charge of
emotionality and irrationality and his plea for institutionally enabled risk
debates, it is further apparent that the psychological attempt at the cognitive mapping of risks suffers from an all too narrow understanding of the
cognitive dimension. Rather than being confined to the minds or mental
factors of individuals, it should rather be extended to include over and
above mental cognitive structures also social and cultural cognitive structures
(Condor and Antaki 1997). Sociologically, it could then be approached in

terms of the social cognitive processes whereby different kinds of (both expert and lay) knowledge are generated and communicatively or discursively related to each other (Strydom 2000). It is only when such an approach is adopted that one could at all begin to appreciate the potential for collective learning inherent in risk debates (Eder 1985; Miller 1986; Rip 1986; Strydom 1987; Wynne 1988, 1989b).

As far as the classification of risks is concerned, this would suggest that one should rather focus on the semantic field of risk debates, if not of the risk discourse as such. The starting point here, which accommodates cognitive structuration through the scheme of safety and danger discussed above, is that a debate or, more broadly, a discourse is in train. In this medium, social actors, agents or groups with distinct perspectives focus on one and the same issue yet play competing and even conflicting interpretations out against one another. Such conflicting interpretations concern both the nature of the risk in question and its possible regulation. In the context of the risk discourse, conflicts of this kind have over time enlarged the field of risk far beyond the traditional limits of what to some appear as calculable risks and to others as clear and present dangers. Both the quality of potential damage or harm and its probability became graded and refined. On the one hand, potential damage was no longer confined to the ecological level and to the individual level of basic values and rights, but broader categories such as social, political and moral damage were also included. On the other, possibilities of damage that are remote and even speculative or hypothetical became a topic of debate. Increasingly, the unforeseen and unknown consequences and side-effects of the new high technologies, or so-called 'second-order dangers' (Bonß 1991: 265; Luhmann 1993: 26; Beck 1999: 153), were included. Adapting and developing Van den Daele (1992a: 327), these two dimensions can be used to construct a cognitive classification of the semantic field of the risk discourse (Table 4.2).

The cognitive space of this classification is opened up by the widely accepted contemporary scheme of safety or security and danger. Its semantic content is shot through with the ambivalence and paradoxical nature of issues that are antagonistically interpreted as at one and the same time a risk and a danger. Important to note is what the twofold tendency toward the broadening of categories of damage and toward decreasing probability of damage indicates. Its thrust is that what we do not know and, indeed, cannot know, hence uncertainty and ignorance, non-knowledge or unawareness (Wynne 1989b; Van den Daele 1992a; Luhmann 1998; Beck 1999; Giddens 1999), come to play an increasingly important role, even the key role, within the cognitive space of risk debates and discursive conflicts.

The universal, global and irreversible quality of new risks

Already in the late 1970s, psychologists included the distinction between old and new among the properties that they investigated from the perspective

Table 4.2 Cognitive classification of the semantic field of the risk discourse

Probability / Damage	Known risks	Suspected risks	Hypothetical risks
Ecological	Pollution through chemicals, gases, radiation, genetic modification, etc.	Irreversible damage to parts of the ecosystem	Collapse of the ecosystem
Personal	Ill health and death through radiation, pathogens, toxins and genetically modified organisms	Involuntary inclusion in state protection programmes	Epidemics and mass deaths through second order dangers
Social	Damage of social relations through technicization	Erosion of social forms of life	Reideologization of western societies and irreversible transmutation of the social
Political	High-technological subpolitical developments beyond democratic legitimation	Erosion of democratic political institutions (e.g. parliaments) and public sphere	Biotechnical regulation and control of social processes
Moral	Erosion of the image of being human	Manipulation, selection and enhancement of human characteristics (e.g. sex, hair colour, brain function)	Genetic transformation of human beings and acceptance of eugenics and human breeding

of the perception of risks (Slovic et al. 1979). In the case of nuclear power, for instance, it proved most significant. The newness correlated highly with properties such as involuntary, catastrophic, dread and invisibility, and thus decisively distinguished nuclear power from other technologies such as conventional electric power. What was true of nuclear power, also applied to chemical and DNA technologies (Slovic 1987). Rather than taking it to be an incontrovertible fact, however, the psychologists attributed this evaluation to the irrationality and emotionality of the public. In effect, therefore, they denied the significance of the distinction between old and new risks. Anthropological cultural theorists (Douglas and Wildavsky 1982; Wildavsky 1994) supported them in this. Not only did these theorists deny that there was any difference between tribal and modern societies and hence the risks they respectively face, but also they made it plain that they were partial by siding with the Promethean risk takers against the new social movements, environmentalists and significant sections of the public. Sociologists who draw on cultural theory to claim that risk debates are simply ritualized symbolic attempts to deal with technology and its danger potential, effectively achieve a comparable result (Conrad 1986; Alexander and Smith 1996).

The thrust of psychological, anthropological and cultural sociological attempts to obliterate the distinction between old and new risks, and thus to deny the unique qualities of the new risks, is readily apparent. They form part of, or at least facilitate, the ineffective and barely legitimate authoritarian strategy that Wynne (1988, 1989a, 1989b) exposed in exemplary fashion in numerous of his publications. Experts, safety officers and government officials, who do not hesitate to regard public opposition to technology as a threat to civilization and even as mob rule, seek to lead people to accept that the risks taken with high technologies today entail no more than the risks we had run in the past. Typically, they offer a laundered, 'white boxed' version of technology that is aimed both at the legitimation of technology and at social closure (Wynne 1988: 160). For sociologists who, by contrast, insist on the necessity of a theory of contemporary society, whether of the 'risk society' (Beck 1992), the 'negentropic order' (Luhmann 1991: 103) or 'radicalized' or 'high modernity' (Giddens 1990: 150; 1991: 4), the distinction between old and new risks are of central theoretical importance. It should be noted that Luhmann's position has the same conservative political intent as those mentioned above who obliterate the distinction between old and new risks. Yet by retaining this distinction and linking it to contingency and paradox, he is able to achieve this effect in a way that is much subtler and less vulnerable to exposure and criticism. This is precisely the sense of his sceptical theory.

In *Risk Society*, Beck operated with a distinction between old and new risks – the latter called 'modernization risks' (1992: 21). Giddens likewise drew a line between the distinct risk environments of pre-modern and modern times, and located what he called 'high-consequence risks' in the latter context (1990: 102, 171). Subsequently, Beck and some authors working closely with him introduced a more refined threefold distinction. Beck distinguished between 'pre-industrial hazards', 'industrial risks' and 'incalculable insecurities in the form of large-scale hazards of late industrialism' (1995: 77), Lau distinguished between 'traditional risks', 'industrial-welfare state risks' and 'new risks' (1989: 420–6), and Bonß, finally, differentiated 'dangers', 'risks' and 'second-order dangers' (1991: 266). Luhmann, surprisingly enough, adopts a comparable position. Whereas danger was emphasized in older societies and risk in modern society, today risk and danger come into conflict in a situation defined by high technology and the cumulation of the effects of decision-making (Luhmann 1993: 24–5, 26, 83). Although adopting the threefold model of traditional cultures, industrial society and high modernity, Giddens continues to distinguish between only two types of risks: 'external risk' and 'manufactured risk' or 'traditional risks' and 'new risks' (1999: 26–7). What matters, however, is the unique quality that these theorists ascribe to the new risks. Without exception, all of them assume that the new risks involve phenomena unknown until the late twentieth century.

Initially, Beck (1992) filled out his distinction between old and new risks by means of a wide range of conceptual pairs such as individual/collective, local/global, sporadic/systematically produced, perceptible/imperceptible, insurable/uninsurable and attributable/non-attributable. They offer a sense of the unique quality of the new risks which he later more systematically and formally tried to capture by means of the statement that they can be delimited neither spatially, nor temporally, nor socially (Beck 1995: 76–7). Mega-hazards of an ecological, nuclear, chemical and genetic kind thus equally affect producers, consumers and all third parties in the broad sense of the word, including living as well as yet unborn beings occupying the biosphere. Giddens stresses that high-consequence risks were unknown in previous eras and have a distinctive quality (1991: 4, 122). Although he does not develop this in a systematic way, it is possible to extrapolate from his relevant writings the very features singled out by Beck. Giddens acknowledges that contemporary risks are faced collectively since they affect virtually everyone (1991: 117, 137). What receives most emphasis in his analyses, however, is the relation between high-consequence risks and the globalized character of high modern social systems (1990: 163–73; 1991: 4, 136–7). Finally, he also lists the irreversibility of these risks (1990: 173).

As regards their unique and distinctive quality, then, we can conclude that contemporary risks are universal, global and irreversible (Halfmann 1988: 14). Socially, they are universal in that they threaten all living beings, from humans through animals to plants. Spatially, they are global in that they know no geographic boundaries and limits, violating political borders and evolutionary niches and penetrating the earth's atmosphere. Temporally, they are irreversible in that they produce adverse effects for future generations of human beings and species of animals and plants. Rather than fixing exclusively on the external or objective features, however, the leading risk theorists are sensitive to the internal or subjective–intersubjective dimension of contemporary risks. In some way, therefore, all of them – Luhmann (1989: 127–32) and Giddens (1990: 131–4) as much as Beck (1992: 49–50) – associate also fear, dread or anxiety with the risks of the late twentieth and twenty-first centuries. For Beck, for instance, the risk society is one in which fear prevails and where the commonality of anxiety provides the basis for a new kind of solidarity and becomes a political force. Fear, dread and anxiety or alarm are interpreted by many, including Douglas and Wildavsky and Luhmann, as an opportunity to discredit those communicating it as being irrational and emotional and serving their own dogmatic or sectarian purposes. A sociological stance does not allow such partiality, however, since it at best leads to the reproduction of the well-known yet ineffective, immature, destructive and barely legitimate authoritarian strategy of denying and excluding from on high public concerns and opposed social judgements. It is a matter, as Beck stresses, neither of 'the dogmatization of expert knowledge', nor of the 'dogmatization of anti-expert [or social movement] knowledge' (1999: 123). An adequate social scientific approach today requires, by contrast, that the multiplicity of competing and conflicting contributions to public communication – including those motivated by anxiety – be located in the discursive process in the medium of which they are related to one another in the working out of the politics of risk.

The reality of risk and its social construction

The idea that risk is something determinable by direct observation, once widely held among natural scientists, risk analysts and environmental sociologists, was effectively put in its place by Douglas in the early 1980s. Inspired by the renaissance in the sociology of knowledge, she argued that risk is a social or collective construct (Douglas 1973; Douglas and Wildavsky 1982). If this claim is taken seriously, as it has to be, then it means that the qualities ascribed to contemporary risks are not simply physical or objective properties of a real, positively given phenomenon. Yearley (1996), for instance, has convincingly demonstrated that the world's environmental problems came to be global through culturally structured social practices and action, from economic activities to promotional, protest and political activities of social movements, NGOs, firms, states and supranational organizations. While containing a reference to reality, whether an event (such as the Chernobyl catastrophe) or what is for the time being accepted as a hard fact (for example, that the carbon dioxide level is on the rise), risks are socially constructed, whether the risk of nuclear radiation or of global warming. As Mannheim (1993: 399–437) pointed out, what is collectively defined and accepted as social reality, the public interpretation of reality, is achieved in public communication. As part of social reality, therefore, risk is a stake rooted in reality over which people compete and conflict in public communication and which becomes collectively interpreted, defined and accepted in and through a mediated discursive process to which the different participants make contributions from their own unique perspectives.

The dynamics of this public discursive process is of cardinal importance for an adequate understanding of risk. Although proposing construction, Douglas's structural anthropology proved too static and anachronistic for the task. The credit has to go to constructivist sociology (Berger and Luckmann 1967; Garfinkel 1967; Blumer 1971; Spector and Kitsuse 1977; Gusfield 1981) and to the new sociology of scientific knowledge (Bloor 1976; Mendelsohn et al. 1977; Latour and Woolgar 1979; Knorr 1981; Knorr-Cetina and Mulkay 1983; Weingart 1983; Aronson 1984; Gilbert and Mulkay 1984; Jasanoff 1987). For they cleared the way for a full-scale social scientific analysis of the mediated discursive processes through which reality – including risk – is socially constructed. Of the major social risk theorists, Beck is the only one who has incorporated this component centrally into his work. He sees risk as being constructed in a process of struggle among different rationality claims in which the admixture or amalgamation of the knowledges of the different agents gives rise to a collectively acceptable definition (Beck 1992: 23, 55, 59). Thus far, however, he has neglected either to state it systematically or to offer a systematic analysis along these lines. Through his appropriation of such notions as the 'knowledgeability' of agents, 'discourse' as the mode of articulation of knowledge and 'frames' as clusters of rules helping to constitute, make sense and regulate activities, Giddens (1984: 87–92) has theoretically opened the way for the acceptance of constructivism. Yet he has not brought it to bear on his account of risk. The social constructivist view is of great importance to Wynne, who focuses on the dialectic between experts and public. Crucial to him is the dynamic interaction of multiple and apparently contradictory discourses in the medium of public discourse, which he evaluates according to whether it is degenerative or allows social and political learning (Wynne 1988: 160–4). But in his writings, too, it makes an unsystematic appearance or is used for the purposes of limited, unsystematic case studies. The most extensive and detailed contributions, both theoretically and empirically, were made by Eder (1988, 1993a, 1996a), Eyerman and Jamison (1991) and Hajer (1995). Eder is a Habermasian who for years worked closely with the master thinker. Eyerman and Jamison align themselves also with Habermas. Hajer, who is associated with Beck, shows some Habermasian influence, but his work rests more on a fusion of Foucault's post-structuralist discourse theory and Harré and Billig's social-psychological argumentative discourse theory.

Eyerman and Jamison took the decisive step in consolidating and transposing to the macro-level the link that tentatively had become established in the course of the 1970s and 1980s among the constructivist, the communicative, the cognitive and the cultural turn in sociology. They gave Habermas's notion of communicative interaction pride of place and by means of his own distinction among technical, hermeneutical and emancipatory cognitive interests reinterpreted it cognitively. Habermas envisaged the linguistically mediated, intersubjective process in the medium of which actors establish interpersonal relations and coordinate their actions through negotiating definitions of the situation and coming to agreement. From Eyerman and Jamison's vantage point, it was the creative, reflexive and discursive cognitive process through which knowledge is collectively produced and society is thus socially constructed. Whereas they still confined themselves to a social movement perspective, Eder (1993a) extended the problematic to the structural context by shifting to public communication. While retaining the emphasis on the discursive nature of the cognitive process, he developed a more sophisticated theoretical and empirical position on both the cognitive structures playing a structuring role in the process and the discursive dynamics in which the resulting cognitive frames of the different actors give rise to a collectively accepted master frame (Eder 1996a; Strydom 1999c, 2000). According to this theoretically most advanced account, social actors or agents draw empirical, moral and aesthetic framing devices from culture to construct cognitive frames for themselves. Once these frames enter public communication, a discursive dynamic of competition and conflict ensues from which emanates a collectively constructed and accepted master frame – for instance, a collectively identified, interpreted, defined, accepted and validated risk. Hajer's socio-cognitive constructivism, which focuses on the political process of struggle for discursive dominance, is broadly comparable to Eder's, but it suffers from a number of theoretical limitations. Although he starts from the 'communicative miracle' (Hajer 1995: 42), he is not sufficiently decisive about the theoretical status of public communication, with the result that the level of generality of his concept of discourse is never clarified and hence remains ambiguous. Since the analysis of the social process of discursive construction for him takes the form of discourse analysis at the level of narrative story-lines, which is indeed important, he underplays the crucial complementary dimension of the analysis of frames and their construction by means of framing devices. One of his strengths, on the other hand, is his notion of discursive dominance or hegemony as socio-cognitive product (Hajer 1995: 60), which brings power into play. Through factors such as credibility, acceptability and trust, the cognitive and the social dimension, particularly cognitive structures and constructs on the one hand and power on the other, become intertwined so as to give rise to a collectively recognized and accepted definition of a risk. What Hajer does not appreciate sufficiently, however, is that such a socially constructed risk is not simply a matter of dominance or hegemony, since trust and social acceptance imply a normative quality of recognition (Honneth 1992) and moral justifiability transcending the exercise of sheer power (Honneth 1991; Habermas 1996). But it would be unwise, of course, to lose sight of the apparently growing potential of professionalized collective agents such as parties, corporations, the media and the state to instrumentalize public communication for their own particularistic interests (Mayhew 1997).

Summary

In this chapter, risk was clarified by considering it at a number of progressively deeper levels. Having gained access to it via the risk semantics prevalent in contemporary public debates, I explored the etymology and lexical meaning of the word as well as attempts to conceptualize it. This led us to penetrate to the level of the cognitive organization of society and, specifically, to attend to the significant contemporary cognitive scheme of safety and danger which accounts for the relevance of the phenomenon of risk today. Approaching the risk discourse from this perspective, it was possible to trace the broadening and deepening of the risk problematic over the last number of decades by cognitively classifying the semantic field of risk. This raised the question not only of the unique quality that is assigned to contemporary risks, but also of the social construction of risk in public discourse. It was suggested that, beyond major risk theorists such as Beck, Luhmann and Giddens, the proposals of Eyerman and Jamison, Eder and Hajer together point toward the possibility of a theoretically sophisticated social scientific understanding of risk that gives prominence to its social construction without losing hold of its reality.

5

Societal production of risk: society as laboratory

During the past few decades, the social sciences increasingly came to recognize that risk is a socially constructed phenomenon. The heavy emphasis on construction and its potential idealistic implications in turn called forth a demand to reassert the reality of risk. When criticized for her pronounced culturalism, even Douglas defended herself by submitting that risks are real, indeed, 'horribly real' (1994: 29). Sociologically, however, it is not sufficient to bring the reality of risk to mind by conjuring up death and destruction. In this vein, Beck submits in his characteristically flamboyant language that 'risk society theory is *not* about exploding nuclear submarines' (2000: 226). Critics of extreme constructivism such as Buttel and Taylor insist that sociology cannot afford to give up its concern with 'science and technology as material-productive forces' (1994: 240). Although differing in their respective emphases, the major risk theorists, including even the sceptical constructivist Luhmann, all dwell on the importance of this dimension in giving reality to risk. Beck stresses science, technology and industry, Giddens capitalism and industrialism, Luhmann high technology, and Burns and Dietz (1997: 55) capitalism, the state, science and technology. A sociology of risk and the risk society must therefore include a sociology of science and technology, industrialism, capitalism and the state. The crucial point, however, is that it cannot simply be a conventional sociology that accounts for the societal production of risk, the facilitation of risk production, and the employment of potentially catastrophic technologies. It has to be a sociology that acknowledges that risks, as disadvantages and threats to collective life, are not merely connected to decisions and human action, but that they are simultaneously dependent on culturally defined processes. Science, technology, industry, capitalism and the state set processes in train that, despite their operation over people's heads and behind their backs, are themselves constituted and guided by cultural models.

Through such models culture plays a fundamental role in the societal production of risks. It is interesting, further, that it is precisely these cultural
models and the role they play that have become a major topic and source
of conflict in the risk discourse over the past number of decades. The
new social movements were instrumental in highlighting these models
by engaging in public risk communication, publicly problematizing high
consequence risks and heightening the degree of reflexivity in society. To
grasp the conditions of the risk society, therefore, it is not sufficient to
look at science, technology, industry, capitalism and so forth. The relation
between society and nature must be taken into account, and a sociology of
culture and of the public sphere is also required.

In this chapter, I propose to consider the conditions of the societal production of high consequence risks by retracing the historical process of
development leading up to contemporary risk society from this culturally
informed perspective. An analysis of the long-term shift from religion to
science will provide the background for a consideration of such culturally
defined phenomena as science, technology, industry, capitalism and the
state and, more broadly, the relation of society and nature. This analysis
will culminate in an account of contemporary society as an experimenting
rather than simply a risk society. In Chapter 6, the shift from science to the
public sphere will be added.

From religion to science

A basic historically significant condition of the societal production of risks
is the modern substitution of science for religion and the consequent
secularization of culture. The decisive step was taken in the seventeenth
century with the state-supported institutionalization of science, which was
consolidated by the scientific revolution of the nineteenth century.

During the medieval period, the religious worldview was the core component of culture, unifying the disparate dimensions of reality and allowing
humans to give meaning to them. Socially, the cultural significance of this
worldview was secured by the institutional dominance of the church, eccle-
siastical organizations and the clergy in everyday life. This privileged hegemonic position was secured by means of the monopolization of religious,
administrative, judicial and educational functions and services as well as
special arrangements and measures such as the separation of the clergy and
laity and the censorship and silencing of heretics and critics. The cumulat-
ive effects of a variety of developments during the Renaissance and Reformation, however, resulted in a fundamental change. These took place in
the context of at least four distinct dynamic forces or logics (Heller 1982:
283–4; Strydom 2000): the centralization of power and the means of violence leading to the formation of the state; second, the development of
technology and science; third, capitalism in the sense of the establishment
of private property, the global extension of the market and an increase in

inequality; and, finally, communication or more specifically democracy in the sense of the project of realizing ever more fully the rights of the members of society and thus decentralizing and rationalizing or civilizing both social and administrative power. Neither the religious worldview could any longer contain the resultant explosion of new ideas, knowledge and communications, nor the church maintain its control over the proliferating practices of new groups such as royalty, technicians, the scientific movement, merchants, humanists, Protestants and, more generally, an increasingly mobile population. Of overwhelming cultural importance was the development of technology and science, but the formation of the state proved to be of the most decisive institutional significance. In turn, the development of capitalism stimulated technology and science as well as the state.

Initially, technology and science developed independently from one another, the relation between them remaining a loose one for a long time. The fact that technology's potential for productivity from a capitalist viewpoint had been apparent from quite early partially accounts for its rapid development compared to science. The development of technology was spearheaded by a new group of specialists who separated from the older category of craftsmen and artisans in the fourteenth and fifteenth centuries. Among them were military technicians, metallurgists, gunpowder millers, chemical technicians, shipbuilders, mining technicians, machine builders, instrument makers and architects. In sixteenth-century Italy, this line of practically oriented men was brought together with learned academics from the universities, for instance through the intervention of the famous Brunelleschi. This provided the basis for the emergence of engineers and their new way of relating to and working in upon nature (Needham 1972; Moscovici 1977; Münch 1984). While furnishing the monarchical states of the period with machines for both war and entertainment, this development eventually culminated, relatively uninfluenced by science, in the seminal innovations of the Industrial Revolution, such as the spinning jenny, Arkwright's water frame, Compton's mule, the water mill and Watt's steam engine.

Science indeed did have its roots in innovations in sixteenth-century Italy, particularly Galileo's mathematization of nature (Heidegger 1978), but it became institutionalized in late-seventeenth-century England and France only on the basis of the philosophical revolution of the seventeenth century. Involving such paradigmatic figures as Bacon and Descartes, it was promoted by the scientific movement that was responsible for the transition to the mechanistic worldview (Toulmin and Goodfield 1968; Webster 1975; Moscovici 1977; Merchant 1990). It is important to note, however, that the actual institutionalization of science under the conditions of Restoration in England and of Absolutism in France depended on the state (Van den Daele 1977; Mandrou 1978). In both cases, the absolutist state opposed and sought to oust the church by monopolizing the means of education to obtain control over the official interpretation of reality (Mannheim 1993: 412). Thus science as a state-monopolized form of thought took the place of religion at the heart of culture. Once given institutional existence in 1662 in the Royal Society and in 1666 in the *Académie des Sciences* and once codified by Newton between 1687 and 1704, science could for the first time be practised as such and undergo internal development.

By 1808, Lavoisier and Dalton had laid down the necessary foundations for the classical synthesis of chemistry and physics, and on this basis a series of astonishing advances followed in the next six decades. Together, they constituted the scientific revolution of the nineteenth century (Toulmin and Goodfield 1968; Moscovici 1977). This achievement consolidated the substitution of science for religion at the core modern culture and the concomitant transformation of an essentially religious culture into a secular one. By the same token, it was also the presupposition for the ascendancy of the scientist over the engineer and the 'scientization of technology' (Habermas 1971: 104), the basing of technology on scientific knowledge. During the period up to and indeed including the Industrial Revolution, science played at best only a secondary role in relation to technical-engineering knowledge. The scientific revolution brought about a reversal of this relationship. The establishment of processes of chemical synthesis and the discovery of electromagnetism, for instance, opened the way for the transformation of technical-engineering knowledge into technology in the modern sense of the word – scientized technology. Henceforth, technology could be developed continuously on the basis of scientific knowledge rather than left to sporadic spurts depending on individual invention.

The scientization of technology provided the basis for a further historically significant step – the fusion of science, technology and industry (Habermas 1971: 104), which in turn had been driven and shaped by capitalism. It allowed the relation between science and technology to be brought to bear on large-scale industrial production for commercial purposes. Germany was the leader in this field in the late nineteenth century. The fusion of science, technology and industry took place first in the chemical industry (Toulmin and Goodfield 1968; Moscovici 1977) where the synthetic method was used for the production of soap, candles and especially colours or dye stuffs. From synthetic colours it was only a short step towards chemo-therapy and the founding of the pharmaceutical industry, from where it rapidly spread to mining, construction, agriculture and food processing. By the early twentieth century, however, the United States had taken over from Germany, as the example of the mass-produced Model T Ford demonstrates. It is important to bear in mind that the scientific revolution and the fusion of science, technology and industry also served as one of the preconditions for the late-nineteenth- and early-twentieth-century turn toward state intervention and the creation of the welfare state. It was widely accepted that the negative consequences and side-effects of the market-based industrial capitalist economic system, particularly the problem of poverty, could be resolved by the state. Invigorating and stabilizing the economy by placing it on a basis of science and technology, which is itself stimulated by means of military research, would make possible both objective wealth and subjective welfare (Ewald 1986; Evers 1987).

Culturally defined processes of risk production: the state and science

The institutionalization of science is a central problem in the understanding of the societal conditions of the production of risks. For here lies the source of the cultural definition of science as a core factor in the process of risk production. One has to go back to this seventeenth-century event in order to grasp science's peculiar mode of objectification of nature without which the typically modern technological manipulation and industrial exploitation of nature remain unintelligible. This event, however, was itself fundamentally shaped by the state. The state took the institutionalization of science under its wing in the course of the process of state formation and thus gave science the form of state-monopolized knowledge. One form of institutional knowledge, that is, religion tied to the church, was displaced by another, that is, science tied to the state. In the following, I give attention first to the state and then to science. In each case, the aim is to isolate the culturally defined processes that serve as conditions of the societal production of risks.

The state: raison d'état

The early modern state, paradigmatically the absolutist state on the continent and the Restoration state in seventeenth-century England, provided the institutional starting point of modern society. Here the long-term process of state-formation, driven by the monopolization of resources and the centralization of power, reached a significant level (Elias 1982). The state set out and indeed proved able to monopolize the means of physical force and violence and the necessary supporting fiscal and administrative resources. Characteristic developments of the time, such as the establishment of armies, the elaboration of legal and bureaucratic systems, the enforcement of taxation, the pacification of territorial populations and mercantilism, are all milestones marking the process of the centralization of power and the formation of the early modern state. At the same time, it was also in the state's interest to monopolize cultural resources through gaining control over the production of culture and cultural products. The central prong of this part of the state's project was the institutionalization of science (Van den Daele 1977; Mandrou 1978). A monopoly of science meant control over the means of relating to the future, of education and of dispensing the official interpretation of reality, which was crucial to the establishment and consolidation first of monarchical and then of state power.

To appreciate the shaping impact of the early modern state on the emerging institutional infrastructure of modern society and, more particularly, the cultural definition of the state, however, it is necessary to consider the original rationality of the state. In a sense, this rationality, and hence the cultural definition of the state pursued here, can be captured by means of the Foucauldian concept of 'governmentality' (Foucault 1988, 1991), but then at least two corrections need to be introduced. In the Foucauldian tradition, first, governmentality is plausibly taken as a deep-seated, collective mentality or understanding serving as a condition of the way that westerners since early modernity up until today have related to the state and the exercise of public power. It is not sufficient to regard this mode of relating to the state only in terms of 'thinking' (Dean 1999: 16), however, since feeling and behaving are equally involved. The cognitive concept of culture by means of which I am trying to clarify the cultural definition of the state requires that the intellectual, aesthetic-conative and moral-practical or normative dimensions all be taken into account simultaneously. Second, Foucault indeed characterizes the modern state as being 'demonic' (1988: 71) and thus approaches the cultural definition of the state I have in mind under the title of reason of state, but he overlooks perhaps the most crucial defining moment. Foucault (1988) stresses a discontinuity between the early modern understanding of the rationality of the state in terms of the doctrine of reason of state, on the one hand, and preceding Christian, judicial and Machiavellian positions, on the other. While there is certainly room for discontinuity, he misjudges the decidedly Inquisitorial and Machiavellian colouration of the doctrine of the reason of state (Skinner 1978). But above all, he neglects the transmission of the subterranean yet characteristic archaic aristocratic rationality of feudal times to the early modern state (Anderson 1980) and, via this latter institutional nodal point, to the modern state (Nederveen Pieterse 1990).

The early modern state, particularly the continental absolutist state and the Tudor and Stuart state in England, was the renewal and perpetuation in a novel political form of the rule of the landowning aristocracy which had existed in feudal times. It exhibited various typically modern features, including a standing army, a permanent administration, diplomacy, national taxation, codified law, trade and an expanding market, so that many were led to regard the early modern state as a bourgeois phenomenon. The fact of the matter, however, is that the early modern state remained feudal in a significant respect. At its very core, it retained a feudal element (Anderson 1980) which, under conditions of a 're-feudalization of European society' (Mannheim 1993: 500), was combined with novel forms of stratification and novel techniques of control. This feudal element was contained in the emphasis on a range of typically aristocratic concerns, from the consolidation of property in land and the centralization of power through *imperium* in the sense of a drive toward expansion and universal domination to extravagantly exhibitionist courts, country houses and lifestyles. Most important, however, was the subterranean archaic aristocratic rationality (Anderson 1980) that underpinned all these various concerns. It consisted of the valuing of, belief in and application of aggression, force, violence and warfare for the purposes of rule or domination, maintenance of power, accumulation of resources, gaining of prestige and territorial aggrandizement.

If one follows the historical vicissitudes of the state, it becomes apparent that it underwent a number of significant changes in the course of time. The constitutionalization of the state through the political or democratic revolutions is undoubtedly the most drastic of these changes. Developments such as these led many to believe that the aristocracy was displaced by the bourgeoisie and, concomitantly, that the feudal element of the state was eradicated. The French Revolution indeed brought an end to the monarchy in France, but in spite of its enormity and significance this historical event did not prevent the European aristocracy from retaining its paramount position. It remained a force to be reckoned with in the economic field and maintained a firm grip on the state, the military and culture. In fact, the aristocracy enjoyed a certain entrenchment in the state apparatus throughout the nineteenth century. Even the crisis of the aristocracy brought about by the depression of the last quarter of the nineteenth century and the reorientation toward an interventionist welfare state did not put a stop to the importance of the aristocracy. State power, including military power, came to serve as the bastion of its influence. This was expressly the case until the First World War, the last ditch stand of the European *ancien régime*, but it was also the mechanism by means of which the aristocracy secured its lasting importance. This continuity meant the retention of the feudal element and hence the archaic rationality at the core of the modern state.

The absolutist state provided the institutional starting point for the emergence of the modern state. The modern state came into being on the ruins of the absolutist state after the latter had been subjected to a revolutionary process of constitutionalization. Despite the breakdown of the absolutist state and its displacement by the modern state, however, the power structure of the state remained largely intact. The feudal core of the absolutist state, its archaic aristocratic rationality, often in functionalized form, stamped the power structure of the modern state in an indelible way. Even such later deep transformations as the democratization and the socialization of the state in the late nineteenth and early twentieth centuries left the power structure of the modern state essentially unaltered. It is in this feudal element, in this archaic aristocratic rationality at the core of the state power structure, that we have to search for the cultural definition of the state and of the processes set in train by it. It is a deep-seated mode of feeling, thinking and acting, which goes back to the absolutist state, that we associate largely unreflectively with the state. According to this collectively accepted mentality, understanding or cultural definition, the state is entitled to proceed in terms of the reason of state. It can occupy a space reserved for matters of state alone and for a kind of reasoning which is focused exclusively on the state itself and is aimed solely at the preservation of the state and the expansion of its power and prestige. Within this space, it is fully and unquestionably in the right to operate politically free from all encumbrance. It can disregard all normative considerations, overriding the ethical, moral and legal norms of society as required. The state is allowed to do anything, whether good or evil, in order to advance what it deems to be in the interest of the state or the common good.

It is this cultural definition of the state, encapsulated by the notion of reason of state, that decisively shaped the institutionalization of science in the seventeenth century. It gave science the character of a state-monopolized or, at least, an instrumental form of knowledge that can be used for any purpose allowed by the state. Yet the structuring force emanating from this definition did not remain confined to early modernity. Due to the continuity of the feudal core of the state power structure, despite frequently being functionalized for other than purely aristocratic purposes, it is this same fundamental understanding that has culturally structured and still structures the state's role in the societal production of risks. The state has historically facilitated the industrial exploitation of nature through its support for science, technology and industry and through intervention in the economy, and it still does so today. But the state does not only facilitate the societal production of risks by providing and stabilizing the necessary conditions for the various processes involved. It also participates directly in the production of risks by itself making political use of risky and even catastrophic technologies, from nuclear to genetic technology in the provision of services, energy, arms manufacture, and so on.

On the basis of the Westphalian model of the international system of states, which held sway between 1648 and the late twentieth century, reason of state became understood as applying to relations between states. Many still think of it in terms of arbitrariness and violence in inter-state relations (Foucault 1988: 74; Dean 1999: 89). Due to various developments, however, this formula has acquired other connotations. Among these developments are the erosion of the Westphalian model in the wake of the emergence of the new world order and the reconstitution of the contemporary state as a result of globalization and localization. Today, we increasingly appreciate that the formula 'reason of state' actually stands for a pervasive and deep-seated cultural structure which goes back to the period before 1648 and affects relations not only between states but also within states. It is this core structure, stamped by absolutism, that culturally defines the state and the various processes it sets in train in the production of risks and the employment of risk-laden or catastrophic technologies. Most commonly, it has come to manifest itself in the form of authoritarian paternalism and an accompanying culture of arrogance.

Science: neutral objectivity and the manipulation and exploitation of nature

Its institutionalization called for science to accommodate to the conditions of Restoration in England and absolutism on the continent (Van den Daele 1977; Mandrou 1978). It took the form of the formal establishment of the Royal Society in London in 1662 and the Académie des Sciences in Paris in

1666. These institutions emerged through a protracted gestation from the meetings of informal learned societies that had been held on a more or less regular basis during the preceding period, but their establishment depended on royal decisions which were decisive for the way in which science became culturally defined. In England during the revolutionary decades of the 1640s and 1650s, different groups representing the scientific movement were actively engaged in devising and promoting a diversity of ideas, schemes and programmes, each being a distinct variant of the new science. Among these culturally creative groups were the Baconian Puritan reform movement conceiving the 'New Learning' as intrinsically possessing moral, educational, social and political dimensions; the chemical philosophy movement proposing a Christian version of magical-religious knowledge of nature; the experimental philosophy movement and the mechanical philosophy movement, each of which put forward its own reductionist concept of science; and the so-called Virtuosi, such as Boyle, Petty, Henshaw, Digby, Winthrop and Ray (Webster 1975; Van den Daele 1977; Groh and Groh 1991). The alternative conceptions of the new science introduced by these competing groups gave rise to controversies in which they were confronted with and played out against each other in a symbolic and cognitive contest. While this contest stretched over decades, in the absence of a scientific tradition, an institutional forum or established criteria, none of the variants could gain the upper hand by demonstrating its cognitive superiority. This was achieved by a selection from among the variants of the new science and the recognition of a corresponding set of cognitively binding criteria by a momentous historical decision in the form of a royal edict issued by King Charles II. The Charter of 1662 entailed the political incorporation of the experimental and the mechanical philosophy to the exclusion of the variants of the new science defended by the remaining groups representing the scientific movement. On the basis of this historical decision, the first formal and permanent scientific institution was established.

Of crucial importance for the definition of science was the particular social context in which it was socially constructed (Van den Daele 1977; Mandrou 1978; Hill 1988; Merchant 1990). The culturally creative period of the generation of a plurality of concepts of the new science coincided with the unsettled years of the Puritan Revolution and Civil War. The historical selection of the experimental and mechanical concept of science by a royal decision and the establishment of the Royal Society took place, however, after the return of Charles II under the conditions of Restoration. This was a period of conservative reaction in all fields, from religion, culture and education to law and social policy. As a consequence, the price that the new science envisaged by the scientific movement had to pay to become institutionalized was high, and the implications for many of the excluded representatives of the scientific movement were severe. Far from separating religion, morality, politics and education from science as was done later, the scientific movement prior to the Restoration, in keeping with Baconianism as the official philosophy of the Revolution, explicitly and actively linked the new science to a programme of radical political, social and educational reform. Being anti-authoritarian, progressive, anti-elitist, educationally idealistic, humanitarian in orientation and for a unity of theological and philosophical knowledge (Van den Daele 1977), the movement devised a wide range of programmes. They included universal education, agricultural innovation, experimental medicine, free health care, employment for the poor, economic reform oriented toward general prosperity, and state intervention in various areas with a view to social amelioration (Webster 1975). The Restoration of 1660 marked not only the end of the Puritan Revolution, but also the curtailment of the reform programme associated with the new science. In order to gain royal recognition, protection and support, and thus to become institutionalized and incorporated into Restoration society, the scientific movement had to demonstrate its conformity by renouncing all cultural, social, political and educational goals and claims which could be regarded as subversive of the new dispensation or could lead to conflict with the regime. It therefore rid itself of those of its representatives who entertained undesirable views, assisted by the repressive machinery of the absolutist Stuart state, particularly during the rule of Clarendon (Mandrou 1978). By means of police measures rather than legislation, supporters and sympathizers of the previous regime, including representatives of the scientific movement, were hunted down during the first years of Charles II's reign, many of whom had to seek safety in exile, either in the United Provinces or the American Colonies.

In France, a comparable yet qualitatively somewhat different process of institutionalization took place (Mandrou 1978). Here, too, we see a multiplicity of informal learned societies meeting regularly over a long period of time, a royal decision giving formal recognition to a certain variety of ideas to the exclusion of others, and the establishment of a scientific institution. But whereas the Royal Society, notwithstanding the royal edict of Charles II, was to a significant degree the outcome of an initiative of the scientific movement itself, the Académie des Sciences was virtually completely created by intervention from above, particularly by Louis XIV's chief minister Colbert. The Académie was founded with the specific intention of exalting the Sun King's glory, but, belonging within the context of strict censorship, active surveillance, firm repression and control over intellectual life, it also had the task of regulating, controlling and disciplining the scientific movement. Encouragement was given to right-thinking savants by pensioning them, yet at the same time the freedom of research was strictly circumscribed, Colbert issuing directives to guide work in areas useful to the absolutist state. Government tutelage was accompanied by the banning of unacceptable points of view, which included Cartesian philosophy and physics as well as the Copernican heliocentric position. As in England, yet more decisively and more completely, the new institution of science was overlaid with an authoritarian institutional form in so far as the absolutist state more or less successfully monopolized the production of knowledge through the exercise of force (Eder 1988; Koselleck 1989).

In both England and France, the scientific movement paid a high price for the institutionalization of science (Leiss 1972; Van den Daele 1977). By royal edict, science was cut loose from its social meaning and normative goals. It had direct implications neither for the organization of different spheres of life nor for the emancipation of human beings or the attainment of a more adequate form of society. Science was defined as a neutral concern involving the pursuit of tightly circumscribed explanatory goals and the growth of knowledge. The potential value of scientific knowledge was identified with the authoritative objectivity of knowledge itself and its progressive potential confined to its technical implications. Its socially institutionalized cultural definition thus fixed science centrally to objectification. In turn, objectification implied a culturally very specific mechanistic, neutral and instrumental orientation to nature.

The basic cultural orientation of science was of fundamental importance for the subsequent fusion of science, technology and industry. Science's cultural orientation entered a mutually supportive relation with technology and industry. Whereas science objectifies nature, technology manipulates objectified nature, and industry exploits for commercial purposes nature objectified by science and rendered manipulable by technology. The fusion of science, technology and industry was itself supported by the state. In fact, this fusion would not have been realized had it not been for military research and production commissioned by the state. In addition to the embodiment of objectification in the state-backed institution of science, of course, the objectification, manipulation and exploitation of nature by science, technology and industry are infused with dynamism – as Giddens (1987) as well as Burns and Dietz (1997) argue – by the capitalist pursuit of profit within a competitive system through the production of commodities for sale on the market. The fusion of science, technology and industry thus gives one a glimpse of the type and quality of the typically modern relation to nature. First, nature is objectified, manipulated and exploited. Second, this is done in a systematic and consistent way in accordance with the pressures of generalized commodification. Finally, the project as a whole draws its confidence and authority from a cultural definition which is backed by the state whose rationality, in turn, had been decisively shaped by absolutism.

The modern relation to nature: organic, mechanical and cybernetic

The above cultural and institutional analysis suggests that a basic condition of the societal production of risks is the particular relation that modern society maintains with nature. This relation is established and maintained through the intermediary of science, in conjunction with technology and industry dynamicized by capitalism, and the state. While science, technology, industry, capitalism and the state, as institutions carrying the activities and processes involved in the production of risks, are of great significance, my argument was that the pervasive and fundamentally important cultural structures defining the state and science must be given special attention. They are responsible for the particular quality of the modern relation to nature. This quality becomes apparent in comparison with the pre-modern relation to nature.

For the greater part of history, but at least since the neolithic revolution, human beings related in an organic way to nature. Thus we can speak of the organic state of nature or, simply, 'organic nature' (Moscovici 1977: 87–90). The contours of organic nature were determined by the close relationship between craftsmanship and natural raw materials in which the immediate qualities of stone, wood, wool and so forth alone were significant for labour – the carpenter, for instance, being in harmony with nature by planing with and not against the grain of the wood. Organic nature was understood as female, a nurturing mother, who provided for the needs of humankind in an ordered, planned universe or cosmos (Merchant 1990). Within the organic framework, the image of mother earth exerted a normative or moral restraint restricting a variety of human activities, for example mining, that could do violence to or denude nature. Working on organic nature requires preparation and skills that are unconscious yet can be developed through the appropriation of techniques. Once this level is reached, the reproduction of knowledge becomes all-important. In its heyday, organic nature found paradigmatic expression in ancient Greek naturalistic art (Clark 1970), astronomy as the science of motion, velocity and duration, and natural philosophy based on cosmological principles (Moscovici 1977; Eder 1996a). In the course of the Renaissance during the sixteenth and seventeenth centuries, however, it underwent such a radical change that it became displaced by a different, even diametrically opposed, state of nature. It is this change, which resulted in 'mechanical nature' (Toulmin and Goodfield 1968: 185; Moscovici 1977: 93–8), that Merchant (1990) has in mind when she talks of 'the death of nature'.

In the early modern period, feelings toward nature, the concept of nature and the rules governing behaviour toward nature were all transformed. The place of the skilled craft worker in harmony with nature was taken by the engineer who uses mathematical knowledge to observe nature objectively from an external viewpoint. No longer did the secondary qualities of raw materials such as form, colour or texture count, since the engineer gave priority to the primary qualities of matter which made it into a source of power or energy – for instance, a flowing stream turning a waterwheel or expanding steam driving a fly-wheel. The machine became the central focus of the human–nature relationship. Rather than a living life-giving force, nature was felt to be an unlimited resource consisting of inert matter. As such, it contained no inherent normative restraints. Inert matter could be approached in a morally neutral way and it could be mastered. It could be objectified, manipulated and exploited at will for whatever human purpose. Craft skills were transformed into a mechanical force, and craftsmanship had to make way for labour connected to mechanical instruments or machines. While the reproduction of knowledge remained important, the modern mechanistic cultural framework prioritized discovery and invention through experimentation. The sense organs and perception were extended and made more sensitive by means of the telescope and microscope and new modes of calculation and estimation in order to probe and reach into the nooks and crannies of inert matter. In a first stage, the transformation of organic into mechanical nature culminated in the seventeenth-century philosophical revolution, which established the mechanistic worldview, and the codification of the resulting new science in Newton's mechanical physics. Through the scientific revolution of the nineteenth century in chemistry, biology and physics, mechanical nature entered a second stage in which it was itself transformed. The scientist took the place of the engineer, and mechanical physics was succeeded by science concerned with the universal structure of nature. Instead of harnessing natural forces by means of machines, the scientist adapted nature to machines. Rather than just focusing directly on nature as object, it was recognized that the scientist is the subject of knowledge who proceeded according to epistemological principles. As discoveries and inventions in chemistry (science of materials), physics (electricity, the splitting of the atom) and biology (genetics) demonstrate (Toulmin and Goodfield 1968), a new synthetic type of knowledge quite different from engineering knowledge had become possible that would in the twentieth century lead beyond mechanical nature. This rendered irrelevant distinctions drawn at the outset of the modern period, such as those between dead and living matter, body and mind, and object and subject.

A new relational and reflexive state of nature was inaugurated by relativity theory, atomic theory and probability theory in the early twentieth century, and subsequently it was strengthened by holomovement or process physics, non-equilibrium thermodynamics, non-linear chaos theory and autopoietic systems biology. Moscovici refers to it as 'cybernetic nature' (1977: 98–108), Halfmann (1986) as 'autopoietic nature', and Merchant associates it with 'a postmodern ecological world view' (1990: xvii). Here nature is understood neither as something substantial nor as something objective, but as a self-organizing system of more or less complex relations in which theoretical knowledge and human beings themselves are implicated. How nature organizes itself also depends on theoretical constructions of nature and corresponding inventions and interventions. Instead of forming (for example, from stone to statue) or transforming natural material (such as from steam to locomotive), the scientist develops new synthetic materials (for example, plastics or transgenic organisms) that have no direct correspondence in nature by combining previously unrelated and unconnected characteristics. Rather than organic substances or mechanical forces, the focus in our emerging state of nature is on the forms of organization of material systems, defined by their physical, chemical or biological characteristics, and the manner in which they can be employed to create new entities and relations possessing the desired features. This relational focus leads far beyond craftsmanship and mechanical or instrumental labour to a new form of regulation or supervision of complex systems. Unlike organic nature but like mechanical nature, cybernetic nature is devoid of inherent normative or moral restraints besides the demand of reflexivity, so that its governance would require moral or ethical considerations to be brought in from elsewhere. Since the Second World War, this has become an increasingly acute problem, particularly since research and human creativity and thus invention, which can be motivated and impelled by any of a wide range of cultural models and social practices, have come to dominate in the field of knowledge.

Since the developments of the twentieth century led to the establishment of a direct relation between nature and society, various authors are convinced that we are today witnessing the beginnings of a new form of human social life in which society is understood to be a form of nature itself. Moscovici conjures up the image of 'post-civilization' or 'culture' (1977: 466) characterized by the unprecedented phenomenon of intensive and wide-ranging cooperative relations, and Merchant, using more conventional contemporary language, speaks of 'an ecologically sustainable way of life' (1990: xviii). The societal production of risks, however, is not only conditioned by a new historical state of nature and society in which humans play an inventive role in directing and regulating highly complex self-organizing systems. It is also, indeed in particular, dependent on the cultural definition of this inventive role, the cultural structures defining and fixing the orientations giving direction to it. Is invention pursued in the name of scientific curiosity, power, wealth or political prestige? As suggested by Mary Shelley's Victor Frankenstein, who ironically was labouring under the delusion that he was motivated by love, modern institutions, organizations, professions and practices are often 'trapped into biases, distortions, half-truths, illusions, and rationalizations' (Burns and Dietz 1997: 55). Cultural dependence of this kind is revealed, for instance, by the phenomenon of counter-expertise in science and conflicts around science in the public sphere. They highlight that the historical cultural definition of both science and the state still retain their relevance today. Despite the contemporary possibility of reflexively relating to nature through a communicative process, science to a significant degree continues to proceed in terms of neutral objectification in conjunction with the technological manipulation and industrial or commercial exploitation of nature. This is strengthened on the one hand by the fact that we are today in a transitional phase between mechanical and cybernetic nature, and on the other by the decisive role of the state in science, technology, capitalism and industry. Culturally defined as it is by its origins in absolutism, the state allows authoritarian paternalism and a culture of arrogance to persist.

The experimenting society: society as laboratory

The contemporary conditions of the societal production of risks reviewed above can be brought together under the title of the 'experimenting society'

(Krohn and Weyer 1989: 349; see also Radder 1986; Wynne 1988; Beck 1992: 204–12, 1995: 122–7; Macnaghten and Urry 1998: 26–7). By contrast with Fuller's (1999) Popperian usage connoting an open society, this title is a different name for the risk society from the viewpoint of the production of risks on the basis of science in the context of the contemporary relation between society and nature. Under the conditions of neo-liberal deregulation, heightened competition and economic globalization, it exhibits a strong tendency toward expansion.

In the seventeenth century, science was established as a clearly circumscribed institution that was by royal privilege disburdened of any social consequences. In contemporary society under the conditions of the cybernetic state of nature, however, science has broken through its legitimate institutional boundaries. Hypotheses and experiments are no longer confined to the laboratory at the heart of the institution of science, as many scientists and some sociologists of scientific knowledge still presume. Both research processes and their attendant risks extend far beyond science itself, reaching deep into society. Research has penetrated and operates to a significant degree in a non-scientific social context. As a result, science has become a form of social action and research has been incorporated in society. Society is now the laboratory (Radder 1986; Wynne 1988; Krohn and Weyer 1989; Beck 1995: 122–7). Science is no longer able to present properly developed and fully tested knowledge, but the very development of knowledge requires the implementation of knowledge. Experimental research and implementation of scientific knowledge coincide. New knowledge and concomitantly new risks are experimentally generated by the implementation of scientific knowledge through technological installations or procedures. Socio-technical processes such as the operation of a nuclear power station, the introduction of medicines or toxic chemicals, and the release of genetically modified organisms assume the quality of experiments beyond the legitimate boundaries of science. Rhetorically, scientists continue to claim that such cases involve the implementation of tested knowledge, but what is common to them – as is clear from increasing media reports about the premature marketing of drugs, and so forth – is in fact the trying out of uncertain implementation or what could alternatively be called experimental implementation, implicit experimentation or real experimentation. Science is no longer able, therefore, to wash its hands of what happens on the outside in the domain of so-called 'trans-science' (Weinberg 1972).

In the case of high-risk technologies, the social experimental quality of scientific research becomes graphically apparent. High-risk technologies, representing complex systems of components, cannot be fully tested in the laboratory before implementation. This means that accidents such as the Chernobyl disaster serve as experiments by means of which theories are empirically tested under real social conditions (Perrow 1984; Krohn and Weyer 1989: 351). Through the experimental implementation of scientific knowledge on the basis of a well-defined research design, which contains also the modelling of risks, scientists learn from accidents and develop scientific

Figure 5.1   Cultural and institutional conditions of the societal production of risks

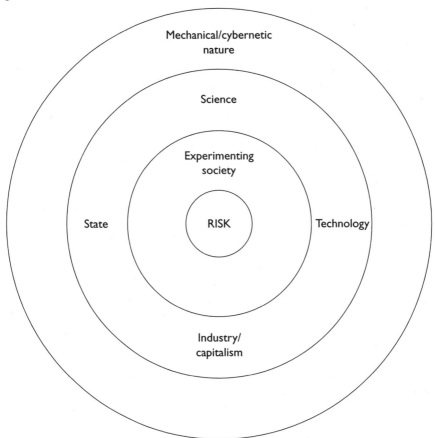

knowledge in a planned manner. This graphic example sociologically focuses the conditions of the genesis of risks in the contemporary world. For some considerable time, we have been living in a political society of a parliamentary nature and in an economic society of a capitalist nature. Under the conditions of a new relation between society and nature, we have recently entered a knowledge society of an experimental nature. In this 'experimenting knowledge society' (Krohn and Weyer 1989: 350), the various conditions of the societal production of risks come together (see Figure 5.1).

Summary

In this chapter, I have offered an overview of the most basic conditions in terms of which a sociological explanation of the production of risks in contemporary society could be offered. The starting point of the analysis was the displacement of religion by science at the beginning of the modern period. The analysis was pursued at an institutional level in two directions. The first was the state, which took the place of the church as the major institutional purveyor of culture, and the second was the institution of science, which was established in the seventeenth century. The major emphasis in the analysis, however, was on the cultural definitions of the state and science and the respective processes to which they give rise. The aim of this was to identify those deep-seated cultural structures that guide and give direction to the institutions and processes that are most directly involved in the production of risks in contemporary society. It was argued that the genesis of risks could be attributed to an intertwined complex of institutional and cultural factors. The first strand of this complex is science with its objectivistic, morally neutral and instrumental orientation which, in turn, became intertwined with the equally instrumentalist manipulative and exploitative orientations of technology and industry respectively. The role of capitalism, it was pointed out, should not be overlooked here. The second strand is the state that in its early modern form determined the cultural and institutional characteristics of science, and in its modern form, indelibly stamped by absolutism, not only continues to provide the conditions for science, technology, industry and capitalism, but also makes use of catastrophic technologies. It was shown, finally, that the articulation of these various conditions of the societal production of risks are best understood today when they are located within the context of the contemporary relation between society and nature. Sociologically, this complex of conditions finds its most paradigmatic expression in the contemporary experimenting society. Here risks are produced on the basis of scientific research caught up in a complex of relations. Motivated and impelled by curiosity, power, wealth, commodification, prestige and such like, it is experimentally implemented in society as laboratory, yet in an arrogant manner deriving from the absolutist core of the state power structure, it insists that it is self-contained and not responsible for any social consequences.

Discursive construction of risk:
the new public sphere

In Chapter 5, we saw how religion was questioned and eventually relativized by the institutionalization of science. It is noteworthy that this process has been duplicated in the recent past, but this time involving science itself. Since the 1960s, science has not merely been questioned increasingly, but it has been pushed off its pedestal. Whereas the scientific movement, in conjunction with the state, originally played a crucial role in relegating religion both institutionally and culturally to the background, it is the new social movements of the late twentieth century that led the way in putting science in its place. Like the institutionalization of science in early modern times, the decisive step was the recent institutionalization of the new social movements in the form of the contemporary public sphere. This resulted in an immense increase in the importance of public communication and the discursive organization of society. Behind this event, of course, lies a long-term process of the development of communication and discourse and the concomitant radicalization of reflexivity. The aim of this chapter, assuming the production of risks covered in Chapter 5, is to analyse the articulation of the problem of risk and its discursive construction in contemporary public communication. Special attention will therefore be given to the new social movements, the public sphere, communication and discourse. Important to keep in mind is that the focus on discursive construction has the methodological sense of shifting the attention away from traditional linear to more fruitful non-linear modes of thought.

The chapter opens with a brief account of the communication revolution and the long-term development of communication. Of interest here is the significance of these developments for the contemporary public sphere. This account will provide a context for establishing the parameters of the phenomenon of reflexivity. The larger part of the chapter, however, will be devoted to the structure, organization and dynamics of public communication and discourse, the focus being on the process of the construction of risk in this medium. In attending to this process, the important topic of the politics of risk will have to be taken into account. To transcend the current tendency to fix on the politics of risk, however, I pursue the analysis of discursive construction to the deeper level of the cultural foundations of contemporary society and their transformation.

The communication revolution and the transformation of the public sphere

The communication revolution of the early modern period involved the penetration of all social relations by communication so that different interpretations of the world could be aired in public (Mannheim 1972). In the feudal period, different social groups or classes such as the free nobility and serfs existed side-by-side, isolated from one another without sustained communication between them. The clergy representing the medieval church enjoyed a monopoly over the interpretation of the world. This official or orthodox interpretation formed the dominant religious-metaphysical worldview of the time. During the Renaissance and Reformation, however, the clergy lost their monopolistic control over intellectual matters, and a free intelligentsia deriving from different social classes made its appearance, producing competing and even conflicting publicly relevant interpretations of reality. Through the ensuing process of the public competition and conflict of interpretations, communication penetrated all social relations so that the different groups were opened up and linked to one another. This communicative leavening of society was further facilitated by the new revolutionary technology, the printing press, as well as by the displacement of the elitist Latin by newly developing national vernacular languages and communication communities.

In subsequent centuries, the communication revolution was carried forward by the classical emancipation movements, including the scientific movement and more generally the bourgeois-Enlightenment movement (Eder 1985; Habermas 1989; Strydom 2000). This development led, on the one hand, to the fall of absolutist domination and, on the other, to the political self-organization of society. Institutionally, this achievement took the form of legally recognized rights, constitutions, parliaments, an independent judiciary and freedom of contract. Central to this whole complex was the 'public sphere' (Habermas 1989, 1996) – a networked space, supported by political institutions, that allowed the taking of positions, the communication of claims, the formation of public opinion and the establishment of collective agreement. In the eighteenth century, the public sphere took a liberal form based on the assumption of the universalization of interests in the medium of discourse. Subsequently, however, the labour movement, motivated by the prevalence of exploitation and poverty, drew attention to the problem of the lack of coordination of collective agents such as the state, industry and labour. Far from all interests being taken into account and collective agreement being attained, workers have no say and are ruthlessly exploited. Through the intervention of the labour movement, the liberal public sphere was further democratized by the addition of political rights to the original basic civil rights. On this basis, procedures of mutual cooperation became institutionalized in the form of the welfare state that was aimed at calculating, insuring and compensating the risks of the capitalist economic system.

The new social movements served as the vehicle of a further spurt in the development of communication and the transformation of the public sphere. In this case, the new communications technology is proving as significant as the movable type in the early modern period. Challenged by the consequences of the integration of science and technology into an economy stabilized by state intervention and stimulated by welfare people processing, the movements emerged in the 1960s and 1970s. As the system of intermediation involving the state, industry and unions had to make room for the new collective agent, this corporatist or semi-corporatist welfare state arrangement started to break down. The new social movements brought with them an immense increase and intensification in communication that could not be accommodated by the existing institutional arrangements. The conditions of the production and reproduction of public communication underwent a change, with the result that the public sphere, first created by the classical emancipation movements and then extended by the labour movement, was drastically transformed. The institutionalized procedures could no longer cope with the intensification of communication and the increase in conflict around issues, and as a consequence the state weakened, became decentred and its conflation with society evaporated.

The new public sphere is no longer characterized by procedurally tightly regulated argumentation and common decision-making, nor by a stable carrier group as Eisenstadt and Giesen (1995) still assume. Instead, it is a fluid social space of competing and conflicting communicative structures in which collective agents struggle over the definition of issues and the making and implementation of decisions (Eder 1995, 1996b). In this new public sphere, experts, scientists and intellectuals as well as privileged historical subjects (for instance, the working class) have all been demythologized. Due to an influx of participants who themselves are heterogeneous, the public sphere became more pluralistic and democratic. This brought with it a proliferation of cultural models (Strydom 1999c), 'good grounds' (Eder 1995: 272) or 'orders of worth' (Boltanski and Thévenot 1999: 368; see also Lafaye and Thévenot 1993), that compel the participants in public communication to orient, think, act and decide differently, thus leading them into competition and conflict. This development obviously changed the very dynamics of public communication. As more cultural models are brought into play, they are more readily questioned, devalued and replaced by or combined with other models. A certain anarchy of cultural forms sets in, indicating that a new level of contingency (Strydom 1999c; Delanty 1999a:

9, 14, 68, 187), uncertainty (Evers and Nowotny 1987) and ambivalence (Bauman 1992) is asserting itself in public communication which itself has become more chaotic and less determinate. The different participants, such as scientists, experts, counter-experts, politicians and social movements, can at best only make contributions that are taken up into the dynamics of the self-organizing discursive process. The only coordination that can be expected, therefore, is dependent on the contingent selection of a cultural model on the basis of the resonant response of the public. A 'communication society' (Eder 1995: 276; Strydom 1999c; Delanty 1999a: 9, 14) or a 'discursive society' (Beck 1997: 128), which emerged from a transformed public sphere organizing itself in a completely new way, has begun to take shape.

Public communication, discourse, and the contemporary public sphere

It is within the context of the society resulting from the communication revolution and the transformation of the public sphere that the social construction of risk takes place. To prepare for an analysis of this process, let us first go in some more detail into a few crucial aspects such as public communication, discourse and the contemporary public sphere.

Public communication as medium of social construction

As we have seen in previous chapters, Douglas ascribes to the view that risk is a collective construct (Douglas and Wildavsky 1982; Douglas 1986, 1994). When one inquires how this occurs and under what conditions, however, it becomes clear that she offers neither an adequate theoretical account nor an empirical analysis in any detail. Her notion of collective construct applies to the modes of perception and corresponding levels of acceptability of risk carried by three distinct institutional cultures. They are the market focusing on economic breakdowns, hierarchy focusing on threats to law and order and national security, and finally community focusing on the deterioration of the environment. But the actual problem is the more complex one of the interrelation of these different positions in a collective process of construction. In a brilliant formulation, she submits that: 'Risk should be seen as a joint product of *knowledge* about the future and *consent* about the most desired prospects', and adds that 'knowledge [i]s the changing product of social activity, always under construction' (Douglas and Wildavsky 1982: 5, 192, original emphasis). Due to her inability to escape from the spell of the psychology of perception, however, she never brings these insights to bear on the joint, dynamic, socio-cognitive process from which the consent results. In fact, the nature of this constructive process remains unaddressed and thus unclear. She understands that it involves social and cultural transformation and she even associates such concepts as 'debate' and 'discourse' with it, yet her anthropological approach does not allow the medium and the historically specific context in which the process takes place to become explicit topics.

Luhmann (1995), by contrast, from the start and throughout stresses the centrality of communication. Yet he understands it in a very specific sense closer to information than communication. Instead of linking it to cognition, action and interaction, as would be sociologically more usual, he conceives it systems theoretically as the autopoietic process of social systems. This means that communication is an independent, autonomous and operationally closed process that functions according to its own requirements. By laying down limits, it allows relations to be established between system operations and thus makes possible the production and reproduction of society. It is unsurprising, therefore, that Luhmann (1989) rejects the concept of public communication deriving from Habermas's (1984, 1987, 1989, 1996) work on communicative action and the public sphere. This, however, is precisely the position adopted by such authors as Beck and Eder. Beck regards risks explicitly as 'social constructions' (1995: 92) that are achieved in a cognitive process of social definition. This process takes place in 'public discussions' in which 'argumentation craftsmen' (Beck 1995: 30, 32) take part. It unfolds through argumentation or the making of 'competing and conflicting claims' and the staging of 'antagonistic definitions and definitional struggles' (1995: 29) and it comes to a temporary closure when the collective accepts a particular social definition of a risk. The medium of this process is communication and the context in which it takes place is the public sphere. Eder, who works this position out in much more detail than Beck, insists on the theoretical significance of public communication for an adequate grasp of constructivism (Eder 1993a, 1996a; Strydom 2000). It is only when public communication is made central that a number of important considerations become clear. First, construction does not entail a concern with particular perceptions and cultural meanings, but rather a demand to focus on the process of generating collectively shared meaning systems. Second, construction is not simply the achievement of one collective actor or agent, whether a social movement, the state or industry, or even a number of them together. Simultaneously, it also involves those who react to these agents, whether supporters and adversaries or observers such as the mass media, the public and social scientists. Finally, the acceptance of public communication compels a refinement of the concept of power. If different kinds of actors or agents are implicated in public communication, it follows that there are different kinds of power. Those who try to impose communicated meanings (for instance, experts or politicians) as well as those who mediate such meanings (that is, the mass media) indeed wield considerable power. But also those who defend meanings and attack dominant meanings are by no means powerless. Above all, however, one should never underestimate the power of those who are in a position in the final analysis to accept or reject communicated meanings, that is, the public, especially in a communication society (Strydom 1999c).

Discourse as a mode of problematizing and reconstituting assumptions

To say that the process of social construction takes place in public communication through argumentative or conflicting claims-making, implies that discourse plays a decisive role in particular historical conjunctures. Discourse, in terms of Habermas's theory (1974: 16–19, 1976: 108–17, 1979: 1–68, 1984: 15–42, 1996: 158–68; Strydom 2000), is the continuation of communication in a different form. It is a special reflexive form of communication. Discourse unfolds in and through communication, yet in opposition to communication. It halts the normal communication of contents by problematizing the implicit claims to validity underpinning and inconspicuously advanced through such communication and allowing them to be pitted against one another. By questioning, bringing out into the open and allowing reflection on and the joint revision of taken-for-granted assumptions, discourse makes possible the re-establishment or creation of a shared background of mutual understanding and the repair of breakdowns in communication. It does this by universalizing interests or value orientations, improving self-understanding by making people aware of deeper consonance in their common form of life, and balancing conflicting interest through compromises. Discourse thus broadens the cultural basis of social action and makes it possible for larger numbers of people to coordinate their orientations and actions. This does not imply that discourse necessarily involves consensus in the strong sense of all the participants and the public fully agreeing on everything. As Foucault (1979, 1981) insists and Habermas is well aware, this is made impossible by the fact that there are power relations present in discourse that cannot easily be neutralized. Besides consensus, the outcome of discourse often consists also of compromise and of 'rational dissent' (Miller 1992: 12) in the sense of the existence side-by-side of contrary interpretations of a collectively accepted fact or issue. A certain compatibility or temporary synthesis is established among the discursively advanced, conflicting claims in a way that cannot fully neutralize power yet is for the time being collectively accepted as morally justifiable (Honneth 1991; Habermas 1996; Strydom 2000).

Under particular historical circumstances, public discourse takes on a more or less coherent and organized form. This is the case when it involves the problematization and articulation of a related set of assumptions or validity claims. The contemporary risk discourse is an organized discourse in this sense. At issue in it is a whole series of typically modern assumptions or validity claims that have for a considerable period been taken for granted, unquestioningly and never spoken about, but in the recent past have become problematic. They include modern assumptions about science, technology, industry, capitalism, the state and above all nature and democracy. Through their ecological or risk communication, the new social movements questioned, brought out into the open, and made these taken-for-granted assumptions or validity claims publicly available for reflection and revision. At the same time, they gave rise to a discourse that drew in also scientists, technologists, industrialists, state officials and politicians as reluctant participants in the public sphere which is continuously being observed by social scientists, the mass media and above all the public. This is the risk discourse that is animated by the vision of an alternative constitution and organization of society according to a new ecological collective identity and a global ethics of collective responsibility (Jonas 1984; Apel 1988, 1991; Dower 1998; Delanty 1999b; Strydom 1999b, 1999d).

Models of the public sphere

The process of social construction, which unfolds in public communication through discourse as a mode of problematization and reconstitution of assumptions, takes place within the framework of the public sphere. The latter is a network of communication structures, supported by institutions such as constitutionally protected rights, that opens up a social space making possible the taking of positions, the communication of claims, the formation of public opinion and the establishment of collective agreement about common problems or issues. Social scientists have introduced a variety of theoretical models of the public sphere for the purposes of the empirical analysis of the making of publicly relevant issues. The theorist who originally introduced the concept of the public sphere in the 1960s (Habermas 1989), however, also seems to be the one who currently has the potentially most fruitful model on offer (Habermas 1996). Before proceeding to the process of social construction of risk, let us briefly consider four of the most interesting available models (Strydom 1993b).

Public arenas, fora, and reference group models

Adopting a constructivist approach in the tradition of symbolic interactionism with a view to analysing the competitive and selective process through which social problems become framed and collectively defined, Hilgartner and Bosk (1988) developed what they call a 'public arenas model'. According to this model, social problems are constructed through public discourse in a number of different arenas embedded in a complex public system of problem formulation and dissemination. The government, courts, the research community, mass media, political campaign organizations and social action groups in some way contribute to the discussion, selection, framing, definition, packaging and dramatization of social problems and their presentation to the public. Subsequently, various authors sought to correct Hilgartner and Bosk's neglect to adequately clarify the competitive process of social construction, the relations among the different arenas and thus their notion of a system of public arenas.

In his 'fora model', Hansen (1991) gave a central place to the mass media to capture the interlinking and dynamic interaction among the different societal fora of meaning production. From that standpoint, he then imposed a structure on them on the basis of the varying strength of the interlinkages and degrees of legitimacy. The result is a hierarchical fora model in which the media establish and activate relations between the top and bottom of the power pyramid. In processes of social construction, therefore, the more powerful, legitimate and strongly linked fora, such as the government, scientific community and courts, possess a certain competitive advantage over weaker and more diffuse fora such as pressure groups, social movements and the public.

Starting from social movement theory, Neidhardt and Rucht (1991) offered a 'model of reference groups', embracing the political-administrative system, agents of control, political parties, interest groups and social movements, the public and the mass media, that is comparable to the above arena and fora models. By contrast with both under- and over-structured conceptions, however, they called for the development of a differentiated process concept to get to grips with the dynamics of constructive processes in a complex public arena. This is exactly what Habermas put forward in his re-examination of the public sphere in 1992 in terms of a core–periphery model representing a constitutionally regulated power circuit (Habermas 1996: 354–84).

Core–periphery model

Habermas sees the public sphere as an elementary social phenomenon taking the form of a complex of networked communicative structures rooted in the lifeworld and activated by civil society. Whereas problems are first experienced and perceived in the privacy of the lifeworld and then thematized, amplified and transformed into issues by associations and institutions belonging to civil society, they achieve publicity in the public sphere. The communicative network of the latter spans three dimensions. This first is the core, consisting of the government, administration, courts and parliament responsible for formal decision-making. The second is the inner periphery, embracing institutions with delegated state functions or self-administration rights such as statutory bodies, insurance systems, foundations, universities and chambers. The third, finally, is the outer periphery, composed of complex networks of negotiation between public administration and private organizations as well as groups, associations, societies and collectivities that perceive, identify, articulate and thematize problems, build and communicate values and identities, form opinions and exert influence on the political system. Rather than regarding the relations among the core, inner periphery and outer periphery as being rigidly structured, Habermas introduces three further sets of distinctions to make the dynamics of communicative action and discourse in the public sphere amenable to empirical analysis. The first, concerning social change and shifts in power along the tracks of the circuitous model, is a distinction between different states of the public sphere and corresponding modes of operation or problem-solving (Habermas 1996: 357–8). Under normal conditions, when the public sphere is in a state of rest, routine decision-making proceeds according to settled procedures on the assumption that the core enjoys priority over the periphery. During periods of mobilization when a crisis consciousness develops and conflict ensues, by contrast, power shifts toward the periphery and an extraordinary mode of problem-solving favouring the constitutional regulation of power comes into force. As a result, civil society obtains the chance to exert influence over the political system. The second set of distinctions concerns the different types of actors who appear in the public sphere (Habermas 1996: 375–6). The basic distinction is between weak yet constitutionally protected actors, such as social movements commanding communicative power, and powerful, well-endowed actors, such as business executives or politicians commanding social and administrative power. While the former emerge from the public to make lifeworld problems into public and political issues and, in so doing, try to keep open and develop the public sphere, the latter appear before the public and use the public to further their own interests or ends. But Habermas also mentions another group of actors – journalists, publicists and press agents commanding both communicative and social power – who report on the former two types while regulating access to the public sphere through the mass media. Although not sufficiently singling out the public as such as observing, commenting upon and evaluating the various types of actors in the public sphere (Strydom 1999c), he does recognize that '[t]here can be no public sphere without a public' since it possesses the 'final authority' over what resonates and is ultimately approved in the public sphere (1996: 364). Habermas's third set of distinctions concerns different types of communication campaigns or forms of communicative agenda-building that are typically employed in processes of the social construction of issues (1996: 379–82), either singly or in combination. In terms of the progressively decreasing weight of the core or, alternatively, the progressively increasing involvement of civil society and the public, there are three distinct analytical types. Inside access, first, refers to a process in which government agencies and groups close to the core pursue goals under deliberate exclusion, besides perhaps identification and attention groups, of public participation. Governmental and other core groups revert to mobilization, second, when they require the support of the mass of the public for the implementation of their policy initiatives or the realization of their goals. Whereas a public sphere in a state of rest favours these two types of agenda-building, the third one becomes more prominent under conditions of communicative conflict, discourse and reflexivity. The outside initiative type of agenda-building applies to a group, typically a social movement, outside the core of formal decision-making institutions. It articulates a grievance or normative innovation and tries to create enough concern about a problem in civil society to make it into a public and political issue which could potentially affect the cultural codes of society.

Having reviewed public communication, discourse and the public sphere, we are now in a position to investigate how risk is socially constructed.

The social construction of risk

The discursive construction of risk is a social process in which different social actors or collective agents compete and conflict with one another in the medium of public communication and discourse to define the risk in question in a way that resonates sufficiently with the public to become accepted as collectively valid. The process commences with the public sphere at rest becoming agitated and crisis consciousness emerging. The normal mode of operation of the public sphere is displaced by a problematizing mode. In the shift from the core to the periphery, administrative and social power has to make room for communicative power. At the periphery, ordinary everyday people's experience and perception of a problem finds articulation. Initially, this takes place in episodic communication in private meeting places, but it soon reaches the level of more structured communication in neighbourhood groupings and voluntary associations. Through the participation of individuals and groups in fora of this kind, organized collective actors in the form of social movements emerge to carry forward the risk communication of the citizenry. Organized as the anti-nuclear, the environmental, the anti-biotechnology patents or the genetic rights movement, for instance, those on the outer periphery take the initiative to make a problem experienced and perceived in the lifeworld into a public and political issue which is collectively identified, defined and dealt with. Their risk communication is therefore of both a moral and a political kind. As moral entrepreneurs, they moralize the problem so as to place it on the public agenda. As collective agents in the field of intermediation between the public, on the one hand, and the political parties and formal decision-making institutions, on the other, they politicize the issue by taking it right up to the core and displaying it as an issue demanding collective political attention and treatment.

Construction is a process of social transformation embracing both transformative action and transformative discursive dynamics. The initiators and first carriers of the process typically are a mobilized public and social movements. Central to their activities as well as to the ensuing discourse is moral–political communication. Such communication intensifies the attention given to a problem and thus highlights differences and stimulates competition and even conflict between actors advancing different interpretations or definitions of the issue. Having sharpened them, however, it sooner or later also decreases the differences between the participants by rendering the object of conflict amenable to social treatment. This not only makes possible agreement about the issue despite divergent interpretations, but also brings about a coordination of the actions of the participants. More broadly, it works against social disintegration in that it stems the tide of uncontrolled consequences and side-effects of risk decisions and the escalation of the attribution of blame. Social transformation does not come about without moral–political communication, which is socially creative, and productive of new ways of feeling, thinking, and acting and hence of new knowledge. In the risk field, this kind of communication is known as 'risk communication' – that is, in a broad sense going beyond its frequent confinement to the information about risks given to the public by experts and governments (Plough and Krimsky 1987; Bechmann 1993b; Fischhoff 1998).

Despite the importance of social movements in the communication of problems, one should not allow oneself to be misled into repeating the persistent social theoretic error of overestimating social movements by ascribing to them the status of subjects of history. Far from being solely responsible for the transformation of society, they should be seen in relation to the other actors or agents participating in a given process of competition and conflict. Since it is a social or communicative and discursive process with collectively or intersubjectively generated outcomes, furthermore, all these actors should be seen in the context of the process of construction of reality to which they contribute. An adequate sociological analysis of any process of construction, including that of risk, must therefore take account of at least five distinct moments.

Social actors or collective agents

Depending on the empirical cross-section of the risk discourse in question, a plurality of social actors or collective agents is involved. The anti-nuclear, environmental and anti-biotechnology patents movements took a leading role in placing and keeping the risk issue in various guises on the public and political agenda. A whole range of other actors or agents, typically forming so-called 'discourse coalitions' (Hajer 1995), were also drawn into the discourse, often against their will. Among them are representatives and branches of different industries, politicians, states and governments, scientists and experts of different kinds, the mass media and others.

Definition or frame of the problem or situation

Each of the actors or agents participating in the risk discourse constructs its own particular definition or frame in a process of communication or collective argumentation among its members. This is achieved by employing the three basic types of cognitive tools or framing devices made available by culture in the form of models or codes – three types conceived in terms of Habermas's theory of culture (Eyerman and Jamison 1991; Eder 1996a; Strydom 2000) a step ahead of its competitors (Gamson and Modigliani 1989; Dickens 1992; Eisenstadt and Giesen 1995; Alexander and Smith 1996). Employing the intellectual framing device, an actor forms a view of the world by mediating conceptualization and empirical knowledge. The moral framing device allows it to regulate how it behaves in relation to the world by laying down certain principles. By means of the aesthetic or conative device, it gives meaning to the world in that it organizes subjective experiences and perceptions in a meaningful way in accordance with its identity. Coming from distinct cultural forms of life and social structural locations, thus representing a particular 'habitus' (Bourdieu 1986), 'positioning' (Davies and Harré 1990; May 2000) or 'institutional culture' (Douglas and Wildavsky 1982; Rayner 1991), the actors or agents construct unique cognitive frames by combining the intellectual, moral and conative framing devices in different configurations. In turn, they give their different frames distinct symbolic forms by putting each into a unique 'symbolic package' (Gamson and Modigliani 1989; Eder 1996a). Such symbolically packaged cognitive frames lend coherence and consistency to the propositions, principles and motivations of each of the actors and also allow them to distinguish themselves from others by well-defined collective identities.

Communication strategy

On the basis of a distinct collective identity and a clear framing of the problem in question, the actors or agents are able to enter in a strategic way into public communication (Bourdieu 1986: 477; Eder 1996a: 168). Strategic communication is aimed not only at the other participants, whether opponents or potential supporters, but also at the observing public. Movement actors communicate a counter-position problematizing claims supporting the status quo, business actors seek to convince the public of their good intentions and progressive ideas, politicians try to create ideological consent and garner public support, scientists sort true and false knowledge, and so on.

Public discourse

Once a number of different actors or agents in the same universe of discourse have framed a common problem or situation in their own unique and hence different ways and begin to communicate their respective frames, a public discourse is generated. Discourse is an open complex of reflexive communication, mutual interpretation, understanding, agreement and rational disagreement with its own logic and dynamics. As such, discourse allows no privileged membership rights and ultimately is withdrawn from the disposal of any participant, irrespective of whether individual or collective. According to its logic of separation and coordination, it first allows the development of different potentially antagonistic interpretations, definitions or frames, and then makes possible their mutual contestation and eventual convergence or coordination. Dynamically, discourse unfolds through a cognitive and symbolic contest in which the participants get embroiled in competition and even conflict. This is what Beck (1992: 29) regards as 'definitional struggles' involving 'competing and conflicting claims', which for Eder (1996a: 169) is more precisely a matter of 'frame competition' in public discourse in which cultural forms mediate the relations among the different actors or agents involved. Such frame competition is at the heart of the ensuing discursive politics – in the present context, risk politics. In the earlier phase of the discourse, when differences among the participants are sharpened, relentless competition and conflict take place among the actor or agent (meso-) frames in a struggle to create resonance among the public and thus to have maximal impact on what eventually becomes accepted as collectively valid. In its later phase, when differences become coordinated, a macro-frame generated by frame competition and conflict emerges gradually from the process of discursive construction.

Emergent and validated definition of reality

The macro-frame to which the discourse gives rise encapsulates the collective definition of the reality constructed in the course of the discursive process. It consists of an amalgam of the frames of the competing and conflicting actors. Rather than a transcendent reconciliation of contradictions, however, it represents a temporary practical synthesis which for the time being relates and normalizes continuing differences and oppositions (Kettler and Meja 1988; Apel and Kettner 1992; Mannheim 1993; Strydom 2000). As an amalgam of frames, on the one hand, it is made up of cognitive structures of a cultural and mental kind, from cultural models to ways of feeling, thinking and behaving. As a practical synthesis, on the other, it is a power-saturated phenomenon. In a given situation, it reflects the relative command of the participating actors over resources and their relative ability to create resonance among the public as well as the power of the observing, evaluating and judging public who ultimately determines what becomes accepted as collectively valid (Strydom 1999c). But far from being exclusively a power phenomenon, as Foucault (1979, 1981) holds, it is more importantly still a normative one, as Habermas (1996; also Honneth 1991) insists. It is in this sense that a macro-frame is socio-cognitively credible, engendering of trust between the public and the powers that be, socially acceptable and able to attain collective validity for a certain time (Miller 1986, 1992; Hajer 1995; Strydom 2000).

The GM food risk

Let us take as an example of the social process of the discursive construction of risk the genetically modified food controversy of the late 1990s and early 2000 (see Table 6.1).

On the basis of scientific claims about new genetic knowledge and its application in genetic engineering, the biotech or so-called 'life industry' (RAFI 1999a), particularly Monsanto, launched a massive GM crop technology and GM foods programme in the 1990s. Not only did they persuade many farmers to plant their genetically modified seeds in a number of countries, but also they succeeded in getting the active support of many governments and financial institutions. The new social movements, represented particularly by such organizations as Greenpeace, Friends of the Earth, Genetic Resources Action International (GRAIN) and Rural Advancement Foundation International (RAFI), often supported by counter-scientific

Table 6.1 The social process of the discursive construction of the GM food risk (1999–2000)

1 Actors or agents	2 Frame	3 Communication strategy	4 Discourse: competition mediated by resonance	5 Emergent collectively accepted definition (or macro-frame)
Science	Potentially useful new knowledge	Scientistic from on high (truth)	Admission of problems	Genetic modification risk is as yet undetermined and thus unacceptable
Biotech industry (e.g. Monsanto)	Increased crop yield, solution to hunger problem	Progressive (profit, development, jobs)	Admission of problems; stock market tumbles; industry in trouble; creation of 'responsible business'; supermarkets ban GM foods	
Governments	Safe, beneficial, worthy of political support (e.g. UK); potentially harmful (e.g. France, Italy)	Political (ambivalent between industry and public)	Admission of potential harmfulness (e.g. Blair); creation of regulatory institutions (e.g. UK, EU)	
Agriculture	Safe, economic and beneficial	Progressive (more food more efficiently produced)	Turn against GM industry and 'bio-serfdom'; law suits	

Banks (e.g. Deutsche Bank)	Potentially high-growth investment	Progressive	Discouragement of and withdrawal from investment
Movements (e.g. Greenpeace, Friends of the Earth, GRAIN, RAFI)	Risks: health, environmental, 'biopiracy' and 'biocolonialism'	Moralize and politicize problems	Continue to press risks home
Counter-science	Risks: health and environmental (e.g. Genetic Genie Report by PEER; GM potato/rat experiment by Dr Pusztai)	Scientistic from below	Continues to press risks home
Mass media	Provide arena, disseminate information, take own position supporting different actors at different times	Mediatize (ambivalent between participants and the public)	Stress changes affecting industry, governments, stock markets and financial institutions
			Public, for precaution, loses trust and rejects GM foods; European consumers refuse to buy GM foods

experts, advanced claims about risks and made the problem of GM foods into a public and political issue. By providing an arena for the various actors and disseminating information about their different positions and interpretations, the mass media helped the emerging controversy about GM foods forming part of the broader risk discourse to culminate in 1999. The discursive interrelation of the antagonistic frames of the different actors, as is clear from media reports at the time, led to a pronounced sequence of competitive and conflictual risk politics in the latter half of that year (Economic and Social Research Council (ESRC) 1999). The European public in particular, who was clearly in favour of precautionary measures, if not a moratorium, anxiously watched and made its evaluation of the issue and its judgement of the various participants known. In the course of the subsequent exchanges, some well-resourced and powerful actors were unexpectedly forced to change their frames quite drastically. Meanwhile, movement organizations and counter-scientific experts (for instance, Dr Arpad Pusztai, Public Employees for Environmental Responsibility (PEER)) continued to emphasize the potential health and environmental risks entailed by GM crops and foods, and growing public concern made itself felt. Often the stupendous resources of the professions, corporations and the state were mustered with the specific intention of discrediting and delegitimizing the questions and criticisms of counter-experts and social movements and of misleading or confusing the public. A good example of this is an industry-based scientist with academic connections, Dr Nigel Poole of the Zeneca Group. Not only did he style himself, some of his colleagues and even his family as willing GM tomato guinea-pigs, but also he tried to paint criticisms of biotechnology as a rerun of 'the Salem witch hunts' (Highfield 1999) – reminding one of a similar public ploy by a British minister in the wake of the BSE crisis which was later officially censured as utterly irresponsible. Yet a consumer backlash against GM foods mounted in Europe and spread to the United States, with the result that industrial activity slowed down, share values on the stock market plummeted, and endless lawsuits against the industry confirmed a producer-consumer rebellion. The biotech industry as well as some of its scientific, governmental, financial and commercial backers were compelled to admit that there are unresolved problems plaguing biotechnology and that the undetermined potential harmfulness of GM foods and crops was sufficient cause for legitimate public concern. For example, Deutsche Bank withdrew from investing in the industry, supermarkets banned GM foods, and Tony Blair (2000: 28) admitted the potential for harm and insisted that 'jobs and profit will never be more important for a responsible government than concern over human health and our environment'. The ill-fated Monsanto had to surrender its vision of a global life industry and seek a merger with a larger concern, Pharmacia Upjohn, which itself upon merging had to curtail its GM foods branch and to style itself as a pharmaceuticals powerhouse in order to avoid a shareholder backlash. By the beginning of the new millennium, then, it was clear that the GM foods controversy had, at least for the time being, given rise to a discursively constructed and collectively accepted reality: the GM food risk, which is as yet undetermined and therefore unacceptable.

The process of discursive construction of risk is of course not exhausted by the production of specific collective definitions of problems or issues. It is a process of social transformation in which discourse plays a central role, neither simply as a matter of economics (that is, competition) nor merely of politics (that is, power play), but rather as a form of social or collective reflexivity (Bourdieu 1986; Latour 1987; Foucault 1991; Beck 1992; Mannheim 1993; Habermas 1996; Pels 1996). Beyond the reflex called forth by the objectivity of real problems (Alexander 1996), it pierces the socio-political dimension (Van Peursen 1970; Beck 1992) and penetrates as deep as the cultural foundations of the risk society (Eder 1996a; Strydom 2000). Initiated by the new social movements, it problematizes implicit claims and taken-for-granted assumptions, questioning them, bringing them out into the open, and allows them to be debated, criticized and jointly revised. Socio-politically, discourse allows reflexivity in the course of the process of construction to problematize modern assumptions underpinning science, technology, industry, capitalism, the state and more generally the experimenting society. They include such assumptions as the following: that science is a morally neutral objectification of nature from an instrumental viewpoint; that technology is a neutral means for the instrumental manipulation of nature; that industrialism should be left to determine the goals of technology and thus to shape science; that capitalism is a benign dynamic force that can be left unchecked running according to its own logic; that the state can legitimately continue to facilitate and employ science, technology, industry and capitalism, irrespective of whether this involves doing good or evil; and, finally, that the experimenting society is an unavoidable outcome of the necessary and unchangeable relation between science, technology, industry, capitalism and the state.

Culturally, discourse allows reflexivity to penetrate to the most basic foundations of modernity. By questioning and generating contestation around taken-for-granted assumptions having a bearing on the relation of society to nature, it reveals the socially constructed character of nature (Moscovici 1977; Eder 1996a; Macnaghten and Urry 1998). It is thus that it became publicly clear that the assumption that nature is a limitless resource of inert matter calling for treatment as a functional object, with nature and society being separate entities, is by no means necessary and unavoidable, but rather one among a number of different options. Many people began to appreciate that it was possible to develop new feelings and ascribe a new meaning to nature, to form a new concept of it and to envisage new rules of behaviour towards it. An increasing number also see that it is urgently necessary to do so under conditions of environmental crisis, the seemingly unstoppable production of universal, global and irreversible risks, and a new cultural justification, legitimation or normatively compelling reason for it.

Summary

In this chapter, I hope to have clarified the social process in which risks are discursively constructed. To make the process intelligible, I started from the communication revolution of early modern times and traced the development of communication with reference to historical waves of social movements and the institutionalization and transformation of the public sphere. This account culminated in a focus on the nature and character of the new fluid public sphere of the late twentieth and twenty-first centuries. A theoretical elaboration of public communication as the medium of construction, of discourse in the sense of the problematization and reconstitution of taken-for-granted assumptions as the central mechanism of the process, and of the circuitous core–periphery model of the public sphere as a fruitful way to conceptualize its context then set us on course for a quite detailed analysis. For analytical purposes, I proposed to divide the process of the discursive construction of risk into five moments – from the participating actors or agents, through their respective frames and modes of strategic communication as well as the discursively organized competition, conflict and resonance creation in which they became embroiled, to the macro-frame or definition of risk as the collective achievement of the process. Substantively, the focus was on the discursive construction of the GM food risk. Finally, I argued that, far from being confined to the production of collective definitions, however, the process of discursive risk construction more deeply and pervasively also reconstitutes the basic assumptions or cultural foundations of modern society. This raises the question of the emergence of a new set of cultural foundations or a new cognitive order for reflexive modernity (Merchant 1990; Lash 1994; Eder 1996a) which provides a basis for the reconstitution of the institutional order of the risk society. The exploration of this question is central to the next chapter.

7

Consensus and conflict in the risk society

The construction of reality in the risk discourse taking place in the new fluid public sphere, as we have seen, not only entails the questioning of core institutions of modern society, but also leads to the transformation of the cultural foundations underpinning them. In this chapter, I propose to go into these changing cultural structures and institutions as well as some of the dynamics involved. I will do so by pursuing a series of closely related topics.

Science, technology, industry, capitalism and the state as well as their institutional interrelation in the experimenting society – all have come under pressure due to the limiting assumptions or cultural models that informed them during the high modern era. The same is of course also true of collective identities such as liberalism and socialism that had been interwoven with these institutional and cultural phenomena. Compensating for the deficiencies of these cultural structures and their institutional embodiments, new cultural forms of legitimation and new institutions, indeed even a new type of institution, have begun to come into being in the late twentieth century. Sustainability and collective responsibility are the most important of the new cultural forms, but comparable developments are also observable in respect of rights and citizenship – for instance, ecological rights, global or ecological citizenship and technological citizenship. At the root of all these cultural forms, however, is nature – a different and more conscious relation to nature. As regards collective identity, a new mode of self-interpretation and self-understanding, environmentalism or ecology, has emerged and begun to take on a post-national and global form. Institutionally, a whole series of new arrangements, from international environmental programmes and national environmental protection agencies to health food shops, have come into being. Of much more interest from the point of view of the society that is currently in the process of formation, however, is the new type of arrangement of our time, namely reflexive institutions. The particular character of these most typical of contemporary institutions points toward the nascent institutional order of our time – what some call 'post-corporatism'.

Considering contemporary developments, the ultimate question that arises concerns the nature of the nascent society of the twenty-first century. Is the society that is at present in the process of coming into being a cultural, deliberative democratic, communicative or discursive society or, by contrast, a genetic, eugenic, authoritarian, bio-society? To account for this basic option in the direction of development during the next number of decades, it is sociologically advisable not only to look at emerging forms of transnational politics but also to inquire what role social class is now playing in the creation and organization of society.

Changing cultural foundations: nature

In previous chapters, I have given attention to different aspects of nature as a cornerstone of the cultural foundations of society. Here it is therefore possible to confine myself to a number of relevant conclusions.

One of the most basic assumptions of the early and high modern periods was that nature and society were separate from one another. Nature was regarded as something given, external, what is not society, something mastered and used by society. In the late twentieth century, however, this cultural cornerstone of modernity became problematized. The dividing line was blurred, so that society became increasingly understood as part of nature and nature as part of society. Beck, for instance, speaks of 'the end of the antithesis between nature and society' (Beck 1992: 80, 1995: 38–40). Enhanced by the depletion and degradation of the organic foundations of life and the consequent appearance of universal, global and irreversible risks, reflexivity penetrated the modern cultural model of nature. The taken-for-granted cultural foundations of modernity became reflexive and discursively available. It was realized that, despite the fact that nature is an abiding reality to which reference is invariably made, there are different interpretations or cultural models of nature. Historically, a distinction can be drawn among the organic, mechanical and cybernetic or reflexive models of the pre-modern, high modern and contemporary periods respectively (Moscovici 1977). Under the syncretic conditions of contemporary communication, discursive and reflexive society, by contrast, all of these models are equally available and actualizable at one and the same time. Culturally, nature has become a problem in that there is no longer just one nature but different natures – or, at least, different constructions of nature (Van den Daele 1992b; Eder 1996a; Macnaghten and Urry 1998).

Today, different options marked by distinct cultural models are available and people are compelled to become active and make choices. Consequently, nature has become a new field of social contestation and conflict (Eder

1993a: 119–40) and we are witnessing a range of 'contested natures' (Macnaghten and Urry 1998). In the risk discourse, the participants as well as the observing, evaluating and judging public draw on different models of nature available in culture and actualize them in competing or conflicting feelings, concepts and modes of behaviour toward nature. Many environmentally minded people, including deep ecologists and some conservationists, are committed to the revival of organic nature. They regard nature as a life-giving force with its own integrity to which we are required to relate organically through the observance of moral restraints inherent in nature itself. The deepest and sharpest conflict in the risk society, however, is between the mechanical and reflexive models. Recent developments in science, the new social movements and more generally the risk discourse have changed the context and thus put pressure on the mechanical model to change in the direction of the reflexive model. Despite this, however, there are many in science, technology, industry and the state who continue to regard nature as a limitless resource of utilitarian significance that we can approach in a morally neutral way and thus objectify, manipulate and exploit with impunity. They are resolutely opposed by those who draw on and activate the reflexive cultural model of nature, among whom is a significant proportion of civil society and the public. For the latter, nature is on a par with an alter ego who demands recognition and respect and, therefore, with whom we are required to tune in properly.

The fact that nature appears only in interpretations informed by different cultural models might lead one to think that the conflict between different models of nature is merely a cultural matter. Since society forms part of nature, however, it is incontrovertible that the contradictions involved also possess an objective dimension. Here the social scientist is required to consider the actors or agents who sponsor the different models and their relations to one another. Sociologically, the concept of social class is the appropriate one. Can contemporary society still be said to be a class society? Traditionally, industrial capitalist society was widely considered to be an economic class society, while the welfare state later added further political conditions of class formation. By contrast, it is not unusual for sociologists to regard contemporary society as having gone beyond the old class divisions (Giddens 1996) and even as tending toward 'individualization', 'classlessness' and a 'post-class society' (Beck 1992: 87, 88, 100). Notwithstanding such developments, however, it is recognized that social inequalities do not disappear, that there are different 'social risk positions', that conflict remains virulent (Beck 1992: 88, 23, 100) and that we are still living in a 'class society' (Giddens 1996: 236). Many authors are emphatic that class has been and still is a central structural feature of social reality which cannot be dismissed without impoverishing the sociological level of analysis already attained (Maheu 1995). In a path-breaking analysis, Bourdieu (1986, 1987) links class and classification, with the implication that the social world should be regarded as being populated by social actors who produce not only classifiable acts (thus the sociologist can determine the different classes to which they belong), but also acts of classification (such as by activating different models of nature) which are themselves classified (that is, by the other participants as well as by the observing public). Eder (1993a) proposes more specifically that we regard nature as the new field of class conflict. According to him, the continuing differentiation and intensification of the exploitation of nature is transforming the class structure of advanced modern societies: 'A new type of society is emerging in which class conflict will be centred on the problem of the exploitation of nature' (Eder 1993a: 120). Merchant (1990) has shown that this new class conflict has a significant gender dimension. Considering the fundamental change in our understanding of nature, it is clear that class is no longer merely a matter of economics or of politics but rather of culture (Touraine 1971; Habermas 1987). While economic and political competition and conflict are by no means of no consequence, as will become clear below, class pertains more properly to the process of the social construction of reality which today is most fundamentally unfolded in dynamics guided by the cultural model of nature. This means that the object of conflict is no longer domination or poverty, as in the two preceding epochs, but nature (Strydom 1990). Instead of being between the absolutist state and the rightless or between capital and labour, therefore, class conflict today transpires above all between those representing a mechanical model and those representing a reflexive model of nature. The classes engaging in conflict are thus aggregates of social positions that share opposing culturally constituted cognitive structures. Not only those directly involved in competition, contestation and conflict are included in these probabilistic constructs, however, but also very importantly today different sections of the observing, evaluating and commenting public. The multiplicity of meeting points between these two classes delineates the site of the creation and organization of the nascent society of the twenty-first century. One could get an idea of this by looking at the stakes at issue in the new class conflict over nature, the reflexively exposed cultural foundations of society.

Considering the cultural interpretations and objective relations sketched above, it is clear that the form and objective characteristics of society increasingly come to depend on which models are culturally available, reflexively accessible and discursively actualized. Against this background, therefore, I now turn to the currently emerging cultural forms of legitimation and institutional arrangements.

Emergent cultural forms of legitimation: sustainability, responsibility, citizenship

All the major cultural forms that have begun to emerge since the 1970s are intelligible only against the background of the new concern with nature through the reflexive penetration and discursive transformation of the cultural foundations of society. Among them are sustainability, collective responsibility and ecological citizenship. As nature was creatively reconstructed in accordance with a reflexive cultural model, the intellectual, moral and aesthetic or conative dimensions of the concurrently emerging ecological macro-frame became gradually clarified. First, a new concept of nature was articulated and differentiated into a cultural form that became officially known in the late 1980s as 'sustainability' or 'sustainable development'. Second, a new principle for relating to nature was developed under the title of 'collective responsibility' which has gained increasing recognition during the 1990s. Finally, a new device for integrating the subject, whether individual or collective, through identification and identity formation was put forward in the form of 'ecological citizenship', which was in turn supported by newly developed ecological rights and articulated in more differentiated forms such as 'technological citizenship'.

Sustainability

The concept of sustainability or sustainable development turns on the idea of a complex of relations among elements that organizes itself which has an affinity with both the concept of ecology and the concept of system. In its early exposition in 1980 in the first World Conservation Strategy (Redclift 1992: 389), the idea was linked to the environment, ecology or nature as a systemic order possessing its own value independently of human beings and social and cultural systems. To articulate this systemic order, biological metaphors were employed. As a consequence, sustainable development was understood in the narrow sense of the maintenance or conservation of life-supporting biological or natural systems. Subsequently, the Brundtland Report (World Commission on Environment and Development 1987) continued to insist on objective necessity in the form of a potential physical penalty entailed by non-compliance with the requirement of sustainability, yet took a different direction. The Commission, established by the UN General Assembly in 1983 and consisting of members from 22 countries, took a more balanced position by shifting some of the emphasis from the environment to human populations. Rather than only biological or natural systems, social and political systems were also seen as objects of efforts to attain sustainability. This direction was later continued by the Second World Conservation Strategy in 1991 (Redclift 1992: 389), but it was essentially the Brundtland Report and the UN Earth Summit of 1992 in Rio de Janeiro that gave international prominence and wide currency to the notion of sustainable development.

The concept was widely discussed and criticized, with many authors questioning its precision and usefulness. Lafferty (1995: 23) is of course quite correct to identify it as a 'contested concept', as is Yearley (1996: 96, 131) to propose resolving the apparent contradictions by defining it as a type of 'socioeconomic advancement' which can be continued indefinitely without exhausting natural resources and impairing the capacity of natural systems to absorb pollution. But there are two things they do not recognize.

First, sustainability or sustainable development is above all a cultural form, consisting of words, concepts, propositions, theories, explanations, justifications, meanings and symbols, that provides legitimation to a range of distinct actors and agents to engage in certain kinds of actions and to create certain kinds of institutions. In this sense, it is neither a sheer negative ideology nor an empty idealistic aspiration, as some authors think, but rather a cultural form with practical efficacy. As such, it coordinates actions and institutions nationally and globally – for instance, by serving as the overriding goal of national policy and international cooperation and hence the shared goal of humankind. Second, this cultural form is generated by a process of social construction in which a number of actors or agents compete and conflict with one another over different interpretations, claims and decisions. This means that it is linear thinking or even a semanticist or idealistic mistake to search for a harmonious concept. In any given situation, sustainability is an amalgam of different elements that do not neatly fit together, a practical synthesis provisionally bringing together continuing oppositions. One way of identifying the elements is to consider the opposing frames advanced by deep ecologists (Sessions 1987), conservationists, political ecologists (Lowe and Rüdig 1986; Eder 1996a), environmental economists of competing neo-Malthusian (Hardin 1968) and neo-Ricardian (Simon and Kahn 1984) persuasions, and so on. Another way is to consider the conflicting interpretations of sustainability offered by ecological modernization and reflexive modernization respectively. These frames, which despite differences are nevertheless able to relate to one another within the cultural form of sustainability, are also reflected in the policy directions and institutional props that are created in support of the realization of sustainability.

Collective or co-responsibility

While sustainability is a new cultural form that has been developed from the intellectual, theoretical-empirical idea of a complex or system to be preserved intact, it is complemented by an emergent cultural form centred on a normative idea of moral obligation. The latter has increasingly been articulated in terms of responsibility or, rather, collective responsibility. An awareness of this normative dimension was clearly signalled by the Brundtland Report (World Commission on Environment and Development 1987). According to the Commission's vision, the earth's resource base must be conserved and enhanced both to meet development goals and as part of our moral obligation to other living beings and future generations. The idea around which the new cultural form of responsibility has been forming, however, was first given proper formulation by authors such as Apel (1980, 1987, 1988, 1991) and Jonas (1973, 1976, 1984). Social scientists, who have already made a wide-ranging contribution to the analysis of sustainability, are also now beginning to give attention to collective responsibility. Among the sociologists, it was authors concerned with the new social movements, such as Melucci (1985, 1996) and Hegedus (1990), who introduced the contemporary concept of responsibility and carried it forward. But it was undoubtedly Beck who, through sociologically linking risk and responsibility, was instrumental, even if in a certain sense by default, in drawing the attention of sociologists more broadly to the phenomenon. Responsibility is a central yet undeveloped concept in Beck (1995, 1999) and Giddens (1996: 237; 1999: 32) also mentions it on occasion, while others have begun to treat it more systematically (Strydom 1999b, 1999d; Delanty 1999a: 156–7, 1999b, 2000: 127–8). Immediately behind this systematic approach to responsibility stands a broader American and, in particular, European intellectual background represented respectively by Jonas and Apel.

From the start, Beck (1992: 28) recognized that the concept of risk presumes a normative horizon. His critical analysis of contemporary society in terms of 'organized irresponsibility' (Beck 1988, 1995: 50–69, 1999: 55, 2000: 227) makes clear how he conceives of this normative dimension. The risk society is characterized simultaneously by the production of dangers, threats and risks and the passing of the responsibility for them from system to system. It is understandable, therefore, why Delanty (1999a: 157) thinks that responsibility is a positive implication and Lash (1994: 201) that it might be the key to Beck's work. But what both suggest is that Beck has not done enough to do justice to this dimension. In his latest work, at least, he now emphatically submits that '[r]isk and *responsibility* are intrinsically connected' (Beck 1999: 6). Already in the late 1960s and early 1970s, both Apel (1980, 1987, 1988, 1991) and Jonas (1973, 1976, 1984) paid attention to the theme of risk and responsibility, and what Beck (1999) conceives as a 'world risk society' finds its complement in what they for many years already call 'collective responsibility', or 'co-responsibility' as Apel (1993; Strydom 1999d) prefers. These two authors introduced and systematically developed the idea of a future-oriented, planetary macro-ethics of responsibility in the face of the unprecedented situation created by both the promise and the risks entailed by science and technology. By contrast with Jonas's metaphysical leanings, Apel (1988) conceives of responsibility in terms of a sociology friendly communication and discourse theory which is sensitive to the contingency, uncertainty and ambivalence of contemporary social life, which explains why he emphasizes co-responsibility rather than simply collective responsibility. It brings into play a public level of responsibility for the effects of collective actions and activities, which demands discursive participation of all those interested and affected, without disburdening individual or collective actors of their personal or agential responsibility.

Apel's reconceptualization of responsibility by means of communication and discourse theory completely transforms the older debates about responsibility and provides the social scientist with the opportunity to conceive and study responsibility in an entirely new way (Strydom 1999b, 1999d). It is a new cultural form, model, code or frame that has become available due to the efforts of a range of different actors or agents participating in the risk discourse to ascribe responsibility and blame to each other in the face of universal, global and irreversible risks. Rather than just a free-floating cultural form, however, this new model strikes roots in the minds of the participants and the observing public. Members of social movements, scientists, politicians, business people, lawyers and citizens – as well as sociologists! – acquire new cognitive structures, including new feelings, concepts and rules of conduct, that are all in some way or another related to the cultural model of responsibility. A mass of quite surprising evidence becomes available, for instance, when one searches the websites of movements, NGOs, governments and even corporations, who began to regard themselves as corporate citizens, by means of the keyword responsibility.

Ecological citizenship

Since early modernity, rights have been a basic means of the creation and organization of society (Strydom 2000). In the context of the contemporary concern with sustainability and responsibility toward nature and future generations, a new category of rights has been conceived in extension of civil, political and social rights. Habermas, for instance, speaks of '[b]asic rights to the provision of living conditions that are . . . technologically and ecologically safeguarded, insofar as the current circumstances make this necessary if citizens are to have equal opportunities to utilize the[ir] civil rights' (1996: 123). Accepting Galtung's (1994) view that rights correspond to human needs, one could argue that new needs have emerged in recent decades that gave rise to this new concept of rights. A cluster of discursively articulated biological (autopoietic, health and reproduction) and socio-cultural (identity) needs led to the concept of environmental or ecological rights.

Considering that citizenship, besides belonging, embraces a status defined by a bundle of rights (Janowitz 1980), these rights to a clean, safe and balanced environment are not merely an extension of the existing system of civil, political and social rights, but in fact have implications for citizenship itself. Whereas the previously established rights centred on the nation-state, the reclassification shifts rights to the global, cosmopolitan and ecosystemic level. In turn, the new rights classification, together with sustainability and collective or co-reponsibility, provided an impetus for rethinking citizenship as 'global' (Turner 1993: 14; Macnaghten and Urry 1998: 152; Delanty 2000), 'ecological citizenship' (Christoff 1996a: 159). Citizenship no longer concerns only sharing in the civic life of ruling and being ruled or collectively exercised self-legislation. Reshaped by an ecological emphasis, it includes the representation of the rights of future generations, other species and the ecosystem and hence taking responsibility for their fate. Once citizens become ecological trustees over and above being members of a political community, a whole range of transnational relationships and alliances open up.

Of particular significance for the theme of this book is what is entailed by being a citizen of a scientific-technological or experimenting society – so-called 'technological citizenship' (Frankenfeld 1992; Zimmerman 1995; Delanty 2001). This new idea, which has yet to find coherent institutional embodiment, starts from the fact that technology, particularly science-based high technology, possesses an unlimited potential for both benefit and harm. It envisages the reconciliation of the freedom to innovate and take risks with citizens' autonomy, dignity and right to a clean, safe and balanced environment. Depending on the scope of the technological regulation regime, the status of technological citizenship could be enjoyed at a range of levels, from the regional through the national to the global. What is clear from the emergence of sustainability, collective or co-responsibility and ecological citizenship, however, is that a technological political community aware of its vulnerability or even victimization by high technology and the need for a more democratic governance of technology is in the process of emergence. This is Beck's 'post-national risk community' (1999: 16) that forms in the wake of the socialization of risk in the context of the world risk society. An interesting point worth developing is that identify-formation under these conditions, and hence increasingly in contemporary society, takes place with reference to victimization rather than through identification with heroes. Be that as it may, technological citizenship as a status embraces both rights and obligations (Frankenfeld 1992: 459). Among the former are the right to information and knowledge, the right to parti-cipate in decision-making, the right to guarantees of informed consent or agreement to certain developments, and the right to the limitation of the total amount of endangerment of individuals and collectivities. The obliga-tions, on the other hand, include the responsibility to learn and use know-ledge about hazards, to participate in activities governing complex hazards, and finally to exercise technological literacy, civic virtue and judgement. These rights and obligations suggest that the currently emerging cultural form of technological citizenship could contribute to the extension of demo-cratic control over the introduction and ongoing management of environ-mental hazards and the self-verification of safety.

Two other cultural forms that arose in the 1990s, which are obviously closely related to ecological and more specifically technological citizenship, are what has come to be called 'environmental justice' (Perrolle 1993; Bryant 1995) and 'environmental victimology' (Williams 1998). The former's emer-gence can be traced to community groups and workers consisting of minorities and the poor in North America who perceive themselves to be unjustly exposed to environmental risks. Rather than the general division between risk-takers and those affected, therefore, it is more specifically conceived in terms of class, ethnicity, race and gender. Starting from the assumption of a stratified society, it draws attention to environmental prob-lems in the community and workplace as issues of justice. Environmental victimology, second, is a cultural form that arose in the wake of victimization resulting from large-scale industrial disasters, beginning in particular with

Bhopal, but besides conspicuous catastrophes it also applies to so-called creeping disasters. It was given a more systematic formulation in criticism and extension of environmental justice, which is reputedly informed by a rich-nation perspective, operates with a traditional notion of stratification and of group identity, and is culturally insensitive. Bringing the global and local – or 'glocal' (Friedman 1994) – level into sharper focus, environmental victimology is thus complementary to environmental justice.

Environmental justice and environmental victimology, like such cultural forms as sustainability, responsibility, ecological rights, ecological citizenship and technological citizenship, have recently also begun to find institutional embodiment, which brings us to the emergent institutions of the risk society.

Emergent institutions: new and reflexive

The process of institutionalization, understood in terms of constructivism as the collective stabilization of reciprocal typifications of subjective frames and actions as something objective (Berger and Luckmann 1967), possesses both a cognitive and a normative dimension (Eder 1996a; Strydom 2000). The construction of shared frames or the establishment of cultural forms such as sustainability and so forth discussed above represents cognitive institutionalization. Normative institutionalization, on which this subsection focuses, concerns the making effective of such frames or forms at the level of social action and practices. Let us briefly review developments of this latter kind at different levels, from legal norms through organizations and institutions to global accords.

New institutions

Until the mid-twentieth century, only a very few organizations (for instance, Zoological Society or the International Council for Exploration of the Seas) addressed environmental issues (fishery, whales and migratory birds) and legal developments were at a comparably low level. It is only since the late 1950s and especially the 1970s that we witness a remarkable efflorescence. Environmental organizations carrying the environmental movement increased rapidly, and the UN, playing a crucial context-setting role, used international law to bring increasing numbers of environmental issues within its scope, despite the fact that its Charter contains no explicit basis for an environmental programme (Birnie 2000). The series of UN conferences since 1972 and the UN Environmental Programme (UNEP 2000), although still in need of being strengthened, are of the greatest importance, as are the moves toward the establishment of an Environmental Council parallel to the UN Security Council (Dolzer 1994) and a permanent UN Second or People's Assembly (NGOs Network 2000). Compared to 7 during the preceding period going back to 1899, some 35 environmental laws were enacted in the United States between 1958 and

1986 (Choucri 1994). A similar legal creativity was exhibited in the European Union and elsewhere. Many of these environmental laws go some way toward institutionally embodying ecological and, more specifically, technological citizenship (Frankenfeld 1992: 477), while in the mean time others such as the Freedom of Information Act has been added in many countries to the same effect. Following the UN Conference on the Human Environment in Stockholm, the 1970s saw the first wave of policy responses to environmental problems in the form of environment departments or agencies charged with protecting the natural environment (Weale 1992). The succeeding second wave brought environmental considerations not only into all government departments and agencies, but also into corporations and business. Since the late 1950s, particularly the 1980s and 1990s, international environmental accords and treaties increased from approximately 5 to more than 120 (Choucri 1994). They include agreements among EU members on reducing acidic gas emissions, ozone-depleting chemicals and marine oil pollution to global accords about sustainable development, the ozone hole, global warming and climate change.

That normative institutionalization is by no means an unproblematic process, however, is demonstrated by any of a number of examples. First, there is the formal vacuity of many legal norms, institutional programmes and international agreements. Second, there are concrete instances such as the failure in late 2000 of the international conference in The Hague to reach an agreement on the emission of greenhouse gases, despite severe floods in many parts of the world linked to global warming. It is at the filling of gaps of this kind that recent institutional developments, such as 'environmental equity justice centers' (Wright 1995), the Permanent People's Tribunal on Industrial Hazards and Human Rights (1998) and the International People's Tribunal on Human Rights and the Environment (2000), are aimed. Environmental justice centres have been created in the United States to address environmetal insult and injustice through collaborative problem-solving involving affected communities and universities. They pursue environmental equity through research, policy formulation, community assistance, and education. The Permanent People's Tribunal, based in Rome and London, was founded in the early 1990s. Between 1991 and 1994 it drafted a 'Charter of Rights against Industrial Hazards' with a view to strengthening national and international systems of prevention, relief and legal accountability in cases of both small and large-scale harmful hazardous events. The International People's Tribunal was convened by NGOs at the second UN Earth Summit in 1997. Basing itself on international conventions and standards, including the Universal Declaration of Human Rights, the Declaration on Victims of Abuse of Power and the 27 Principles adopted at the Rio Earth Summit, it provides a global forum for the consideration of environmental risks, victimization and rights violations as well as the mobilization of global solidarity. By hearing cases of human rights violations in connection with environmental destruction, it seeks to hold corporations and governments accountable.

Reflexive or discursive institutions

Many of the institutions mentioned above, although new or emerging, answer to the traditional concept according to which an institution consists of four components: an idea recognized and upheld by those involved, personnel fulfilling different roles, norms governing internal and external relations, and finally a material apparatus. More characteristic of contemporary society, however, and therefore more interesting, is a new type of institution and, by extension, a new type of institutional order. This new type of institution is what has come to be called 'reflexive institutions'.

Apel (1987: 30–2) introduced the idea of reflexive institutions in the context of considering the problem of institutionalizing responsibility for the future in the case of science, technology and medicine. In his view, it could be achieved by the discursive organization of collective responsibility. It requires the embedding of science, technology and medicine in practical discourses that unfold between public debates and legislative deliberation and thus incorporate expert knowledge within an appropriate social, ethical and practical framework. Eder, who regards 'reflexive institutions' (1996a: 212) or 'discursive institutions' (1998) as a characteristic feature of our time which is yet to be adequately understood and explained, together with a number of associates at the Munich Social Science Research Group conducted a two-year research project on this new phenomenon in the environmental field funded by the German Research Community (Eder 1993b). Whereas under modern conditions institutions had become more formal, organizational and goal-oriented, according to him, in contemporary modernity they are becoming more reflexive, which entails greater informality and orientation toward the appropriateness and reasonableness of action and the generation of an implicit understanding and agreement among those involved. As examples, Eder (1993b: 3, 10–11) lists commissions of inquiry, technology assessment commissions, talks in search of dialogue and consensus, self-restricting agreements between industry and environmental groups – all flexible and even fleeting institutional arrangements with only a temporary existence. Beck (1994: 28–9) sees 'intersystemic mediation' or reflexive institutions existing in rudimentary form in round tables and in investigative, ethical and risk committees. They fulfil the demand for forms and fora of consensus-building cooperation among politics, science, industry and citizens. As such, they demonopolize expertise, informalize jurisdiction, open the structure of decision-making and create at least partial publicity (Beck 1997: 122–3). Yearley envisages flexible, self-aware, knowledge-making institutions that are capable of correcting the practical shortcomings of universalizing discourses such as science and expertise (Yearley 1996: 149, 151). What Dryzek (1990: 43, 1997: 199) discusses under the title of 'discursive designs' can also be interpreted as reflexive institutions. He takes as examples the mediation of national, international and environmental disputes, alternative dispute resolution, regulatory and principled negotiation, policy dialogue and problem-solving workshops. These institutions are 'fluid and transient, lasting no longer than a particular problematic situation' (Dryzek 1990: 44), make possible 'understanding across different frames of reference [yet] allow continued differences' (1990: 54), and since they are 'not bound up in constitutional and formal rules, they allow their own supercession' (1990: 56). Whereas Dryzek stresses a normative concept of reflexive institutions as authentically democratic ones, Hajer (1995) points out that they operate within certain limits, so that they could not be assumed necessarily to be more effective, more productive of consensus, less time-consuming and less expensive than other institutions. Hajer nevertheless insists that 'reflexive institutional arrangements' (1995: 286) are most suitable to deliberate decision-making in the risk society. He regards them as 'institutional forms that could accommodate the increase in cognitive reflexivity, argumentation and negotiated social choice' (Hajer 1996: 266). They are of course not going to make the environmental dilemma of contemporary society go away. However, by contrast with the paternalist techno-corporatist Windscale Inquiry, for instance, a 'societal inquiry' (Hajer 1995: 288–92) such as the Canadian Berger Inquiry can serve as an instrument for the creation of open structures to determine collectively and consciously in what kind of nature and society we really want to live.

Post-corporatism

The emergence of reflexive institutions has far-reaching effects. It involves a transformation of the institutional order that prevailed for most of the twentieth century. Eder thus regards reflexive institutions as being characteristic of a new institutional order to which he refers as 'post-corporatism' (Eder 1996a: 212, 1998; see also Lash 1994: 207–8). The key to this transformation is to be found in the close relation between reflexive institutions and the generation of communication and discourse.

In the fairly typical tripartite corporatist arrangement of the postwar period (Beck 1992: 48), the state, employers and unions engaged in conflicts and negotiations about the equitable distribution of the wealth of the nation. The emergent institutional order carried by reflexive institutions, by contrast, not only makes room for other social actors, such as NGOs, social movements and the media, but also has a much looser structure. It is an institutional order penetrated by communication. Rather than being connected through formally organized relations, therefore, actors and institutions relate through communication. Public communication and discourse, the mass media and the public thus play a much more prominent role in it. The centrality of communication explains why culture as the source of models, standards and criteria comes to weigh more heavily on actors, agents and organizations, and why the public, the soundboard of cultural choice, gains in authority (Strydom 1999c). In the post-corporatist order, consequently, the conflict over distribution is no longer central. Its place is taken by a struggle among social movements, the state, industry, science and so forth that is fought out via the media and plays off before the observing public. Rather than a normative conflict, the post-corporatist order harbours the process of the social construction of reality (Lash 1994). Within its confines, the participants are struggling over the form and object-ive characteristics of society by conflicting over which culturally available and reflexively accessible models, standards or criteria are going to be dis-cursively actualized and collectively validated. In the same way that cor-poratism in the past took a variety of forms under different conditions, post-corporatism differs depending on whether it is realized under the con-ditions of the American competition model, the British compromise model, the French etatist model or the German synthesis model, and so on (Münch 1996).

The nascent society of the twenty-first century: world government and bio-society?

If the cultural and institutional forms discussed above are factors in the process of the constitution and organization of society, the question arises as to what objective features the nascent society of the twenty-first century is likely to assume. At one level, there is little doubt that some form of regulation will follow upon the deregulation of the late twentieth century. Some form of a world political dispensation is going to be attached to the emerging global economic and world risk society. In fact, it is a hotly discussed topic at present. The question is what form we can expect it to take. Besides transnational politics, however, the current stage of the pro-duction and construction of risks suggests that society is faced by a basic option. In what direction will we go? In addition to being threatened and ravaged by global environmental problems, the possibility of a bio-society is the spectre haunting us today. It is doubly risky from a social scientific viewpoint, for its realization would entail the displacement of sociology by sociobiology and, more generally, the transformation of the social sciences into sociobiological sciences. Could we avoid the bio-society by going in the direction of a cultural society instead?

The transnational political form of society

In opposition to economic globalization as an opening up and liberalization process, environmental problems and challenges, as many have observed (Held 1996: 351; Yearley 1996: 151; Habermas 1998: 121, 157), are provid-ing the strongest impetus thus far toward processes of cultural, social and political globalization. Among them are a globalizing movement, a globaliz-ing discourse, a global awareness, a global frame, closely related planet-wide identities and transnational institutions and negotiation systems. Not only do these developments give the clearest coherent indication of a global shift in human affairs (Held 1996: 351), but also they hold out the promise of renewed closure and regulation under drastically changed conditions

(Habermas 1998: 125–30). This is precisely the significance of phenomena such as sustainability, responsibility, citizenship, the UN Environment Programme, and reflexive institutions discussed above. As against an experimenting society feeding a process of economic deregulation and globalization, all these phenomena point in the direction of an interdependent world or global society with a transnational political dispensation capable of catching up with and delimiting global networks.

What neo-liberalism and postmodernism celebrate as a relentless process of opening up that does not admit of any closure, has in fact already been forced to begin to close by the emergence of what Beck calls the 'world risk society' constituted by 'post-national risk communities' (1999: 16). To the latter, of course, one could also add accompanying developments, such as the UN acquiring the task of averting ecological disaster over and above its traditional focus on securing peace and later concern with avoiding humanitarian catastrophes (Birnie 2000). Although only reactively through shared feelings of indignation in the face of the societal production of universal, global and irreversible risks and the concomitant violation of human rights, people all over the world have begun to regard themselves as world citizens and to form a new kind of solidarity. This solidarity has both a cosmopolitan and an ecological dimension (Archibugi et al. 1998; Habermas 1998: 163; Beck 1999: 1–18; Delanty 2000). Unlike the solidarity of state citizens, which could found the constitutional state and the welfare state, however, the solidarity of world citizens neither implies nor would make possible the formation of a world government, as some predict and others fear (Zolo 1997). The establishment of something like the 1995 proposal of the then G7 to consolidate its power in a new form of geopolitical governance, which would realize Zolo's horror scenario of a new hierarchical and monocentric 'cosmopolitan Holy Alliance', can of course not be excluded. But the emerging interdependent world society of the twenty-first century, which can be adequately organized on the basis neither of the global market nor of a world state, is much more likely to call for a form of world politics or global governance devoid of world government.

In contrast to a static, monocentric hierarchy, Held (1996: 357) sees it as a political order of democratic associations, cities, nations and regional and global networks in which an intensive participatory democracy at local level is complemented by deliberative assemblies at the global level. Habermas (1998: 165) emphatically rejects the static model of multilevel politics within a world organization in favour of a dynamic model of interaction and interference among autonomous political processes on national, international and global level. Global governance would entail that international negotiation systems enabling agreements between states communicate with democratic processes within states on which governments depend, on the one hand, and relate to the politics of a world organization such as a revitalized United Nations, on the other. It is obvious that what was discussed above under the title of reflexive institutions would be an integral and vital part of transnational institutions and negotiation systems at the heart of such an arrangement. As the 'epistemic function' (Habermas 1998: 166) of democracy expands, the significance of reflexive institutions as 'knowledge-making institutions' (Yearley 1996: 151) will increase. The legitimacy of global governance, therefore, would depend not only on participatory and expressive rights, but also on general access to deliberative processes. For instance, NGOs could be included in international negotiations and the UN could be given the right to demand referenda on important issues in all member states to ensure their public consideration (Habermas 1998: 166–7). Above all, however, the realization of global governance would require that citizens, associations and movements in civil societies all over the world adequately articulate the awareness of a cosmopolitan solidarity that has started the emerge under the compulsion of environmental problems, risks and challenges.

Bio-society or cultural society?

A potential set of objective features of twenty-first-century society other than its transnational political form comes into view when one considers it from the more specific viewpoint of environmental problems and challenges. The emergent society is not merely a risk society, but also at the same time an experimenting society. It involves both the production and construction of risks. The production of risks entails the bundling of the logics of scientific-technological advancement, industrialism, capitalism and statecraft. The social construction of risks, on the other hand, draws more strongly on the logics of culture and democracy. What objective features society is going to exhibit in the first third or half of the twenty-first century depend on where the emphasis falls in the next number of decisive years.

The production of risks in the experimenting society is closely tied to the process of deregulation and economic globalization. Such production could be expected to be encouraged, therefore, under either of two conditions – the first perhaps more encouraging than the second. The first is the neo-liberal dream of an unregulated or minimally regulated global marketplace. The second is the vision, if not of a world state, then at least of a new form of world government, what – following Zolo (1997) – may be called a new 'Holy Alliance'. Of particular importance as a realizable possibility here is the hierarchicist political perspective of international geopolitical government as envisaged by the then G7. Irrespective of whether the one or the other takes effect, the production of risks can be expected to continue on a significant scale. Current conditions suggest that it will assume a particular character. Neither the risk of nuclear radiation nor the risks of global warming, climate change and reduced ozone protection will disappear, of course. But the extraordinary contemporary focus on genetic engineering, biotechnology and in particular so-called 'bioethics' (that is, human genetic engineering and biotechnology) makes clear that this will be the major area of productive activity. In the next decade and more, by far the largest number and by far the most significant risks – so-called 'bio-hazards' – will undoubtedly emerge here. Indeed, if either a global marketplace or a new Holy Alliance comes to prevail, society is likely to be so thoroughly transformed and so deeply restructured by biotechnology that it assumes the form of a 'bio-society' (Jäger et al. 1997: subtitle) and, by extension, a 'eugenic civilisation' (Rifkin 1998: 116).

Shaped by the latest technology revolution based on the fusion of genetics and computers, the possibility of a bio-society is already discernible in the emergence of certain material conditions. Among the indicators are in vitro fertilization, surrogate wombs, bio-industrial factories, genetically modified organisms (GMOs), GMO releases, GM crops and foods, cloned animals, transgenic species, fabricated human organs, the patenting of life, commercialized genes and gene pools, human somatic cell and germ line therapies, stem cell research, genetic screening technologies and tests, genetic readouts, genetic databanks, bio-informatics, and so on. These conditions contain pointers towards a range of features that could potentially become characteristic of society. Indeed, some of them are already observable, particularly but not only in the United States (Rifkin 1998). As microbiologists and geneticists reorganize life at the genetic level, society at large becomes fundamentally restructured. Instead of a social reality, it becomes a bio-society possessing its own profile (Van den Daele 1992a; Paul 1994; Jäger et al. 1997; Habermas 1998; Rifkin 1998). Its information basis is altered and, consequently, a different understanding of society, its building blocks and processes develops. Not nurture but nature counts, not the environment but genes determine personality, behaviour, groups, institutions and society at large. The solution of social problems such as underachievement, unemployment, poverty, deviance, crime and conflict require, therefore, a much more fundamental attack than the modification of rules of conduct and institutions. The treatment of serious genetic disorders by somatic therapy or, even more desirable, their elimination by means of germ line therapy as well as the correction of cosmetic defects to enhance well-being, are central to the new approach. Upon this follows the increased use of genetic screening in all spheres of life, from the family and school through health and insurance to the workplace. Child development and family relations are rethought on a genetic model, and genetic responsibility is imposed on parents, with the result that parental eugenics takes hold and changes beyond recognition parenthood as well as the relation between parent and child. Educational systems are geneticized on the basis of the view that individual abilities are genetically rather than socially determined, and as a result of the medicalization of pedagogy the mentor role and the relation between teacher and student are transformed. Courts rely increasingly on the results of genetic screening and brain scans in sentencing and bail and parole decisions. Due to the new information basis of society and the distinctions it allows, genetic discrimination and genetic stigmatization become a standard feature of everyday life, education, health, insurance and work. A loss of solidarity with disabled people occurs, the choice of marriage partner is determined by a genetic readout, genetic stereotyping of racial and ethnic groups becomes common, and an expanding untreatable, uneducable, uninsurable, unemployable genetic underclass emerges. Over and above this underclass as well as the majority of ordinary people, a small genetocracy, a new genetic aristocracy able to afford enhancement with synthetic genes, occupies leadership roles in all spheres of life. Comparable to the eugenic movement of the first part of the twentieth century in the United States and Germany in particular, society becomes thoroughly reideologized in terms of genes, genetic engineering, biotechnology and bioethics. Correspondingly, a new politics proceeding from genetic causality and exerting 'bio-power' (Foucault 1981: 140), what has been called 'genetically correct politics' (Rifkin 1998: 153) or 'biopolitics' (Féher and Heller 1994; Jäger et al. 1997; Delanty 1999b), becomes the generally accepted approach to collective problems. Finally, this bio-society becomes embedded in a 'eugenic civilization' (Rifkin 1998: 116–47). In order to conceptualize and theorize the new understanding of society, a paradigm change in sociology in particular and the social sciences in general can be observed (Jäger et al. 1997: 340; Rifkin 1998: 148). The aberrant eugenic sociology of the early twentieth century is being reinvented. In the form of sociobiology it not only helps to shape the climate of ideas favourable to the emergence of the bio-society, but also becomes an indispensable political instrument for the biotechnical regulation and control of societal processes.

Whether these developments will actually become objective features of society, however, is by no means a fait accompli. It is only one possible option that is at present being sponsored by what may be called the 'new eugenics movement' (Rifkin 1998: 128). This movement is the impetus behind the 'sub-politics' (Beck 1992: 204) of biotechnology and bioethics, which entails the experimental implementation of epoch-making decisions on the future, while trying to bypass the public sphere and parliaments. It is represented by an increasingly identifiable group that derives from microbiology, genetics, medicine and bioethics (Paul 1994). Some of its members openly attack democratic institutions (Byk 1992: 371, 1999: 157–8), advocate genetocratic views (Engelhardt 1977; Silver 1997), work against human rights (Milani-Comparetti 1993) and even deliberately violate the rules governing research (Meek 2000; RAFI 2000). It is disturbing that these views are not exclusive to this group, but through its leading figures are also central to the Council of Europe, the G7 and G8 and even Unesco. Among large sections of the information-starved citizens of many countries, however, a significant degree of public unease about this movement and the democratic deficit of key institutions is observable. Out of this unease an opposition has been growing, sometimes linking with the anti-globalization movement. It is spearheaded by the anti-genetic engineering (Gottweiss 1995) and the anti-biotechnology patents movements (McNally and Wheale 1999), and evidence of the emergence of what may be called a 'genetic rights movement' (Rifkin 1998: 168) is also mounting (GRAIN 1997, 1999; Greenpeace 1999; RAFI 1999b).

Whether a bio-society is going to be established is dependent on the definitional struggles of these forces and the response of the public. The direction of the constitution and organization of society is tied up with the construction of reality in the risk discourse. Like the nuclear project, therefore, it is entirely possible that the biotechnology project could also be significantly circumscribed and limited. In this case, the society of the twenty-first century could acquire the character of a 'cultural society' (Moscovici 1977: 466; Lash 1994: 208; Eder 1996a) rather than that of a bio-society. From one viewpoint, this is a cosmopolitan, participatory and deliberative democratic society in which reflexive institutions make possible circumspect and responsible dealings with ineradicable uncertainty and ambivalence as well as our equally unavoidable 'non-knowledge' (Beck 1999: 109–32). From another deeper perspective, it is a society that allows the reflexive exposure, symbolic communication and discursive articulation and mediation of semantic backgrounds, cultural models, taken-for-granted primitive classifications or deep-seated culturally constituted cognitive structures. A cultural society is one, therefore, in which the process of social construction of reality has sufficient room to unfold despite obstacles, making it possible for a culture of contradictions manifested in public communication to guide and shape decision-making in a basic and dynamic yet not over-specific way. It is obviously this eventuality that we should expect and work towards today – a society discursively setting cultural and normative limits to dominant epistemic communities and neoliberal economic and political regimes.

Summary

In this chapter, which brings Part two to a close, the focus was on some of the most significant cultural and institutional developments and dynamics in contemporary society. I attempted to show that a transformation in the cultural foundations of society, which is intimately tied to a new social or class conflict, brought nature as a cultural cornerstone to awareness. This provided the starting point for the rise of a range of cultural forms, from sustainable development and collective or co-responsibility through environmental rights to ecological and technological citizenship, which are all stakes in the new class conflict. While these cultural developments provide legitimation for and find institutional embodiment in a whole series of new institutions, the most conspicuous new departure of our time is the appearance of reflexive or discursive institutions. As regards the nature and character of the social reality that is thus being constituted and organized, I have argued that at the beginning of the twenty-first century, society is faced with some basic options. Politically, we are haunted by the spectre of a new Holy Alliance and socially by a bio-society. Fortunately, we are still at a stage where sensitive individuals, an active civil society, an agitated public sphere and a critical public can take us in the direction of a cosmopolitan form of global governance and a reasonable, humane society instead. The emergence of a transformed public sphere and a post-corporatist institutional order, carried by a process of the constitution and organization of society in which class conflict plays a role, suggests that such a development is by no means far fetched.

PART THREE

Rethinking the risk society

8

Towards a new critical theory

In Parts one and two, I offered an overview and analysis of some of the most important literature on the theme of risk, environment and society. Drawing on my theoretical and research experience in the field, I made my own selection of material – within the limits of a book such as this – and structured it according to my own understanding. In this final chapter, which is reserved for an original view, I wish to draw together the threads in such a way that I highlight my own position and make a contribution to the rethinking of the risk society. Sociologically, I hope to open new possibilities for both theorizing and researching contemporary society and, politically, I like to think that it would be in line with a more democratic mode of governance. Above all, however, I want to underline the importance of the public role of sociology.

The explicit aim of the chapter is to outline a new critical theory of the nascent society of the twenty-first century. On the one hand, it turns on a conception of society in terms of communicative or discursive modernity rather than simply reflexive modernity. On the other, it proceeds from the assumption that sociology is today vitally dependent on a combination of pragmatic (that is, communication, network, relational) sociology and critical theory. The first step in the presentation is a rethinking of the risk society as a knowledge and a communication society. The theoretical rationale of this proposal is the cognitive turn in sociology. This provides a basis for also rethinking constructivism in terms of the new cognitive sociology. To clarify the epistemological assumptions of this position, a brief foray is made into the new theory of evolution that is at present emerging in sociology. Under the title of the experimenting society and collective or co-responsibility, the resulting social theory of cognitive frames then provides an opportunity for opening up social scientifically neglected areas for potentially wide-ranging research. The basic cognitive sociological assumption here is that both risk and responsibility, while having roots in reality, are discursive constructions that on the one hand emerge from intersubjective processes of attribution and on the other require critical intersubjective testing. Finally, therefore, a critical theory to which the concept of social critique is central is presented. This new theory, which is impossible without a reference to the cognitive dimension, forms the theoretical and methodological basis of the public role of sociology.

Risk society, knowledge society, communication society

The self-understanding of contemporary society as the risk society arose, on the one hand, due to the manifestation of the failure of core institutional practices in an ecological crisis and, on the other, the emergence of a wide-ranging discourse. Through discourse, the complex of science, technology and industry together with their taken-for-granted cultural assumptions were problematized. The result of this was that it became apparent that contemporary society is simultaneously also an experimenting society. The fact that discourse entailed the epistemic penetration of both epistemic and non-epistemic practices revealed something of great significance. It became apparent that the risk society is at one and the same time also what some authors call a 'knowledge society' (Böhme and Stehr 1986; Stehr 1994; Böhme 1997). By considering the risk society as a knowledge society, one is able to identify a deeper and more pervasive dimension both of the production and the construction of risk. Risk society involves both the production of knowledge in the experimenting society and the construction of social reality through the conflict of different knowledges.

It seems as though Beck is aware of this, for he regards his theory and political sociology of the risk society as 'in essence *sociology of knowledge*' (1992: 55, translation modified) and sees risks as being socially effective only within knowledge (1992: 23). Like Böhme (1997) and Stehr (1994), he clearly operates with a sociological concept of knowledge, rather than with an epistemological or logical concept as the propositional content of true statements. Not only are there different kinds of knowledge, sociologically, but also the different types are carried by social actors or collective agents who possess distinct competences, power resources and opportunities yet are interdependent. As a knowledge society, therefore, contemporary society cannot be reduced to a 'science society' (Kreibich 1986), as though it could be characterized by one dominant type of knowledge. For the same reason, it cannot be equated with a postindustrial knowledge or service economy (Bell 1974) either. Nor is it reducible to an 'information society' (Webster 1995; Castells 1996), an objectivistic concept which loses sight of the subjective and intersubjective dimension of knowledge. Contemporary society is a knowledge society to the extent that it is characterized by the proliferation of different kinds of power-based knowledge and, consequently, by knowledge politics and the construction of reality in and through knowledge.

The question, however, is whether it is theoretically and methodologically sufficient to conceive society in terms of the concept of knowledge. Epistemologically, it certainly makes sense (Böhme 1997: 449–50). The concept 'knowledge society' allows one to characterize society in one particular way, so that certain features can be highlighted. It could also be useful in historically contrasting the present epoch with the preceding one. It further makes possible the pinpointing of developmental tendencies and the identification of alternatives that could be important for political action and policy. Considered more closely, however, it becomes clear that the substantive and static nature of the concept calls for compensation, all the more so under current conditions. This may look like an argument in favour of 'information society', but, as the difference between the objectivistic concept of information and the intersubjective concept of communication suggests, this is better done by the concept of 'communication society'. This conception appears in the work of different contemporary theorists, but goes back to Habermas. For instance, some speak of a 'discourse society' (Beck 1997: 128), while others prefer 'communication society' (Eder 1995: 276; Delanty 1999a: 9, 14, 69; Strydom 1999c; see also Münch 1991). The extension and support of knowledge by communication is necessary for various reasons. Communication captures better the process nature of the production, promotion and transmission of knowledge, and without it we cannot get a grip on the generalization, networking and globalization of knowledge. Neither knowledge politics, nor the discursive construction of reality could be grasped without reference to public communication. In a time when it is less knowledge as such than knowledge of knowledge that counts, communication as the medium of knowledge above all allows us to come to terms with the phenomenon of reflexivity. In is in this sense that the approach to the risk society I am proposing focuses on public communication rather than simply on reflexivity (also Delanty 1997: 138).

The new cognitive sociology

The decisive paradigm change required to rethink the risk society, however, is the adoption of the cognitive perspective implicitly contained in the above concatenation of risk, knowledge and communication. A shift of emphasis from knowledge to the communicative or discursive processes of its generation and structuration brings into view this important yet largely neglected dimension in sociology. Not only knowledge in the sense of content and organized branches or bodies of what is known requires structure, but also communicative processes are likewise structured. In both cases, the structuration is provided by cognitive structures of different levels and scope.

The neglect of the cognitive dimension in sociology is lamentable. Böhme (1997: 455, 457–8), for instance, conceives knowledge sociologically as 'sharing in cultural capital', and for Stehr (1994: 95) it is a 'capacity for social action'. Beck (1992: 154, 168) also sees knowledge and related action competences as having become more generally available, with the result that a politics and subpolitics of knowledge have emerged which are changing society beyond recognition. Significantly, he has also become conscious of the fact that knowledge is in principle accompanied by non-knowledge or 'unawareness' (Beck 1999: 109–32), and that the latter is actually the key to the definitional struggles in the risk society. What all these theorists of knowledge touch on yet leave unmentioned and undeveloped, is the more pervasive cognitive dimension that embraces acts of recognition and knowing, processes of the generation of knowledge and the micro, meso and macro cognitive structures shaping, forming and containing knowledge from the outset and throughout. Bourdieu, unlike Böhme who depends on him, is acutely aware of the dimension of 'cognitive structures' (Bourdieu 1986: 468; Strydom 1999a: 61–3). They take the form of classificatory schemes of perception, experience, thought, appreciation and expression that figure as stakes in the struggles of the different social classes and are implemented by them in their own particular competing ways. Stehr (1994) likewise remains oblivious of the cognitive connotations of talking of capacities or competences for social action. Despite submitting that 'knowledge and unawareness are separated within knowledge', Beck (1999: 127) also fails to appreciate that this compels him to adopt a cognitive approach. The recurring expression 'cognitive sociology' in Beck's (1992: 55, 1999: 121, 127, 129) writings, it should be noted, is an artefact of translation, since in the original German he consistently uses the expression *Wissenssoziologie* (sociology of knowledge) instead.

Since its founding by Mannheim, the sociology of knowledge has never given any serious or sustained attention to the distinction between knowledge and the cognitive dimension (Wolff 1993: 27). It is only relatively recently that its significance has started to become clearer, and sociologists are yet to appreciate its theoretical and research potential. Central here is the little noticed, late-twentieth-century 'cognitive turn in sociology' (Fuller 1984) against the background of the rise and development of the cognitive sciences since the 1950s (De Mey 1982; Varela et al. 1993; Bechtel and Graham 1998). Authors such as Schutz, Piaget, Wittgenstein, Kuhn, Berger and Luckmann, Garfinkel, Habermas, Foucault, Cicourel, Bourdieu, Douglas, Luhmann and Giddens helped to inaugurate this turn (Knorr-Cetina and Cicourel 1981), but they either did not pursue it as such or confined themselves to the micro-level. If anyone played a part in giving wider currency to the cognitive turn, then it is some representatives of the post-Mertonian sociology of scientific knowledge or social studies of science (Nowotny 1973; Bloor 1976; Mendelsohn 1977; Knorr-Cetina and Mulkay 1983; Knorr-Cetina 1988; Jasanoff et al. 1995). By and large, however, the sociologists of science have declined to include the wider society in their treatment of science, as is suggested by their willingness to regard science as a laboratory-based practice while overlooking society as laboratory. This has prompted Pels (1996), who is critical of the Wittgensteinian and Kuhnian leanings of the sociology of science yet borrows from it the expression 'social epistemology', to return to Mannheim to develop a comprehensive sociopolitical theory of knowledge. But it is theorists who link up with Habermas (1972, 1984, 1987, 1996) who have taken the decisive step.

Eyerman and Jamison's (1991) 'cognitive approach', for instance, is a more interesting, more widely synthetic and potentially more fruitful departure than that of Pels. Drawing on Habermas in particular, but also on Foucault, Bourdieu and Giddens, they develop a broad contextual theory not only of knowledge but also, based on the notion of 'cognitive praxis', of knowledge production through cognitive processes such as social movements and public communication. A few years earlier, Eder (1988: 300–6), who works in the Habermasian tradition, proposed a structural theory on the level of the production of society partially inspired by Bourdieu and Giddens. In the early 1990s, he articulated it in an analysis of environmentalism through a constructivist-structuralist theory of cognitive frames carried in communication (Eder 1996a). Since the late 1980s, finally, I have sought to extrapolate and develop what I provisionally call the new cognitive sociology from the cognitive turn in sociology and subsequent advances (Strydom 2000; see also Delanty 1999a; Domingues 2000). Rather than concentrating on practices as such, whether communication (Habermas), discourse (Foucault, Habermas), negotiation (Knorr-Cetina), strategizing (Bourdieu), competition, conflict or networking (Latour and Woolgar), none of which is of course jettisoned, the focal concern here is the variable structural models of practical action. Of particular interest from the cognitive sociological perspective, is the interrelation among the micro, meso and macro levels. This involves the mediation, in particular situations, of cognitive structures in the minds of individuals, collective cognitive structures such as collective actor identities, organizational frames and ideologies, and finally cultural cognitive structures such as cultural models of all sorts.

In the wake of the turn whereby the traditional normative paradigm was displaced by the cognitive paradigm, a whole range of assumptions and concepts has gained a high profile in contemporary sociology and, more broadly, the social sciences. The cognitive turn centrally questioned the function of norms in social action and interaction by rejecting the traditional assumption of norms as being consistent and exerting a determining influence. Instead, it emphasized the need to develop a sensitivity for and an ability to identify the whole range of culturally defined alternatives available to practices and the constitution and organization of society. Casualties of this change were such core modernist notions as the unitary concept of modernity, the linear concept of progress, the progressivist or developmental concept of evolution, the identification of modernity and universalism, and so forth. Alternative concepts which arose as these notions broke down include, for example, knowledgeable agent, organization of experience, uncertainty, frame, master frame, paradigm, world model, classification system, scheme, code, script, network and construction. It is ironic that there is hardly more than a handful of social scientists who are aware that these are all cognitive concepts. Having emerged at identifiable points in time, they can actually be related to one or another of the phases in the development of the cognitive sciences and, hence, the cognitive approach. This development stretches from the initial narrow cognitivism or structuralism through connectionism or emergentism to enactivism or pragmatic cognitivism (De Mey 1982; Varela et al. 1993; Bechtel and Graham 1998). In the recent past, these and related concepts have come to play a central theoretical and methodological role in the social sciences, yet few appreciate that their potential could be much better exploited if their rootedness in the cognitive approach were recognized. Today, social scientists exhibit a strong tendency to revitalize symbolic analysis and to appropriate these concepts for that purpose. However indispensable symbolic analysis may be, and I accept that it is, it should not be allowed to conceal or even displace the equally if not more important dimension of cognitive processes and cognitive structures. To arrive at an adequate conception of constructivism, not to mention critique, such a cognitive emphasis is essential.

Constructivism

The significance of the cognitive approach for the analysis of contemporary society can be demonstrated with reference to the central phenomenon of the discursive construction of risk. One can certainly learn from the available types, such as social (Berger and Luckmann 1967), communications (Watzlawick et al. 1967), representational (Moscovici 1977), empirical (Knorr 1981) and radical (Schmidt 1987) constructivism, but new developments (Eyerman and Jamison 1991; Eder 1996a; Strydom 2000) point towards a more focused cognitive version.

The social process of the discursive construction of reality is a transformative cognitive process. On the one hand, it draws on existing knowledge and cognitive structures and, on the other, it generates new knowledge and new cognitive structures and brings about their selective coordination. Most typically, a mobilized citizenry taking the form of a social movement initiates the process. Engaging in and being carried by cognitive praxis (Eyerman and Jamison 1991), a movement is not just a collective actor, but rather a creative cognitive process in which new knowledge, new cognitive structures and a new cultural model are produced and communicated. Undoubtedly, social movements are typically the first to identify problems, articulate new irritating objects of indignation and communicate cognitive and normative innovations. Yet other actors or agents who participate in the process of social construction, such as industry, the state, science, the legal profession and the media, should likewise be regarded as vehicles of cognitive processes. Each one not only possesses a certain type of knowledge, but also has an orientation to the world. The latter can be analysed in terms of basic micro-level cognitive construction devices of a theoretical-empirical, a moral and a conative kind. With reference to these devices, it is possible to identify the meso-level cognitive frame – or definition of the situation – that each actor or agent constructs for itself and communicates in public. If one further follows the competition and conflict of the frames of the different participants in a particular cross-section of the risk discourse, it is possible to disentangle their cognitive-symbolic contest and to register the degree to which the different frames resonate with the observing, evaluating and judging public. Once this stage has been reached, analysis reveals the macro-level cognitive frame, consisting of a selective alignment and combination of the competing frames, which results from the process of social construction and is given collective validity by the final cognitive or epistemic authority, the public (Strydom 1999c). By such analysis, we can thus grasp the way in which the collective cognitive process of construction not only transforms society but also serves it in creatively dealing through problem-solving and coordination with an open history, contingency, uncertainty and ambivalence.

Constructivism, in my view, is best seen from a cognitive theoretical point of view that acknowledges both intersubjective understanding and the objectivity of reality with which we maintain pragmatic relations. Epistemologically, this entails something like a pragmatic-realist constructivism on a weak naturalistic basis. For this conception, which differs sharply from both Quinean naturalism in North American and British sociology (Fuller 1992; but see Fuller 2000) and from Bhaskarian ontological realism in British sociology (Outhwaite 1987), I am indebted to Habermas (1999a). On the one hand, constructivism pertains to the communication and action of actors or agents who evaluate conflicts and actions in view of a yet to be realized world of well-organized social relations which they seek to bring into being. On the other, the organic development and the sociocultural form of life of these actors and agents have a natural origin that is accessible to an evolutionary explanation. The cognitive structures at the centre of constructivism, that is, those making possible and framing the perception, experience, explanation and interpretation of reality, can therefore be regarded as having been given rise to by natural historical or evolutionary learning processes. This is what gives them their cognitive import in the first instance. This continuity between an ontologically prior nature and an epistemically prior intersubjective world is not such, however, that it can be interpreted in a strong naturalistic sense. On the contrary, the objective world is not simply ontologically given, but one to which we relate pragmatically through our instrumental, linguistic and communicative practices. And the constructive engagement of actors and agents is and remains subject to the problem of self-referential moral-political action and thus the choice of appropriate criteria of justification. In the wake of the breakdown of past sources, such as natural law and the philosophy of history, authoritarian paternalism has for decades in many societies provided the necessary criteria. But it has itself now definitively broken down, leaving us with an open history, contingency, uncertainty and ambivalence. These conditions shove the problem of the social construction of reality to the forefront and compel social scientists to give more focused attention to modes of perception, modes of framing, cognitive structures and the collective processing of cultural models of reality.

It is interesting to note that the pragmatic-realist constructivism on a weak naturalistic basis put forward here is at present finding support in the convergent development of the theories of evolution of the German Darwinian school, the Uppsala school and the Habermas school (Strydom 1999e). The convergence is taking place on the basis of Darwinism becoming more cultural (Giesen 1991; Burns and Dietz 1992, 1997) and culturalism becoming more Darwinian (Eder 1988, 1992). In each case, a selectionist or situationalist theory is formulated that articulates the Darwinian threefold model of variation, selection and stabilization or reproduction with interactionism, communication and discourse theory or constructivism. Burns and Dietz (1997), for instance, speak of the combination of 'environmental constraint and selectivity (physical as well as social) with bounded constructivism (through human agency)' (1997: 2).

Responsibility in the experimenting society

The cognitive sociological approach opens up a range of neglected and new research areas. Here I want to emphasize two closely related areas that were discussed in previous chapters and can be considered urgent topics in the study of contemporary society: the experimenting society and collective or co-responsibility. Given the current state of the art, real progress is promised by intensive cognitive sociological research in these two vital yet neglected areas.

What is of interest from a cognitive sociological perspective are the transcendental structures possessing cognitive import that guide and give direction to the construction and organization of society. These cognitive ordering principles are not directly observable, but become apparent only from the relations and tensions among a variety of individual phenomena. Within the context of a discursively organized process of social construction, attention is first given to different sets of cognitive practices and then the competition and conflict between the distinct cognitive frames they produce are disentangled. In contemporary society, where we are witnesses of a profound transformation of the cognitive organization of social life, this competition and conflict have taken on a graphic profile in the context of the risk discourse. Here it manifests itself as a new form of class conflict, possessing also a gender dimension, which takes shape around the issue of risk. The culturally constituted cognitive structures guiding science, technology, industry, capitalism and the state, which culminate in the experimenting society, are confronted by another set. The latter was introduced into the public sphere by a mobilized public and the new social movements and is currently pursued by citizens in many capacities in the direction of participatory or deliberative democracy and a cosmopolitan democratic form of governance.

The competition and conflict point to a new evolutionary departure. The production of risks as well as the authoritarian paternalism by means of which they are institutionally being dealt with have both been revealed as being guided by structures that indeed originated from evolutionary learning processes yet do not possess the universal cognitive import we have assumed until recently. Since those cognitive structures have contributed to both the generation of the environmental crisis and to its poor management, they are in need of revision and fine-tuning. The limits around science, technology, industry, capitalism and the state or, more generally, the experimenting society must be redrawn in a more precise manner by a new set of guiding and direction-giving structures developed in practical discourse. Collective responsibility, or co-responsibility, stands for this set of cognitive structures. Responsibility in this sense, as the constructivist approach suggests, does not imply an absolute prohibition against potentially harmful research and experimentation, but rather a reasonable and balanced arrangement based on new cognitive structures arising from the latest evolutionary spurt. Research should be conducted at a slower pace and be accompanied by constant reflection on critical threshold values by both science and a critical public. Second, it should be monitored and regulated by global reflexive institutions that operate at a level coextensive with the impact of the potential risks produced. Practices giving rise to the new macro-ethic of global responsibility are already for some time in evidence on the part of social movements, politicians, scientists and lately even corporations or so-called corporate citizens. Yet social scientists have been very slow indeed to give attention to these new cognitive practices and the concomitant politics of responsibility, not to mention the new cultural model of responsibility of our time (Strydom 1999b, 1999d; Delanty 1999a: 156–7, 1999b, 2000: 128).

It is within sociology's reach to make a contribution to the transformation of the cognitive organization of modern society and, thus, to the constitution and organization of the emerging society of the twenty-first century. This would require intensive cognitive sociological research on both the currently still predominant experimenting society and the emerging cultural model of collective or co-responsibility which holds out the promise of its fundamental transformation.

Socio-cognitive critique

The cognitive constructivist position advanced above implies a relational conception of the social world, with the emphasis therefore being less on

static substances and entities than on dynamic differences, relations, networks and processes (Emirbayer 1997). The fact that it is obviously close to
a pragmatic sociology raises the question of how critique is possible within
such a framework. For critique is apparently not easily reconcilable with
constructivism or relationalism. On the one hand, constructivist or pragmatic sociologists on the whole are not inclined towards critique, since
their focus is on the process of realization through concretization transpir-
ing within the existing institutional order. On the other hand, critical theorists typically latch onto a particular social actor, collective agent or entity,
such as the bourgeoisie, capitalism or the system, and its putative ideology
or one-sided mode of reasoning. This is why the Marxian 'ideology critique' of Lukács and Marcuse, but also Horkheimer and Adorno's 'critique
of instrumental reason' and Habermas's 'critique of functionalist reason'
leave one with the impression of substantialist rather than relational assumptions. The same goes for Benjamin's very different redemptive critique
that, instead of playing the ideal off against reality, seeks to redeem a
unique experience from the past to illuminate the present. Despite the apparent difficulty highlighted by these entrenched positions, I am convinced
that critical theory and constructivist or pragmatic sociology can be recon-
ciled in a way that allows a new and timely form of critique – one that is
both a critique of the status quo and a critique of utopianism. This is what
I have proposed to call 'socio-cognitive critique' (Strydom 2000: 263, 279,
301; also 1999c).

Starting points for such a concept of critique are available in various
authors. The most powerful impetus towards a new concept was provided
by the growing realization that critical theory's concept of critique is inadequate. Here critique was based on opposing a normative ideal to a de-
formed reality, Habermas being best known for his vision of the realization
of moral universalism through the completion of the project of modernity.
What the critical theorists overlooked was that they were in fact engaging
in moralization from a particular position within society which was by no
means without consequences for society. Others appreciated that the social
sciences form part of the very social reality they analyse and, therefore,
both proceed from assumptions and have unintended consequences that
call for reflection. Touraine (1981) treated social scientific knowledge as
being part of a system of historical action and saw its social significance as
inhering in its relation to other forms of knowledge. Reflecting on the
study of social class and the unintentional embroilment of the social sciences in the reproduction of the existing class structure, Bourdieu (1986)
proposed a reflexive sociological concept of critique – what he called 'vulgar' or 'social critique'. Rather than offering an objective description of
society or opposing an ideal to it, sociology considers the relevant relations
involved and seeks to uncover illusions about reality.

Taking cues from the French authors, Eder (1993a: 76–80, 98–100) dis-
tances himself from Habermas by means of a 'social critique of morality'
and adopts the idea of sociological de-illusionment in the sense of critically

and self-critically dissolving fallacies or uncovering and destroying illusions about social reality. Beyond Bourdieu's static class perspective, however, he links social critique to Habermas's concern with learning processes, so that the uncovering of illusions serves the opening up of possibilities for change and transformation. Burns and Dietz (1997: 55) acknowledge the need for a critical perspective in view of the fact that most modern collectivities, communities, professions, organizations and institutions entertain definitions of reality that are shielded against contrary evidence, so that they are often trapped into biases, distortions, half-truths, illusions and rationalization. Beck (1999: 79–81) rejects critical theory's application of well-justified standards to society and the concomitant condemnation of particular actors or groups even against their own self-understanding. Adopting relationalism comparable to Touraine and Bourdieu's, he sees critique as being democratized to the extent that the risk society develops into a conflictual and self-critical society. Through their competing, contradictory and conflicting rationality claims, the different actors or agents, such as science, politics, industry, insurers and social movements, engage in a reciprocal critique. This societal self-critique forms the reference point for sociology's critical contribution to a new framework for the reinvention of society and politics.

None of the concepts of critique advanced by Beck, Burns and Dietz, and Eder reaches the proposed socio-cognitive level. This also goes for Calhoun (1996: 462–3), despite his clarification of the different dimensions of critique. Beck focuses so strongly on the risk society as a self-critical society that he has little to say on the critical role of sociology as such and, as I have argued above, even though there is a cognitive dimension to his work, he largely neglects to bring it out. There is indeed a suggestion of a link between distorted cognitive orders and critique in Burns and Dietz, yet it is left unexplored and undeveloped. Eder exhibits a clear grasp of both the critical task of sociology and of the cognitive dimension in much of his work, yet he does not rethink critique in contemporary cognitive terms. It essentially remains Bourdieuean social critique. It is interesting to note that Habermas (1999b: 98), in response to criticisms rejecting the strategy of supporting critique by a normative reference point outside society, has recently refined his position by locating critique within society itself. To the extent that he sees the social movements criticizing society as its vehicle, however, it is apparent that he still does not assume a relational position. Rather than constructivism, which demands that all the participants be accorded equal attention, he adopts a legitimationist procedure which involves judging the participants according to the criterion of good and bad and then identifying with one particular participant deemed to be good or legitimate (Strydom 1999c: 19–20, 2000: 89–90).

In order to make room for critique in constructivism, it is necessary to bring out the cognitive dimension of the social process of the discursive construction of reality and to conceive critique as working on cognitive structures. The normative reference point making critique possible can neither be projected beyond society nor tied to the frame or normative code of any one participant. It forms part of and is carried by the communicative or discursive process as such. The basis of critique is to be found in the various cognitive structures that become objective features structuring the situation within which the different discourse participants relate to one another. Far from judging and condemning the ideology of a particular actor or agent, therefore, it is a matter of closely studying a variety of related cognitive processes and structures. Included are the frames and normative codes of all participants, irrespective of whether one likes them or not, and the macro-frame that emerges from their discursive transformation and is eventually collectively accepted by the participants, despite their competing interpretations of it. To fulfil the requirements of sociocognitive critique, the whole network of different cognitive processes and structures is investigated in relation to the strategic actions of the actors or agents in order to distinguish both the negative and positive impacts of each. Similar attention is given to the role of the public in the collective acceptance of a macro-frame. On the one hand, the illusions carried by the cognitive structures are exposed and, on the other, starting points for potential learning processes are ferreted out. For instance, the instrumentalism, hostility to democracy and authoritarian paternalism of experts, corporations and governments are uncovered no less than the fundamentalism, medievalism, political authoritarianism, and wishful thinking of some of their critics. Sociologists' own illusions are similarly treated. At the same time, all contributions to new cultural and political forms, irrespective of their source, are registered as possible ways of correcting the exposed errors or of moving from the problematic to the more adequate. The decisive question is whether they keep open and extend the public sphere within the given relational context and, hence, whether they might lead to a mode of governance free from a logic of control and commensurate to the global level.

An important step that can be taken to advance an understanding of the critical task of sociology and thus to clarify matters well beyond authors like Beck and Eder, is to distinguish different types of cognitive structures or models. In this respect, the distinction among representational, operational and explanatory models (Caws 1973; Strydom 1999c: 17–18) could be useful. The members of society, or the participants in social construction, dispose over cognitive structures that could function either as representational or as operational models or, indeed, as both at the same time. Whereas a representational model corresponds to the more conscious part of an actor or agent's intellectual, moral and conative orientation to the world, an operational model concerns its more unconscious practical dealings. In so far as the sociologist is able to critically reflect the whole relational context, a set of cognitive structures forming an explanatory model can be attributed to him or her. But the sociologist has no exclusive possession of epistemic authority. Observers and commentators as well as the observing, evaluating and judging public to varying degrees enjoy this same privilege. In fact, often the epistemic authority of the sociologist depends on such a third point of view. This is increasingly the case as society becomes more communicative, discursive and reflexive. It should also be borne in mind that, in such a society, participants themselves are increasingly acquiring the competence of observation. Therefore, explanatory models even on their part cannot be excluded. Be that as it may, by means of the distinction of representational, operational and explanatory models it is possible to clarify, in terms of cognitive structures of different levels and scope, the relations among the participants in society, the observing, evaluating and judging public, and the sociologist or social scientist. Finally, this raises the question of the public role of sociology.

The public role of sociology

In the wake of sociology's renewed breakthrough in the 1960s, its public role – if one could here call it thus – was decisively shaped by the formation of a reform and development coalition in which social scientists joined with political and economic decision-makers in pursuit of social improvement. Social scientific knowledge was expected to be politically and practically useful by providing tools required in policy interventions and the governance of economy and society. Strong pressure was exerted over social scientists to redefine their self-understanding from intellectuals dealing with society in its complexity to experts serving policy- and decision-makers. Even after its most recent political crisis under conservatism in the 1970s and 1980s, demands to be politically useful have steadily increased. This pressure is often mediated through EU research budgets and is clearly observable in research programmes on risk and the environment.

Simultaneously, however, this particular understanding of political usefulness has been questioned by various developments. Among them are the increase in the complexity of society, the pluralization of relations, the transformation of the public sphere due to the new social movements and the shift of the social scientific focus from stable, causal and linear relations to complex non-linear ones occurring over time and depending on cultural structures. As a consequence, the earlier assumed direct relation between theory and practice or between justification and application broke down (Apel 1988; Beck and Bonß 1989; Stehr 1994). Under these conditions, sociology on the one hand has to remain open to the possibility of the transformation of cultural, social and political assumptions and structures. On the other, since politics extends from the formal decision-making system to value- and will-formation in civil society, it cannot restrict the usefulness of its knowledge to political and economic elites and decision-makers, but is required to communicate it also to those subject to decision-making processes and decisions. Besides objectifying its subject matter and producing empirical and policy relevant knowledge, sociology has the task of opening communication processes that assist public discursive reflection

on the implications and consequences of the full spectrum of social practices. It is here where sociology, as part of a communication society and of
public discourse, assumes the form of a 'discursive practice' (Delanty 1997:
139) that its public role in the proper sense of the word enters (Eder 1993a;
Calhoun 1996; Delanty 1997; Strydom 1999c, 2000).

In order to fulfil its public role, sociology has to avoid affirming existing
relations by subjecting taken-for-granted cultural categories, concepts and
interpretations constitutive of social practices to critical scrutiny. Rather
than just reproducing existing representational cognitive structures, to put
it in theoretical terms, it is required to discover both operative and explanatory models. In adopting a critical stance, however, it can no longer proceed
from the older assumption that the intellectual is in possession of the truth
and is therefore able to provide the correct answers or even to bring about
enlightenment and emancipation single-handedly. Although not taking such
a stance, Giddens (1996) nevertheless adopts a problematic position in
his depiction of the role of sociology and its transformative impact on
the social world. On the one hand, he underestimates the creativity of
social actors and social movements who first sense, perceive and identify
problems and hence, vice versa, he overestimates the originality of social-
scientific concepts (1996: 75–7). On the other, Giddens attributes too much
weight to sociological knowledge when he asserts that the 'reappropriation
of expert knowledge . . . is the very condition of the "authenticity" of everyday life' (1996: 46). The public significance of sociological knowledge does
not inhere in sociology as such. Forming part of a relational complex in a
structured social setting, its significance must be sought in the relation of
sociological knowledge to other knowledges in the context of public communication and discourse. Sociological knowledge does not exist beyond
society, but is constructed and takes on form only in the discursive interrelation of the different types of cognitive structures and knowledges carried
by a plurality of participants (Strydom 2000). Under these conditions, the
public role of sociology commences with the making visible of the whole
spectrum of different experiences, perceptions, frames and knowledges.
This is achieved by locating and heightening the tensions and relating the
intersecting lines of creativity and conflict to each other. By adopting such
a minimalist mediating role, sociology's aim is to break down the ethno-
centricity of perspectives and to contribute to the development of reciprocal
perspectives or an alignment of frames. A basic assumption here is that a
self-reflexive and self-transformative public discourse worthy of a democratic society presupposes a culture of differences or even a 'culture of
contradictions' (Eder 1993a: 194). The public role of sociology, therefore,
is by no means confined to linking up with social creativity to stimulate the
development of a diverse culture of reflexively and discursively available
cognitive structures and cultural models. A central question for it at this
stage is how the different actors or agents and their frames are recognized
and incorporated in the public sphere (Calhoun 1996: 456; Strydom 2000).
This question comes to a head in the sociological dissection of the emergent

macro-frame which, in addition to credibility, acceptability and trust, bears all the hallmarks of power in discourse, whether competition, hegemony or exclusion. In any event, democratic legitimacy can be attained only under conditions where communication is sufficiently open to allow an adequate discursive mediation of all the participants as well as the observing, evaluating and judging public. Ultimately, the rationale of a public role for sociology is to be found in contributing to democratic public discourse and the attainment of the highest degree of democratic legitimacy possible.

9

Conclusion

In this book, I sought to open up the theme of risk, environment and society by offering a historically informed analysis of the risk discourse regarded as a public process of communication about a problem of societal significance. In keeping with this approach, I located the problem of risk as it relates to the environment at the centre of the process of public communication, since it represents the reality reference of all those involved, irrespective of how much their respective interpretations differ from one another. At the same time, I considered the participants (that is, experts, industry, the state and social movements) and their different interpretations and claims regarding risk as well as the audience of observers, evaluators and commentators (that is, the public, media and social scientists) and their orientations and reactions. This allowed me to identify a range of dimensions, spelled out in Table 1.1 in Chapter 1, some of which were selected for further development in the individual chapters of the book. They include frameworks of understanding of risk (Chapter 2), theories of risk and the risk society (Chapter 3), the characteristics of the contemporary phenomenon of high consequence, technological-ecological risks (Chapter 4), the material conditions of the production of risks in contemporary society (Chapter 5), the social construction of risks in public communication through discursive competition, conflict and consensus formation (Chapter 6), the cultural and institutional dynamics through which contemporary risk society is being (re)constituted and (re)organized (Chapter 7), and finally the culturally constituted cognitive dimension of risk and the risk society and ways of dealing with it (Chapter 8).

From the analysis of contemporary epistemological frameworks of understanding, which varies between realism and constructivism, we learned that it would not be advisable to adopt either the former or the latter position on its own for the purposes of coming to terms with the phenomenon of risk. The more fruitful contemporary approaches all cluster in the space between these two extremes, taking the form of some variety either of weak critical or reflexive realism, as represented by Dickens, Burns and Dietz, and Nowotny, or of weak constructivist realism, as represented by Beck, Giddens and Eder (see Table 2.1). In distinction to these various authors, I proposed to proceed from a pragmatic realism based on a weak naturalism that gives priority to nature over culture yet nevertheless sees enough of a distinction between the two to allow the mediation of realism and constructivism.

The analysis of the two major theoretical directions in the field of risk, environment and society brought home a number of important insights. Theoretically, all the major social theorists – Beck, Luhmann, Giddens, Eder – underscored the necessity of adopting a theory of modernity and, related to it, process and non-linear thinking to account for the nature and prominence of risk in contemporary society. In varying degrees, the theoretical literature also stressed the importance of systematically considering such matters as science and technology, contingency, decision-making, communication and contradiction or structural conflict in contemporary society. An interesting outcome of the juxtaposition of opposing theorists such as Catton and Dunlap, Beck, and Luhmann was the insight that the risk society cannot be led back solely to the environment and the ecology crisis. While the threats and dangers of nuclear disaster, pollution, global warming, climate change and biotechnology played a special role in focusing the central problem of risk, the risk society is also attributable to the fact that society has become increasingly functional, differentiated, complex and relationally constituted. A subtle aspect that is present in the writings of a wide range of authors – Beck, Luhmann, Giddens, Eder, Burns and Dietz, Nowotny, Dickens, Dean, Douglas, Esser – yet is not given the profile it deserves, is the cognitive dimension. It is of the utmost importance, in my estimation, and therefore I made it the central plank of my own contribution in this book. Coming at it from a modified Habermasian tradition, I proposed to make sense of the theoretical diversity in the field of risk, environment and society by adopting a theoretical approach that is centred on a communication and discourse theory of society incorporating a relational pragmatist and a cultural cognitive emphasis.

Politically, the risk theorists with whom we dealt took extreme positions, ranging from conservative through neo-liberal to radical democratic. These political positions were reflected in arguments recommending such different strategies as an elitist and paternalistic risk politics, either a fatalistic or an opportunistic acceptance of the risk society, and a discursive approach to dealing with the consequences and complexity of society in ways that are seen to be legitimate. My response to this was to locate myself closer to the democratic and discursive pole, and to attempt to revitalize the critical function and public role of sociology. This implies that I regard the contingencies of the risk society less as leaving us in a paradoxical or double-bind situation calling either for fatalism or for decisionism than as confronting us with a situation of uncertainty in which learning in necessary – as assumed, for instance, by Beck, Wynne and Eder.

We have seen that risk is a compound phenomenon consisting of different dimensions. On the one hand, it is a culturally constituted cognitive scheme according to which people not only experience, interpret and understand their world, but also orient their actions. I have argued that, due to various developments, this scheme has acquired a special significance in contemporary society, with the result that large numbers of people today relate to their world in terms of it. On the other hand, risk refers to dangers or threats, which means a reality that entails potential adverse effects. Environmentally speaking, the adverse effects entailed by contemporary risks include negative impacts on ecosystems, cycles, the climate and the biosphere at large embracing human, animal and plant species and their various forms of life. Depending on the particular interpretation adopted according to socioculturally circumscribed structural position, both individuals and groups treat such dangers or threats either as an opportunity to be cultivated with a view to potential benefits or as a problematic, questionable and even unacceptable endangerment. At this fault-line is located a – if not the – characteristic structural conflict of contemporary society that can be regarded as a new form of class conflict. Taking shape around the issue of risk, it ultimately concerns the manner in which society relates to nature. I have argued that it is because of the fact that science, technology and industry, driven by capitalism and supported by the state, have become central to the mediation of this relation in the contemporary period that risk has assumed significance today for society as a whole. For those who are willing to take risky decisions because they see risk largely as a measure of probability and magnitude of events with potentially adverse effects that could nevertheless deliver large benefits, high technology based on science and realized in industry therefore holds out the big promise. For those who, by contrast, regard high technology and large-scale sociotechnical systems as inherently hazardous, risky decisions and practices involving technology, science and industry not only threaten the organic foundations of all forms of life, but also are foisted on the majority without public debate or their consent. I have argued that the public discourse about risk which civil society and the social movements were nevertheless able to generate became the medium for opening up, exposing and reflecting upon the cultural models and cognitive structures informing the risk politics of our time. My major methodological point was to stress the need for the social sciences – as well as interested citizens! – to link up with this collective achievement and, by extension, to self-critically analyse the illusions, irrespective of whether they derive from biases, distortions, half-truths or rationalizations, embodied in the culturally constituted cognitive structures of all those involved. Of particular importance are the illusions of experts, safety officials, corporations and state officials, yet those of voluntary associations, social movements and the public should by no means be excluded.

Here enters the new cognitive sociology, particularly in so far as it is able to provide a foundation for and sharpen sociology's critical function by the addition of a novel form of socio-cognitive critique.

One of the main arguments of the book was that risk has assumed a significance in contemporary society that it has never enjoyed before. This has much to do with the fact that science, technology and industry have come to play a vital role in social life and have achieved expansion on a global scale. But it is above all the centrality and pervasive impact of the cultural cognitive scheme of safety and danger that indicates just how significant risk is for contemporary society. I have argued that this scheme or frame is having the effect of dividing people and mobilizing them to take part in public communication and discourse, to form new identities, to engage in competition and conflict and the achievement of collective agreement or, at least, rational disagreement on the basis of which new institutions could be built. This means that risk is becoming a major mode of the constitution and organization of society. The competition, contestation and conflict that we have come to associate with the issue of risk and the risk discourse should therefore be reduced neither to economic nor to political competition and conflict, nor even to both. Involved are cultural and institutional dynamic processes that cut much deeper. I have argued that a thorough investigation of the risk discourse leads us to the deep-seated process of the construction of reality. Fulfilling the requirements of a multilevel approach, this constructive process of the constitution and organization of society was accordingly analysed from a number of different perspectives, including a material, a sociocultural and a dynamic one.

As we have seen, risk theorists, especially those defending constructivism in one form or another, are often taken to task for neglecting the material dimension of risk or the material practices by which it is produced in the first place. Although I take constructivism seriously, I am convinced that this criticism does not apply to the analysis offered in this book. In accordance with my position, which incorporates a realist dimension (that is, a pragmatic rather than an ontological or even a naive realism), it was necessary to give attention to the conditions of the societal production of risks. These conditions are overwhelmingly of a material nature. Rather than offering a selective account of the material conditions in terms of such factors as capitalism, science, technology, industry or the state, however, I sought to develop a more comprehensive and integral account that is commensurate with the current global order. The experimenting society, in my view a central concept in the analysis of contemporary society, was the concept used for this purpose. Through this concept, I explicitly sought to bring together all the material conditions making possible the societal production of high consequence, technological-ecological risks so characteristic of our time. Since I am not simply a realist but rather take a position that simultaneously makes room for constructivism, however, I insisted that it is not sufficient to approach these material conditions exclusively from the outside. In addition to a materialist analysis, I proposed to gain critical access to them through the culturally constituted cognitive structures that give them direction as well as those confronting and opposing them and making them amenable to observation. This is the sense of the new cognitive sociological approach and its critical function at this particular level of analysis.

Besides the production of risks, we have also considered the social or discursive construction of risks. It was necessary to introduce the constructivist perspective since realism by itself is not sufficient. Specifying only the material conditions of risks as it does, realism does not allow us to understand how risks become collectively identified, selected and defined and why their collective treatment goes in particular directions. Realism remains too general, since it fails to specify over and above material conditions the particular conditions of uncertainty and ambivalence that come to permeate society when the structures making possible the experience, perception, interpretation and evaluation of the natural, social and psychological world break down. I have argued that the construction of risk, which implies the collective handling of uncertainty and ambivalence, is best dealt with in terms of processes of communication and discourse in the transformed public sphere of the late twentieth and twenty-first centuries. This new context I tried to make intelligible by tracing the historical shift from a religious culture to a scientific culture to a communicative culture which were institutionally carried by the church, by the state and by the public sphere respectively. A major theoretical point I sought to make here was that communicative and discursive processes in the contemporary public sphere are structured by cultural models and cognitive structures which call for painstaking analysis. This is one of the major tasks of the new cognitive sociology. Once these structures are acknowledged, it becomes apparent that the discursive treatment of risk is not just a covert economic and an overt political phenomenon, but also a process of construction that penetrates to the very cultural foundations of society underpinning its institutional organization.

I investigated the transformed cultural foundations of contemporary society with reference to nature in so far as it has become reflexive and discursively available and thus an object of contestation and even class conflict. This conflict involves aggregates of people who advance antagonistic constructions of nature on the basis of alternative culturally constituted cognitive structures. In contemporary society where communication is of central significance, the different social classes are not only found in aggregates of people directly engaged in competition, contestation and conflict, but also especially importantly in distinct sections of the observing, evaluating and commenting public. It is in terms of the changed foundations that such characteristic emergent cultural forms of legitimation of our time as sustainability, collective or co-responsibility and ecological citizenship become comprehensible. I have argued that responsibility has thus far received much less attention than sustainability and even ecological citizenship, but that it is a key concept deserving different treatment. For this to happen, however, the widespread misconception according to which it is an instrument of conservative thinking has to be overcome. The field of risk, environment and society is perhaps the most fitting crucible in which this prejudice could be tempered.

The most interesting institutional development in line with the transformed cultural foundations of society is the novel phenomenon of reflexive or discursive institutions which seem to be a characteristic feature of the risk society. This type of institution represents a new mechanism of democratic decision making that stimulates the assumption of co-responsibility and thus generates a high level of legitimacy. As such, it promises to be an indispensable component of a future reasonable and humane society. Not only would reflexive institutions be required by a new global political form of governance that is able to avert the dominance of both the global market and a new Holy Alliance in the guise of a monocentric, hierarchical world state. Simultaneously, they would also be central to a culturally diverse democratic society that is able to avoid succumbing to the inescapably inhumane and authoritarian, eugenic and genetocratic bio-society envisaged by the new eugenics movement and its expert, corporate and political bedfellows who resist the ecological or, more generally, the discursive taming of the experimenting society.

As the risk discourse unfolded between the 1950s and the present, as we have seen, various human or social scientific disciplines emerged to take up aspects of the debates, seeking to make a contribution to the clarification of the issues and to overcoming the risk problem. Among these disciplines, in chronological order as they emerged concurrently with the risk discourse, were economics, innovation and diffusion studies, survey research, psychology, anthropology and sociology, with which is associated also political theory. Sociology entered the scene at that late moment when the various risk debates broadened into a fully fledged public risk discourse. In the hands of the leading risk theorists since Short's incisive intervention, therefore, sociology took on the broad perspective that had been associated with it from the start and through its classical period and was later again forcefully reasserted by C. Wright Mills under the title of 'the sociological imagination'. It is in this very tradition that Beck stands when he regards risk as being of significance for society as a whole and defends the age-old sociological task of developing a diagnosis of the times. Sociology's link with public discourse and its broad yet historically focused perspective are thus of great importance. They explain why sociology is exceptionally well placed to make a constructive contribution to the risk discourse, to the mature handling of the risk issue, and thus to the constitution and organization of the emerging society of the twenty-first century.

As we know all too well today, sociology's contribution can no longer naively be conceived in terms of a direct and unproblematic relation between theory and practice, irrespective of whether the translation of scientific knowledge into policy decisions and administrative measures or into revolutionary action. Sociology's contribution should rather be seen as finding its focal point in the public definition of issues – in this case, risk issues. This is why I have consistently argued for developing a new cognitive sociology that is able to play a meaningful public role. To do so, it should be able to shed light on the full range of culturally constituted cognitive structures that come into play in processes of public communication and discourse, and to critically puncture across the board the illusionary projections attached to those structures. Under the conditions of the current risk-laden experimenting society, the sense of such critique is to pinpoint not only false notions of universalism, as for instance represented by science, state and community, but also the consequences and side-effects of the economic and political organization of society. Critique, as I have argued, is not a matter of playing off against the present an alternative, as yet lacking state that would be realized fully once the impediments are removed. It is a permanent attempt to identify steps toward learning or ways of dealing with impediments that in some form or another come into play to make a movement toward less problematic and more adequate conditions of existence difficult. Besides analysis and critique, however, sociology should simultaneously be able to shed light on newly emerging cultural forms of legitimation and concurrent cognitive structures, and to imagine appropriate institutional arrangements. One of these is a discursive democratic dispensation as a vital component of a reasonable and humane society in the twenty-first century. For the very rationale of sociology, which coincides with the most basic problem that we are facing today, is the attainment of a civilization that is characterized less by its failures – for example self-endangerment, self-injury and potential self-destruction – than by its mode of dealing with its obstacles and failures.

References

Adam, B., Beck, U. and van Loon, J. (eds) (2000) *The Risk Society and Beyond*. London: Sage.

Aggleton, P., Davies, P. and Hart, G. (eds) (1995) *Aids: Safety, Sexuality and Risk*. London: Taylor and Francis.

Alexander, J.C. (1996) Critical reflections on 'Reflexive Modernization', *Theory, Culture and Society*, 13(4): 133–8.

Alexander, J.C. and Smith, P. (1996) Social science and salvation, *Zeitschrift für Soziologie*, 25(4): 251–62.

American Journal of Sociology (1996) Symposium on market transition, 101(4).

Anderson, P. (1980) *Lineages of the Absolutist State*. London: Verso.

Apel, K-O. (1967) *Analytic Philosophy of Language and the 'Geisteswissenschaften'*. Dordrecht: Reidel.

Apel, K-O. ([1973] 1980) *Towards a Transformation of Philosophy*. London: Routledge and Kegan Paul.

Apel, K-O. (1987) The problem of a macroethic of responsibility to the future in the crisis of technological civilization, *Man and World*, 20: 3–40.

Apel, K-O. (1988) *Diskurs und Verantwortung*. Frankfurt: Suhrkamp.

Apel, K-O. (1991) A planetary macroethics for mankind, in E. Deutsch (ed.) *Culture and Modernity*. Honolulu, III: University of Hawaii Press.

Apel, K-O. (1993) How to ground a universalistic ethics of co-responsibility for the effects of collective actions and activities, *Philosophica*, 52(2): 9–29.

Apel, K-O. and Kettner, M. (eds) (1992) *Zur Anwendung der Diskursethik in Politik, Recht und Wissenschaft*. Frankfurt: Suhrkamp.

Archibugi, D., Held, D. and Köhler, M. (eds) (1998) *Re-Imagining Political Community*. Cambridge: Polity.

Aronson, N. (1984) Science as claims-making activity, in J.W. Schneider and J.I. Kitsuse (eds) *Studies in the Sociology of Social Problems*. Norwood, NJ: Ablex.

Axelrod, R. (1984) *The Evolution of Cooperation*. New York: Basic Books.

Barnes, B. (1982) *T.S. Kuhn and Social Science*. London: Macmillan.

Barnett, H.J. and Morse, C. (1963) *Scarcity and Growth*. Baltimore, MD: Johns Hopkins University Press.

Bauman, Z. (1992) *Modernity and Ambivalence*. Cambridge: Polity.

Bechmann, G. (ed.) (1993a) *Risiko und Gesellschaft.* Opladen: Westdeutscher.
Bechmann, G. (1993b) Risiko als Schlüsselkategorie der Gesellschaftstheorie, in G. Bechmann (ed.) *Risiko und Gesellschaft.* Opladen: Westdeutscher.
Bechtel, W. and Graham, G. (eds) (1998) *A Companion to Cognitive Science.* Oxford: Blackwell.
Beck, U. (1988) *Gegengifte.* Frankfurt: Suhrkamp.
Beck, U. ([1986] 1992) *Risk Society.* London: Sage.
Beck, U. (1994) The reinvention of politics, in U. Beck, A. Giddens and S. Lash (eds) *Reflexive Modernization.* Cambridge: Polity.
Beck, U. ([1988] 1995) *Ecological Politics in an Age of Risk.* Cambridge: Polity.
Beck, U. (1996) World risk society as cosmopolitan society?, *Theory, Culture and Society,* 13(4): 1–32.
Beck, U. (1997) *The Reinvention of Politics.* Cambridge: Polity.
Beck, U. (1999) *World Risk Society.* Cambridge: Polity.
Beck, U. (2000) Risk society revisited, in B. Adam, U. Beck and J. van Loon (eds) *The Risk Society and Beyond.* London: Sage.
Beck, U. and Bonß, W. (1989) *Weder Sozialtechnologie noch Aufklärung?* Frankfurt: Suhrkamp.
Beck, U., Giddens, A. and Lash, S. (1994) *Reflexive Modernization.* Cambridge: Polity.
Beckerman, W. (1974) *In Defence of Economic Growth.* Milan: Credito Italiano.
Bell, D. (1974) *The Coming of Post-Industrial Society.* London: Heinemann.
Benton, T. (1985) Realism and social science, in R. Edgley and R. Osborne (eds) *Radical Philosophy Reader.* London: Verso.
Berger, P.L. and Luckmann, T. (1967) *The Social Construction of Reality.* Harmondsworth: Penguin.
Bernstein, P.L. (1998) *Against the Gods.* New York: Wiley.
Bhaskar, R. (1978) *A Realist Theory of Science.* London: Harvester Wheatsheaf.
Bhaskar, R. (1989) *The Possibility of Naturalism.* London: Harvester Wheatsheaf.
Birnie, P. (2000) The UN and the environment, in A. Roberts and B. Kingsbury (eds) *United Nations, Divided World.* Oxford: Oxford University Press.
Blair, T. (2000) The key to GM is its potential, both for harm and good, *Independent on Sunday,* 27 February.
Bleicher, J. (1980) *Hermeneutics, as Method, Philosophy and Critique.* London: Routledge and Kegan Paul.
Bloor, D. (1976) *Knowledge and Social Imagery.* Chicago: University of Chicago Press.
Bloor, D. (1983) *Wittgenstein.* London: Macmillan.
Blühdorn, I. (1997) A theory of post-ecological politics, *Environmental Politics,* 6(3): 125–147.
Blumer, H. (1971) Social problems as collective behaviour, *Social Problems,* 18: 298–306.
Böhme, G. (1997) The structures and prospects of knowledge society, *Social Science Information,* 36(3): 447–68.
Böhme, G. and Stehr, N. (1986) *The Knowledge Society.* Dordrecht: Reidel.
Boltanski, L. and Thévenot, L. (1999) The sociology of critical capacity, *European Journal of Social Theory,* 2(3): 359–77.
Bonß, W. (1991) Unsicherheit und Gesellschaft, *Soziale Welt,* 42: 285–77.
Borger, J. (1999) How the mighty fall, *Guardian,* 22 November.
Bourdieu, P. (1986) *Distinction.* London: Routledge and Kegan Paul.
Bourdieu, P. (1987) What makes a social class?, *Berkeley Journal of Sociology,* 32: 1–17.
Breuer, S. (1989) Das Ende der Sicherheit, *Merkur,* 8: 710–15.

Brock, D. (1991) Die Risikogesellschaft und das Risiko soziologischer Zuspitzung, *Zeitschrift für Soziologie*, 20(1): 12–24.

Brown, J. (1989) *Environmental Threats*. London: Belhaven.

Bryant, B. (ed.) (1995) *Environmental Justice*. Washington, DC: Island.

Burns, T.R. (1986) Actors, transactions and social structure, in U. Himmelstrand (ed.) *Sociology: From Crisis to Science?*, Vol. 2. London: Sage.

Burns, T.R., Baumgartner, T. and Deville, P. (1985) *Man, Decisions, Society*. New York: Gordon and Breach.

Burns, T.R. and Dietz, T. (1992) Cultural evolution, *International Sociology*, 7(3): 259–83.

Burns, T.R. and Dietz, T. (1997) Evolutionary sociology. Paper read at ISA Conference, Zeist, Netherlands.

Burns, T.R. and Ueberhorst, R. (1988) *Creative Democracy*. New York: Praeger.

Burton, I., Kates, R.W. and White, G.F. (1978) *The Environment as Hazard*. New York: Oxford University Press.

Buttel, F.H. (1986) Sociology and the environment, *International Social Science Journal*, 38(109): 337–56.

Buttel, F.H. (1987) New directions in environmental sociology, *Annual Review of Sociology*, 13: 465–88.

Buttel, F.H. and Taylor, P. (1994) Environmental sociology and global environmental change, in M. Redclift and T. Benton (eds) *Social Theory and the Global Environment*. London: Routledge.

Byk, C. (1992) The human genome project and the social contract, *Journal of Medicine and Philosophy*, 17(4): 371–80.

Byk, C. (1999) Law and the cultural construction of nature, in P. O'Mahony (ed.) *Nature, Risk and Responsibility*. London: Macmillan.

Calhoun, C. (1996) Social theory and the public sphere, in B.S. Turner (ed.) *The Blackwell Companion to Social Theory*. Oxford: Blackwell.

Castel, R. (1991) From dangerousness to risk, in G. Burchell, C. Gordon and P. Miller (eds) *The Foucault Effect*. London: Harvester Wheatsheaf.

Castells, M. (1996) *The Information Age*, Vol. 1. Oxford: Blackwell.

Catton, W.R. and Dunlap, R.E. (1978) Environmental sociology, *The American Sociologist*, 13: 41–9.

Caws, P. (1973) Operational, representational, and explanatory models, *American Anthropologist*, 76: 1–10.

Choucri, N. (ed.) (1994) Special issue: global environmental accords, *Business and the Contemporary World*, 6(2).

Christoff, P. (1996a) Ecological citizens and ecologically guided democracy, in B. Doherty and M. de Geus (eds) *Democracy and Green Political Thought*. London: Routledge.

Christoff, P. (1996b) Ecological modernization, ecological modernities, *Environmental Politics*, 5(3): 476–500.

Clark, K. (1970) *The Nude*. Harmondsworth: Penguin.

Claval, P. (1992) Nature, environment, ecology, and social systems in advanced industrialized societies, in M. Dierkes and B. Biervert (eds) *European Social Science in Transition*. Frankfurt: Campus.

Coleman, J.S. (1993) The rational reconstruction of society, *American Sociological Review*, 58: 1–15.

Condor, S. and Antaki, C. (1997) Social cognition and discourse, in T.A. van Dijk (ed.) *Discourse Studies*, Vol. 1. London: Sage.

Conrad, J. (1986) Risikoforschung und Ritual, in B. Lutz (ed.) *Technik und sozialer Wandel*. Frankfurt: Campus.

Cottle, S. (1998) Ulrich Beck, 'Risk Society' and the media, *European Journal of Communication*, 13(1): 5–32.

Covello, V.T. and Mumpower, J. (1985) Risk analysis and risk management, *Risk Analysis*, 5(2): 103–20.

Covello, V.T., Menkes, J. and Nehnevajsa, J. (1982) Risk analysis, philosophy, and social and behavioural sciences, *Risk Analysis*, 2(2): 53–8.

Daly, H.E. (1977) *Steady-State Economics*. San Francisco, CA: Freeman.

Darier, E. (1996) Environmental governmentality, *Environmental Politics*, 5(4): 585–606.

Davies, B. and Harré, R. (1990) Positioning, *Journal of the Theory of Social Behaviour*, 20(1): 43–63.

Dean, M. (1999) *Governmentality*. London: Sage.

Delanty, G. (1997) *Social Science*. Buckingham: Open University Press.

Delanty, G. (1999a) *Social Theory in a Changing World*. Cambridge: Polity.

Delanty, G. (1999b) Biopolitics in the risk society, in P. O'Mahony (ed.) *Nature, Risk and Responsibility*. London: Macmillan.

Delanty, G. (2000) *Citizenship in a Global Age*. Buckingham: Open University Press.

Delanty, G. (2001) *Challenging Knowledge*. Buckingham: Open University Press.

De Mey, M. (1982) *The Cognitive Paradigm*. Dordrecht: Reidel.

Dickens, P. (1992) *Society and Nature*. London: Harvester Wheatsheaf.

Diekmann, A. and Jaeger, C.C. (eds) (1996) *Umweltsoziologie*. Opladen: Westdeutscher.

Dierkes, M. and Wagner, P. (1992) European social science in transition, in M. Dierkes and B. Biervert (eds) *European Social Science in Transition*. Frankfurt: Campus.

Dietz, T., Burns, T.R. and Buttel, F.H. (1990) Evolutionary thinking in sociology, *Sociological Forum*, 5: 155–71.

Dolzer, R. (1994) Institutional issues and global agreement, in N. Choucri (ed.) Special issue: global environmental accords, *Business and the Contemporary World*, 6(2): 102–6.

Domingues, J.M. (2000) Creativity and master trends in contemporary sociological theory, *European Journal of Social Theory*, 3(4): 467–84.

Douglas, M. (ed.) (1973) *Rules and Meanings*. Harmondsworth: Penguin.

Douglas, M. (1986) *Risk Acceptability in the Social Sciences*. London: Routledge and Kegan Paul.

Douglas, M. (1994) *Risk and Blame*. London: Routledge.

Douglas, M. and Wildavsky, A. (1982) *Risk and Culture*. Berkeley, CA: University of California Press.

Douvan, E. and Withey, S. (1954) Public reactions to nonmilitary aspects of atomic energy, *Science*, 119: 1–3.

Dower, N. (1998) *World Ethics*. Edinburgh: Edinburgh University Press.

Downs, A. (1972) Up and down with ecology, *Public Interest*, 28: 38–50.

Dryzek, J.S. (1990) *Discursive Democracy*. Cambridge: Cambridge University Press.

Dryzek, J.S. (1997) *The Politics of the Earth*. Oxford: Oxford University Press.

Dubiel, H. (1988) *Kritische Theorie der Gesellschaft*. Weinheim: Juventa.

Dunlap, R.E. and Catton, W.R. (1994) Struggling with human exceptionalism, *The American Sociologist*, 25: 5–30.

Dunlap, R.E. and Mertig, A.G. (1996) Weltweites Umweltbewusstsein, in A. Diekmann and C.C. Jaeger (eds) *Umweltsoziologie*. Opladen: Westdeutscher.

Dunlap, R.E. and van Liere, K. (1978) The 'new environmental paradigm', *Journal of Environmental Education*, 9: 10–19.

Eder, K. (1985) *Geschichte als Lernprozeß?* Frankfurt: Suhrkamp.

Eder, K. (1986) Soziale Bewegungen und kulturelle Evolution, in J. Berger (ed.) *Die Moderne: Kontinuitäten und Zäsuren*. Gottingen: Schwartz.

Eder, K. (1988) *Die Vergesellschaftung der Natur*. Frankfurt: Suhrkamp.

Eder, K. (1992) Contradictions and social evolution, in H. Haferkamp and N.J. Smelser (eds) *Social Change and Modernity*. Berkeley, CA: University of California Press.

Eder, K. (1993a) *The New Politics of Class*. London: Sage.

Eder, K. (1993b) Reflexive Institutionen? Research proposal, Deutsche Forschungsgemeinschaft Project Ed 25/7. Munich: Munich Social Science Research Group.

Eder, K. (1995) Die Institutionalisierung sozialer Bewegungen, in H-P. Müller and M. Schmid (eds) *Sozialer Wandel*. Frankfurt: Suhrkamp.

Eder, K. (1996a) *The Social Construction of Nature*. London: Sage.

Eder, K. (1996b) The institutionalisation of environmentalism, in S. Lash, B. Szerszynski and B. Wynne (eds) *Risk, Environment and Modernity*. London: Sage.

Eder, K. (1998) Taming risks through dialogues, in M.J. Cohen (ed.) *Risk in the Modern Age*. London: Macmillan.

Eder, K. (1999) Societies learn and yet the world is hard to change, *European Journal of Social Theory*, 2(2): 195–215.

Ehrlich, P. (1968) *The Population Bomb*. New York: Ballantine.

Eisenstadt, S.N. and Giesen, B. (1995) The construction of collective identity, *European Journal of Sociology*, 36(1): 72–102.

Elias, N. (1982) *State Formation and Civilization*. Oxford: Blackwell.

Ellul, J. ([1954] 1964) *The Technological Society*. New York: Vintage.

Elster, R. (1989) *The Cement of Society*. Cambridge: Cambridge University Press.

Emirbayer, M. (1997) Manifesto for a relational sociology, *American Journal of Sociology*, 103: 281–317.

Engelhardt, H.T. (1977) Some persons are humans, some humans are persons, and the world is what we persons make of it, in S.F. Spicker and H.T. Engelhardt (eds) *Philosophical Medical Ethics*. Dordrecht: Reidel.

Erskine, H.G. (1963) The polls: atomic weapons and nuclear energy, *Public Opinion Quarterly*, 2: 155–90.

ESRC Global Environmental Change Programme (1999) *The Politics of GM Food*, special briefings, October.

Esser, H. (1990) 'Habits', 'frames' und 'rational choice', *Zeitschrift für Soziologie*, 19(4): 231–47.

Esser, H. (1996) Die Definition der Situation, *Kölner Zeitschrift für Soziologie und Sozialpsychologie*, 48(1): 1–34.

Evers, A. (1987) Die Armutsdebatte in der Zeit der Formierung der Industriegesellschaft, in A. Evers and H. Nowotny, *Über den Umgang mit Unsicherheit*. Frankfurt: Suhrkamp.

Evers, A. and Nowotny, H. (1987) *Über den Umgang mit Unsicherheit*. Frankfurt: Suhrkamp.

Ewald, F. (1986) *L'Etat-Providence*. Paris: Grasset.

Ewald, F. (1989) Die Versicherungs-Gesellschaft, *Kritische Justiz*, 21: 385–402.

Ewald, F. (1991) Insurance and risk, in G. Burchell, C. Gordon and P. Miller (eds) *The Foucault Effect*. London: Harvester Wheatsheaf.

Eyerman, R. and Jamison, A. (1991) *Social Movements*. Cambridge: Polity.

Féher, F. and Heller, A. (1994) *Biopolitics*. Aldershot: Avebury.

Fischhoff, B. (1998) Risk perception and communication unplugged, in R.E. Löfstedt and L. Frewer (eds) *The Earthscan Reader in Risk and Modern Society*. London: Earthscan.

Foucault, M. (1979) *Discipline and Punish*. Harmondsworth: Penguin.

Foucault, M. (1981) *The History of Sexuality*, Vol. 1. Harmondsworth: Penguin.

Foucault, M. (1988) *Politics, Philosophy, Culture*. London: Routledge.
Foucault, M. (1991) Governmentality, in G. Burchell, C. Gordon and P. Miller (eds) *The Foucault Effect*. London: Harvester Wheatsheaf.
Frankenfeld, P. (1992) Technological citizenship, *Science, Technology, and Human Values*, 17(4): 459–84.
Fréchet, G. and Wörndl, B. (1993) The ecology movements in the light of social movements' development, *International Journal of Comparative Sociology*, 34: 56–74.
Friedman, J. (1994) Being in the world, in M. Featherstone (ed.) *Global Culture*. London: Sage.
Fuller, S. (1984) The cognitive turn in sociology, *Erkenntnis*, 74: 439–50.
Fuller, S. (1992) Epistemology radically naturalized, in R.N. Giere (ed.) *Cognitive Models of Science*. Minneapolis, MN: University of Minnesota Press.
Fuller, S. (1999) *The Governance of Science*. Buckingham: Open University Press.
Fuller, S. (2000) *Thomas Kuhn*. Chicago and London: University of Chicago Press.
Galtung, J. (1994) *Human Rights in Another Key*. Cambridge: Polity.
Gamson, W.A. and Modigliani, A. (1989) Media discourse and public opinion on nuclear power, *American Journal of Sociology*, 95(1): 1–37.
Garfinkel, H. (1967) *Studies in Ethnomethodology*. Englewood Cliffs, NJ: Prentice-Hall.
Georgescu-Roegen, N. (1971) *The Entropy Law and the Economic Process*. Cambridge, MA: Harvard University Press.
Giddens, A. (1984) *The Constitution of Society*. Cambridge: Polity.
Giddens, A. (1987) *The Nation-State and Violence*. Cambridge: Polity.
Giddens, A. (1990) *The Consequences of Modernity*. Cambridge: Polity.
Giddens, A. (1991) *Modernity and Self-Identity*. Cambridge: Polity.
Giddens, A. (1996) *In Defence of Sociology*. Cambridge: Polity.
Giddens, A. (1999) *Runaway World*. London: Profile Books.
Giesen, B. (1991) Code, process and situation in cultural selection, *Cultural Dynamics*, 4: 172–85.
Gilbert, G.N. and Mulkay, M.J. (1984) *Opening Pandora's Box*. London: Cambridge University Press.
Goldblatt, D. (1996) *Social Theory and the Environment*. Cambridge: Polity.
Gordon, C. (1991) Governmental rationality, in G. Burchell, C. Gordon and P. Miller (eds) *The Foucault Effect*. London: Harvester Wheatsheaf.
Gottweiss, H. (1995) German politics of genetic engineering and its deconstruction, *Social Studies of Science*, 25(2): 195–235.
Gould, L.C., Gardner, G.T., DeLuca, D.R. *et al.* (1988) *Perceptions of Technological Risks and Benefits*. New York: Russell Sage.
GRAIN (1997) Towards our sui generis rights, *Seedling*, December, http://www.grain.org/publications
GRAIN (1999) Spouting up: selling Iceland's human heritage, *Seedling*, March, http://www.grain.org/publications
Gramling, R. and Freudenberg, W.R. (1996) Environmental sociology, *Sociological Spectrum*, 16(4): 347–70.
Greenpeace (1999) Biosafety protocol, http://www.greenpeace.org/~geneng/
Groh, R. and Groh, D. (1991) *Weltbild und Naturaneignung*. Frankfurt: Suhrkamp.
Gusfield, J.R. (1981) *The Culture of Public Problems*. Chicago: University of Chicago Press.
Habermas, J. (1971) *Toward a Rational Society*. London: Heinemann.
Habermas, J. (1972) *Knowledge and Human Interests*. London: Heinemann.
Habermas, J. (1974) *Theory and Practice*. London: Heinemann.

Habermas, J. (1976) *Legitimation Crisis*. London: Heinemann.
Habermas, J. (1979) *Communication and the Evolution of Society*. London: Heinemann.
Habermas, J. ([1981] 1984, 1987) *The Theory of Communicative Action*, Vols. 1–2. London and Cambridge: Heinemann and Polity.
Habermas, J. (1986) The new obscurity, *Philosophy and Social Criticism*, 11: 1–19.
Habermas, J. ([1962] 1989) *Structural Transformation of the Public Sphere*. Cambridge: Polity.
Habermas, J. ([1988] 1992) *Postmetaphysical Thinking*. Cambridge: Polity.
Habermas, J. ([1992] 1996) *Between Facts and Norms*. Cambridge: Polity.
Habermas, J. (1998) *Die Postnationale Konstellation*. Frankfurt: Suhrkamp.
Habermas, J. (1999a) *Wahrheit und Rechtfertigung*. Frankfurt: Suhrkamp.
Habermas, J. (1999b) *The Inclusion of the Other*. Cambridge: Polity.
Hacking, I. (1990) *The Taming of Chance*. Cambridge: Cambridge University Press.
Hajer, M.A. (1995) *The Politics of Environmental Discourse*. Oxford: Oxford University Press.
Hajer, M.A. (1996) Ecological modernization as cultural politics, in S. Lash, B. Szerszynski and B. Wynne (eds) *Risk, Environment and Modernity*. London: Sage.
Halfmann, J. (1986) Autopoiesis und Naturbeherrschung, in H-J. Unverferth (ed.) *System und Selbsproduktion*. Frankfurt: Lang.
Halfmann, J. (1988) Risk avoidance and sovereignty, *Praxis International*, 8(1): 14–25.
Hansen, A. (1991) The media and the social construction of the environment, *Media, Culture and Society*, 13: 443–458.
Hardin, G. (1968) The tragedy of the commons, *Science*, 162: 1243–8.
Hegedus, Z. (1990) Social movements and social change in self-creative society, in M. Albrow and E. King (eds) *Globalization, Knowledge and Society*. London: Sage.
Heidegger, M. ([1954] 1977) *The Question Concerning Technology and Other Essays*. New York: Harper and Row.
Heidegger, M. (1978) *Basic Writings*. London: Routledge and Kegan Paul.
Held, D. (1980) *Introduction to Critical Theory*. London: Hutchinson.
Held, D. (1996) *Models of Democracy*. Cambridge: Polity.
Heller, A. (1982) *A Theory of History*. London: Routledge and Kegan Paul.
Hencke, D. and Evans, R. (2000) How US put pressure on Blair over GM food, *Guardian*, 28 February, http://www.newsunlimited.co.uk
Hewitt, K. (1997) *Regions of Risk*. London: Addison-Wesley-Longman.
Highfield, R. (1999) We have had GM tomatoes for years, *Daily Telegraph*, 18 February.
Hilgartner, S. and Bosk, C.L. (1988) The rise and fall of social problems, *American Journal of Sociology*, 94(1): 53–78.
Hill, C. (1988) *The World Turned Upside Down*. Harmondsworth: Penguin.
Hobbes, T. ([1651] 1973) *Leviathan*. London: Dent.
Hohenemser, C., Kasperson, R. and Kates, R. (1977) The distrust of nuclear power, *Science*, 196: 25–34.
Honneth, A. (1991) *Critique of Power*. Cambridge, MA: MIT Press.
Honneth, A. (1992) *Kampf um Anerkennung*. Frankfurt: Suhrkamp.
Huber, J. (1982) *Die verlorene Unschuld der Ökologie*. Frankfurt: Fisher.
Huber, J. (1995) *Nachhaltige Entwicklung*. Berlin: Sigma.
Inglehart, R. (1977) *The Silent Revolution*. Princeton, NJ: Princeton University Press.
International People's Tribunal on Human Rights and the Environment (2000) Information, http://www.ngos.net/ipt
Jacobs, M. (1997) The limits of neoclassicism, in M. Redclift and T. Benton (eds) *Social Theory and the Global Environment*. London: Routledge.

Jäger, M., Jäger, S., Ruth, I., Schulte-Holty, E. and Wichert, F. (eds) (1997) *Biomacht und Media*. Duisburg: DISS.

James, P. and Thompson, M. (1989) The plural rationality approach, in J. Brown (ed.) *Environmental Threats*. London: Belhaven.

Jänicke, M. (1985) *Preventive Environmental Policy as Ecological Modernization and Structural Policy*. Berlin: Wissenschaftszentrum.

Janowitz, M. (1980) Observations on the sociology of citizenship, *Social Forces*, 59(1): 1–24.

Japp, K.P. (1990) Das Risiko der Rationalität für technik-ökologische Systeme, in J. Halfmann and K.P. Japp (eds) *Riskante Entscheidungen und Katastrophenpotentiale*. Opladen: Westdeutscher.

Japp, K.P. (1992) Selbstverstärkungseffekte riskanter Entscheidungen, *Zeitschrift für Soziologie*, 21(1): 31–48.

Japp, K.P. (1993) Risiken der Technisierung und die neuen sozialen Bewegungen, in G. Bechmann (ed.) *Risiko und Gesellschaft*. Opladen: Westdeutscher.

Jasanoff, S.S. (1987) Contested boundaries in policy-relevant science, *Social Studies of Science*, 17: 195–230.

Jasanoff, S.S., Markle, G.E., Petersen, J.C. and Pinch, T. (eds) (1995) *Handbook of Science and Technology Studies*. London: Sage.

Jaspers, K. (1955) *Vom Ziel und Ursprung der Geschichte*. Frankfurt: Fischer.

Jessop, B. (1994) Post-Fordism and the state, in A. Amin (ed.) *Post-Fordism*. Oxford: Blackwell.

Johnson, B.B. and Covello, V.T. (eds) (1987) *The Social and Cultural Construction of Risk*. Dordrecht: Reidel.

Jonas, H. (1973) Technology and responsibility, *Social Research*, 40(1): 31–54.

Jonas, H. (1976) Responsibility today, *Social Research*, 43(1): 77–97.

Jonas, H. ([1979] 1984) *The Imperative of Responsibility*. Chicago: University of Chicago Press.

Kasperson, R.E. et al. (1988) The social amplification of risk, *Risk Analysis*, 8(2): 177–87.

Katz, E., Levin, M.L. and Hamilton, H. (1963) Traditions of research on the diffusion of innovation, *American Sociological Review*, 28: 237–52.

Kettler, D. and Meja, V. (1988) The reconstitution of political life, *Polity*, 20(4): 623–47.

Knorr, K. (1981) *The Manufacture of Knowledge*. Oxford: Pergamon.

Knorr-Cetina, K. (1988) The micro-social order, in G.N. Fielding (ed.) *Actions and Structure*. London: Sage.

Knorr-Cetina, K. and Cicourel, A.V. (eds) (1981) *Advances in Social Theory and Methodology*. Boston, MA: Routledge and Kegan Paul.

Knorr-Cetina, K. and Mulkay, M. (eds) (1983) *Science Observed*. London: Sage.

Kölner Zeitschrift für Soziologie und Sozialpsychologie (1998) Die Diagnosefähigkeit der Soziologie, special issue.

Koselleck, R. (1989) *Vergangene Zukunft*. Frankfurt: Suhrkamp.

Kreibich, R. (1986) *Die Wissenschaftsgesellschaft*. Frankfurt: Suhrkamp.

Kriesi, H. and Giugni, M.G. (1996) Ökologische Bewegung im internationaler Vergleich, in A. Diekmann and C.C. Jaeger (eds) *Umweltsoziologie*. Opladen: Westdeutscher.

Krohn, W. and Weyer, J. (1989) Gesellschaft als Labor, *Soziale Welt*, 40: 349–73.

Kuhn, T.S. (1962) *The Structure of Scientific Revolutions*. Chicago: University of Chicago Press.

Lafaye, C. and Thévenot, L. (1993) Une justification écologique?, *Revue française de sociologie*, 34: 495–524.

Lafferty, W.M. (1995) The implementation of sustainable development in the European Union, in J. Lovenduski and J. Stanyer (eds) *Contemporary Political Studies 1995*, Vol. I. Belfast: Political Studies Association of the UK.

Lash, S. (1994) Expert-systems or situated interpretation?, in U. Beck, A. Giddens and S. Lash (eds) *Reflexive Modernization*. Cambridge: Polity.

Latour, B. (1987) *Science in Action*. Buckingham: Open University Press.

Latour, B. and Woolgar, S. (1979) *Laboratory Life*. London: Sage.

Lau, C. (1989) Risikodiskurse, *Soziale Welt*, 3: 418–36.

Leiss, W. (1972) *The Domination of Nature*. New York: Braziller.

Leiss, W. (1996) Three phases in the evolution of risk communication practice, *Annals of the American Academy of Political and Social Science*, 545: 85–94.

Löfstedt, R.E. and Frewer, L. (eds) (1998) *The Earthscan Reader in Risk and Modern Society*. London: Earthscan.

Lowe, P.D. and Rüdig, W. (1986) Political ecology and the social sciences, *British Journal of Sociology*, 16: 513–50.

Luckmann, T. (ed.) (1978) *Phenomenology and Sociology*. Harmondsworth: Penguin.

Luhmann, N. ([1986] 1989) *Ecological Communication*. Cambridge: Polity.

Luhmann, N. (1990a) Technology, environment and social risk, *Industrial Crisis Quarterly*, 4: 223–31.

Luhmann, N. (1990b) The cognitive program of constructivism and a reality that remains unknown, in W. Krohn, G. Küppers and H. Nowotny (eds) *Self-Organization*. Dordrecht: Kluwer.

Luhmann, N. (1991) Das Moderne der modernen Gesellschaft, in W. Zapf (ed.) *Die Modernisierung moderner Gesellschaften*. Frankfurt: Campus.

Luhmann, N. (1992) *Die Wissenschaft der Gesellschaft*. Frankfurt: Suhrkamp.

Luhmann, N. ([1991] 1993) *Risk: A Sociological Theory*. Berlin: de Gruyter.

Luhmann, N. ([1984] 1995) *Social Systems*. Stanford, CA: Stanford University Press.

Luhmann, N. (1998) *Observations on Modernity*. Stanford, CA: Stanford University Press.

Lupton, D. (1999) *Risk*. London: Routledge.

McGinty, L. (1976) Whose acceptable risk?, *New Scientist*, 71: 582–3.

MacKenzie, D. and Wajcman, J. (eds) (1985) *The Social Shaping of Technology*. Buckingham: Open University Press.

Macnaghten, P. and Urry, J. (1998) *Contested Natures*. London: Sage.

McNally, R. and Wheale, P. (1999) Bio-patenting and innovation, in P. O'Mahony (ed.) *Nature, Risk and Responsibility*. London: Macmillan.

Maheu, L. (ed.) (1995) *Social Movements and Social Classes*. London: Sage.

Mandrou, R. (1978) *From Humanism to Science 1480–1700*. Harmondsworth: Penguin.

Mannheim, K. ([1936] 1972) *Ideology and Utopia*. London: Routledge and Kegan Paul.

Mannheim, K. (1993) *From Karl Mannheim*, edited by K.H. Wolff. New Brunswick, NJ: Transaction.

Marcuse, H. (1964) *One Dimensional Man*. Boston, MA: Beacon.

Marx, K. ([1867] 1977) *Capital*, Vol. 1. London: Lawrence and Wishart.

Mauss, A.L. (1975) *Social Problems as Social Movements*. New York: Lippincot.

May, T. (2000) A future for critique? Positioning, belonging and reflexivity, *European Journal of Social Theory*, 3(2): 157–73.

Mayhew, L.M. (1997) *The New Public*. Cambridge: Cambridge University Press.

Mazur, A. (1987) Putting radon on the public's risk agenda, *Science, Technology, and Human Values*, 23(1/2): 86–93.

Meadows, D.H., Meadows, D.L., Randers, J. and Behrens, W.H. (1972) *The Limits to Growth*. New York: Universe Books.

Meek, J. (2000) Bad genes, *Guardian*, 8 February, http://www.newsunlimited.co.uk

Melucci, A. (1980) The new social movements, *Social Science Information*, 19(2): 199–226.

Melucci, A. (1985) The symbolic challenge of contemporary movements, *Social Research*, 52(4): 789–816.

Melucci, A. (1996) *Challenging Codes*. Cambridge: Cambridge University Press.

Mendelsohn, E., Weingart, P. and Whitley, R. (eds) (1977) *The Social Production of Scientific Knowledge*. Dordrecht: Reidel.

Merchant, C. (1990) *The Death of Nature*. San Francisco, CA: Harper and Row.

Milani-Comparetti, M. (1993) From genetics to gene-ethics, *International Journal of Bioethics*, 4(2): 99–101.

Miller, M. (1986) *Kollektive Lernprozesse*. Frankfurt: Suhrkamp.

Miller, M. (1992) Discourse and morality, *Archives Européennes de Sociologie*, 33(1): 3–38.

Miller, M. (1994) Intersystemic discourse and co-ordinated dissent, *Theory, Culture and Society*, 11: 101 21.

Mol, A.P.J. (1996) Ecological modernization and institutional reflexivity, *Environmental Politics*, 5(2): 302–23.

Mol, A.P.J. and Spaargaren, G. (1993) Environment, modernity and the risk society, *International Sociology*, 8(4): 431–59.

Monbiot, G. (2000) Just say no to biotech business, *Guardian*, 2 March, http://www.newsunlimited.co.uk

Morrison, D.E. (1980) The soft cutting edge of environmentalism, *Natural Resources Journal*, 20(2): 275–98.

Moscovici, S. (1977) *Essai sur l'Histoire Humaine de la Nature*. Paris: Flammarion.

Münch, R. (1984) *Die Struktur der Moderne*. Frankfurt: Suhrkamp.

Münch, R. (1991) *Dialektik der Kommunikationsgesellschaft*. Frankfurt: Suhrkamp.

Münch, R. (1996) *Risikopolitik*. Frankfurt: Suhrkamp.

Nederveen Pieterse, J.P. (1990) *Empire and Emancipation*. London: Pluto.

Needham, J. (1972) Mathematics and science in China and the West, in B. Barnes (ed.) *Sociology of Science*. Harmondsworth: Penguin.

Neidhardt, F. and Rucht, D. (1991) The analysis of social movements, in D. Rucht (ed.) *Research on Social Movements*. Frankfurt and Boulder, CO: Campus and Westview.

Nelkin, D. (ed.) (1992) *Controversy*. London: Sage.

Non-Governmental Organizations (NGOs) Network (2000) A people's assembly – is in sight?, http://www.ngos.net/plpassem.html

Nowotny, H. (1973) On the feasibility of a cognitive approach to the study of science, *Zeitschrift für Soziologie*, 2(3): 282–96.

Nowotny, H. (1987) Die wiederkehrende Aktualität von Verunsicherung, in A. Evers and H. Nowotny, *Über den Umgang mit Unsicherheit*. Frankfurt: Suhrkamp.

Nowotny, H. (1996) Umwelt, Zeit, Komplexität, in A. Diekmann and C.C. Jaeger (eds) *Umweltsoziologie*. Opladen: Westdeutscher.

Offe, C. (1986) Die Utopie der Null-Option, in J. Berger (ed.) *Die Moderne: Kontinuitäten und Zäsuren*. Gottingen: Schwartz.

Onions, C.T. (ed.) (1976) *The Oxford Dictionary of English Etymology*. Oxford: Clarendon.

Otway, H. (1987) Experts, risk communication, and democracy, *Risk Analysis*, 7(2): 125–9.

Otway, H.J. and Cohen, J.J. (1975) Revealed preferences, RM-75-5. Laxenburg: International Institute for Applied Systems Analysis.

Otway, H.J. and Fishbein, M. (1976) The determinants of attitude formation, RM-76-80. Laxenburg: International Institute for Applied Systems Analysis.

Otway, H.J. and Pahner, P.D. (1976) Risk assessment, *Futures*, 8: 122–34.

Otway, H.J. and Thomas, K. (1982) Reflections on risk perception and policy, *Risk Analysis*, 2(2): 69–82.

Outhwaite, W. (1987) *New Philosophies of Social Science*. London: Macmillan.

Park, R.E. (1936) Human ecology, *American Journal of Sociology*, 42(1): 1–15.

Paul, J. (1994) *Im Netz der Bioethik*. Duisburg: DISS.

Pels, D. (1996) Karl Mannheim and the sociology of scientific knowledge, *Sociological Theory*, 14(1): 30–48.

Permanent People's Tribunal on Industrial Hazards and Human Rights (1998) Charter of rights against industrial hazards, in C. Williams (ed.) *Environmental Victims*. London: Earthscan.

Perrolle, J.A. (ed.) (1993) Special issue on environmental justice, *Social Problems*, 40(1).

Perrow, C. (1984) *Normal Accidents*. New York: Basic Books.

Perry, A.H. (1981) *Environmental Hazards in the British Isles*. London: Allen and Unwin.

Pinch, T. and Bijker, W. (1984) The social construction of facts and artifacts, *Social Studies of Science*, 14: 399–441.

Plough, A. and Krimsky, S. (1987) The emergence of risk communication studies, *Science, Technology, and Human Values*, 12(3/4): 4–10.

Radder, H. (1986) Experiment, technology and the intrinsic connection between knowledge and power, *Social Studies of Science*, 16: 663–83.

RAFI (1999a) Pharma-gedon, *Genotypes*, 21 December, http://www.rafi.org/news

RAFI (1999b) Biopiracy Project Chiapas, Mexico, denounced by Mayan indigenous groups, http://www.rafi.org/news

RAFI (2000) Phase II for human genome research, http://www.rafi.org/news

Rapoport, A. (1996) Die systemische Ansatz der Umweltsoziologie, in A. Diekmann and C.C. Jaeger (eds) *Umweltsoziologie*. Opladen: Westdeutscher.

Ravetz, J. and Brown, J. (1989) Biotechnology, in J. Brown (ed.) *Environmental Threats*. London: Belhaven.

Rayner, S. (1991) A cultural perspective on the structure and implementation of global environmental agreements, *Evaluation Review*, 15(1): 75–102.

Rayner, S. and Cantor, R. (1998) How fair is safe enough? The cultural approach to societal technology choice, in R.E. Löfstedt and L. Frewer (eds) *The Earthscan Reader in Risk and Modern Society*. London: Earthscan.

Redclift, M. (1992) The meaning of sustainable development, *Geoforum*, 23(3): 395–402.

Renn, O. (1984) *Risikowahrnehmung der Kernenergie*. Frankfurt: Campus.

Rifkin, J. (1998) *The Biotech Century*. London: Gollancz.

Rip, A. (1986) The mutual dependence of risk research and political context, *Science and Technology Studies*, 4(3/4): 3 15.

Rogers, E.M. (1963) *The Diffusion of Innovations*. New York: Free Press.

Roth, E., Morgan, M.G., Fischhoff, B., Lave, L. and Bostrom, A. (1998) What do we know about making risk comparisons?, in R.E. Löfstedt and L. Frewer (eds) *The Earthscan Reader in Risk and Modern Society*. London: Earthscan.

Rothschild, Lord (1978) Risk, *The Listener*, 30(November): 715–18.

Rucht, D. (1990) Campaigns, skirmishes and battles, *Industrial Crisis Quarterly*, 4: 193–222.

Rustin, M. (1994) Incomplete modernity, *Radical Philosophy*, 67: 3–12.

Sayer, A. (1984) *Method in Social Science*. London: Hutchinson.

Schmidt, S.J. (ed.) (1987) *Der Diskurs des Radikalen Konstruktivismus*. Frankfurt: Suhrkamp.

Schnaiberg, A. (1983) Redistributive goals versus distributive politics, *Sociological Inquiry*, 53: 200–19.

Schneider, J.W. (1985) Social problems, *Annual Review of Sociology*, 11: 209–29.
Schulze, G. (1997) *Die Erlebnisgesellschaft*. Frankfurt: Campus.
Scott, A. (2000) Risk society or angst society?, in B. Adam, U. Beck and J. van Loon (eds) *The Risk Society and Beyond*. London: Sage.
Sessions, G. (1987) The deep ecology movement, *Environmental Ethics*, 8: 105–25.
Short, J.F. (1984) The 1984 presidential address: the social fabric at risk, *American Sociological Review*, 49(6): 711–25.
Silver, L.M. (1997) *Remaking Eden*. New York: Avon.
Simmons, I.G. (1991) *Changing the Face of the Earth*. Oxford: Blackwell.
Simon, J.L. (1996) *The Ultimate Resource 2*. Princeton, NJ: Princeton University Press.
Simon, J.L. and Kahn, H. (eds) (1984) *The Resourceful Earth*. Oxford: Blackwell.
Sismondo, S. (1993) Some social constructions, *Social Studies of Science*, 23: 515–53.
Skinner, Q. (1978) *The Foundations of Modern Political Thought*, Vol. 1. Cambridge: Cambridge University Press.
Slovic, P. (1987) Perception of risk, *Science*, 236: 280–5.
Slovic, P., Fischhoff, B. and Lichtenstein, S. (1979) Rating the risks, *Environment*, 21(3): 14–39.
Smart, B. (1998) *Facing Modernity*. London: Sage.
Smith, J.M. (1982) *Evolution and the Theory of Games*. Cambridge: Cambridge University Press.
Spaargaren, G. (1996) *The Ecological Modernization of Production and Consumption*. Wageningen: Landbouw Universiteit.
Spaargaren, G. and Mol, A.P.J. (1991) Ecologie, Technologie en Sociale Verandering, in A.P.J. Mol, G. Spaargaren and A. Klapwijk (eds) *Technologie en Milieubeheer*. The Hague: SDU.
Spaargaren, G. and Mol, A.P.J. (1992) Sociology, environment, and modernity, *Society and Natural Resources*, 5(4): 323–44.
Spector, M. and Kitsuse, J.I. (1973) Social problems, *Social Problems*, 21: 145–59.
Spector, M. and Kitsuse, J.I. (1977) *Constructing Social Problems*. Menlo Park, CA: Cummings.
Starr, C. (1969) Social benefit versus technological risk, *Science*, 165: 1232–9.
Stehr, N. (1994) *Knowledge Societies*. London: Sage.
Strydom, P. (1987) Collective learning, *Philosophy and Social Criticism*, 13(3): 265–81.
Strydom, P. (1990) Habermas and new social movements, *Telos*, 85: 156–64.
Strydom, P. (1992) The ontogenetic fallacy, *Theory, Culture and Society*, 9(3): 65–93.
Strydom, P. (1993a) Sociocultural evolution or the social evolution of practical reason?, *Praxis International*, 13(3): 304–22.
Strydom, P. (1993b) Agenda-setting and agenda-building, European University Institute, Project 42, research paper 10.
Strydom, P. (1999a) Hermeneutic culturalism and its double, *European Journal of Social Theory*, 2(1): 45–69.
Strydom, P. (1999b) The civilisation of the gene, in P. O'Mahony (ed.) *Nature, Risk and Responsibility*. London: Macmillan.
Strydom, P. (1999c) Triple contingency, *Philosophy and Social Criticism*, 25(2): 1–25.
Strydom, P. (1999d) The challenge of responsibility for sociology, *Current Sociology*, 47(3): 65–82.
Strydom, P. (1999e) The theory of evolution in contemporary sociology: a new European rapprochement? Protocol of graduate seminar, University College, Cork, 1999–2000.
Strydom, P. (2000) *Discourse and Knowledge*. Liverpool: Liverpool University Press.

Szerszynski, B., Lash, S. and Wynne, B. (1996) Introduction: ecology, realism and the social sciences, in S. Lash, B. Szerszynski and B. Wynne (eds) *Risk, Environment and Modernity*. London: Sage.

Theory and Society (1995) Special issue on circulation versus reproduction of elites during the postcommunist transformation of Eastern Europe, 24(5).

Toulmin, S. and Goodfield, J. (1968) *The Architecture of Matter*. Harmondsworth: Penguin.

Touraine, A. (1971) *The Post-Industrial Society*. New York: Random House.

Touraine, A. (1981) *The Voice and the Eye*. Cambridge: Cambridge University Press.

Touraine, A. (1983) *Anti-Nuclear Protest*. Cambridge: Cambridge University Press.

Tuchman, G. (1978) *Making News*. New York: Free Press.

Turner, B.S. (ed.) (1993) *Citizenship and Social Theory*. London: Sage.

Turner, R.H. (1969) The public perception of protest, *American Sociological Review*, 34(6): 815–31.

United Nations Environmental Programme (2000) http://www.unep.org

Van den Daele, W. (1977) The social construction of science, in E. Mendelsohn, P. Weingart and R. Whitley (eds) *The Social Production of Scientific Knowledge*. Dordrecht: Reidel.

Van den Daele, W. (1992a) Scientific evidence and the regulation of technical risks, in N. Stehr and R.V. Ericson (eds) *The Culture and Power of Knowledge*. Berlin: de Gruyter.

Van den Daele, W. (1992b) Concepts of nature in modern societies and nature as a theme in sociology, in M. Dierkes and B. Biervert (eds) *European Social Science in Transition*. Frankfurt and Boulder, CO: Campus and Westview.

Van Peursen, C.A. (1970) *Strategie van de Cultuur*. Amsterdam: Elsevier.

Varela, F.J., Thompson, E. and Rosch, E. (1993) *The Embodied Mind*. Cambridge, MA: MIT Press.

Watzlawick, P., Beavin, J. and Jackson, D.D. (1967) *The Pragmatics of Human Communication*. New York: Norton.

Weale, A. (1992) *The New Politics of Pollution*. Manchester: Manchester University Press.

Webster, C. (1975) *The Great Instauration*. London: Duckworth.

Webster, F. (1995) *Theories of the Information Society*. London: Routledge.

Weinberg, A. (1972) Science and trans-science, *Minerva*, 10: 209–22.

Weingart, P. (1983) Verwissenschaftlichung der Gesellschaft, Politisierung der Wissenschaft, *Zeitschrift für Soziologie*, 12(3): 225–41.

Weingart, P. (ed.) (1989) *Technik als sozialer Prozess*. Frankfurt: Suhrkamp.

Wheale, P. and McNally, R. (1993) Biotechnology policy in Europe, *Science and Public Policy*, 20(4): 261–79.

White, G.F. (1945) *Human Adjustment to Floods*. Chicago: University of Chicago Press.

Wildavsky, A. (1994) *But is it True?* Chicago: University of Chicago Press.

Williams, C. (ed.) (1998) *Environmental Victims*. London: Earthscan.

Wolff, K.H. (1993) Introduction: a reading of Karl Mannheim, in K.H. Wolff (ed.) *From Karl Mannheim*. New Brunswick, NJ: Transaction.

World Commission on Environment and Development (1987) *Our Common Future* (Brundtland Report). Oxford: Oxford University Press.

Wright, B. (1995) Environmental equity justice centers, in B. Bryant (ed.) *Environmental Justice*. Washington, DC: Island.

Wynne, B. (1988) Unruly technology, *Social Studies of Science*, 18: 147–67.

Wynne, B. (1989a) Frameworks of rationality in risk management, in J. Brown (ed.) *Environmental Threats*. London: Belhaven.

Wynne, B. (1989b) Building public concern into risk management, in J. Brown (ed.) *Environmental Threats*. London: Belhaven.

Wynne, B. (1996) May the sheep safely graze? A reflexive view of the expert–lay knowledge divide, in S. Lash, B. Szerszynski and B. Wynne (eds) *Risk, Environment and Modernity*. London: Sage.

Yearley, S. (1996) *Sociology, Environmentalism, Globalization*. London: Sage.

Zimmerman, A.D. (1995) Toward a more democratic ethic of technological governance, *Science, Technology, and Human Values*, 20(1): 86–107.

Zolo, D. (1997) *Cosmopolis*. Cambridge: Polity.

Index

SOCIAL SOLIDARITIES
THEORIES, IDENTITIES AND SOCIAL CHANGE
Graham Crow

- What is the significance of social solidarity?
- Has social change undermined the potential for people to come together and act coherently?
- What can we learn from comparing the solidarities of families, communities and wider societies?

Social solidarity is important in many areas of our lives, or at least in how we wish our lives to be. Family and kinship relationships, community life, trade union activity and the identity politics of new social movements are just some of the numerous ways in which social solidarity features in contemporary social arrangements. This book explores the ways in which people strive to come together and act as a coherent, unified force. It considers the arguments of those who claim that solidarity is increasingly fragile, and of those who are concerned to revitalise solidarities in our unsettled societies. The author shows how social change can be understood in the context of the limitations as well as the potential of the pursuit of solidarity, drawing on research findings on social relationships in families, communities, and the post-communist world. Written with undergraduate students and researchers in mind, *Social Solidarities* will be an invaluable text for those studying social theory, and family, community or comparative sociology.

Contents
Introduction – Part One Classical theories of social solidarity – Contemporary theories of social solidarity – Part Two Family solidarities – Community solidarities – The solidarity of Solidarity *– Part Three Making sense of social solidarities in unsettled societies – References – Index.*

c.160pp   0 335 20230 6   (Paperback)   0 335 20231 4   (Hardback)